Gamestar Mechanic

FOR

DUMMIES®

A Wiley Brand

by Jacob Cordeiro

FOR

DUMMIES®

A Wiley Brand

Gamestar Mechanic For Dummies®

Published by: **John Wiley & Sons, Inc.,** 111 River Street, Hoboken, NJ 07030-5774, www.wiley.com

Copyright © 2014 by John Wiley & Sons, Inc., Hoboken, New Jersey

Published simultaneously in Canada

No part of this publication may be reproduced, stored in a retrieval system or transmitted in any form or by any means, electronic, mechanical, photocopying, recording, scanning or otherwise, except as permitted under Sections 107 or 108 of the 1976 United States Copyright Act, without the prior written permission of the Publisher. Requests to the Publisher for permission should be addressed to the Permissions Department, John Wiley & Sons, Inc., 111 River Street, Hoboken, NJ 07030, (201) 748-6011, fax (201) 748-6008, or online at http://www.wiley.com/go/permissions.

Trademarks: Wiley, For Dummies, the Dummies Man logo, Dummies.com, Making Everything Easier, and related trade dress are trademarks or registered trademarks of John Wiley & Sons, Inc. and may not be used without written permission. Gamestar Mechanic is a trademark of E-Line Media. All other trademarks are the property of their respective owners. John Wiley & Sons, Inc. is not associated with any product or vendor mentioned in this book.

For general information on our other products and services, please contact our Customer Care Department within the U.S. at 877-762-2974, outside the U.S. at 317-572-3993, or fax 317-572-4002. For technical support, please visit www.wiley.com/techsupport.

Wiley publishes in a variety of print and electronic formats and by print-on-demand. Some material included with standard print versions of this book may not be included in e-books or in print-on-demand. If this book refers to media such as a CD or DVD that is not included in the version you purchased, you may download this material at http://booksupport.wiley.com. For more information about Wiley products, visit www.wiley.com.

Library of Congress Control Number: 2013954110

ISBN 978-1-118-83212-7 (pbk); ISBN 978-1-118-83213-4 (ebk); ISBN 978-1-118-83214-1 (ebk)

Manufactured in the United States of America

10 9 8 7 6 5 4 3 2 1

Contents at a Glance

Table of Contents

Introduction

*U*sing the online program Gamestar Mechanic, users can design and publish their own video games, and they can play and review video games created by other users. This friendly creative community has built a database of more than 350,000 games created by its users all over the world.

No programming experience is required in order to design these video games, but they have a deep creative art behind them. Games can take as little as 5 minutes to complete and publish, and elaborate games can take many hours of work. Because no programming is involved, designing games in Gamestar Mechanic focuses almost entirely on the pure creative process, making it the perfect game design tool for all ages.

Gamestar Mechanic, at `www.gamestarmechanic.com`, can also be used as an educational program, and more than 4,000 schools are using this website to teach students to learn through play. The site alone offers players the opportunity to design, play, and review games by participating in a digital community — these activities are not only great fun but also effective teachers of critical thinking, systems thinking, media literacy, and creative skills.

About This Book

Gamestar Mechanic For Dummies, which supplements your Gamestar Mechanic experience, contains information for readers of every skill level. You can see the basic principles of navigating and using the site, teaching classes, publishing games that are fun to play, and understanding the core concepts of game design.

If you have never used Gamestar Mechanic, you can find introductory information in the first few chapters of this book. Later on, I describe more advanced concepts, so I recommend that you practice publishing a few games as you read. In Gamestar Mechanic, practice is vital to improving your skills — as long as you learn about yourself as a designer from your published games, you may notice the quality of your productions dramatically improving over time.

This book can show you how to

- Find your way around the Gamestar Mechanic website and interface
- Play games from the huge collection that's available for free
- Use the toolbox to design games
- Become a member of the Gamestar Mechanic community

- ✔ Master the elements and metrics of fun games
- ✔ Compete in game design contests
- ✔ Teach (or learn from) Gamestar Mechanic classes

Don't worry if you have trouble mastering some of the concepts in this book. *Gamestar Mechanic For Dummies* can help you become aware of these concepts so that you can improve your skills more efficiently.

Foolish Assumptions

To be able to write this book for all different types of readers, I've made certain assumptions about you. First, I assume that you have

- ✔ A computer — and you know how to use it
- ✔ An e-mail address — and you can receive e-mail
- ✔ A functioning keyboard and computer mouse

I also assume that

- ✔ You know what a web browser is, and you can surf the web.
- ✔ Your computer can run Flash programs, or download the necessary application to do so.
- ✔ You are allowed (if you're a younger reader) to use a site that supports online communication, which contains strong filters against inappropriate content.

Icons Used in This Book

I've placed various icons in the margins of this book to point out specific information that you may find useful while working on Gamestar Mechanic:

You can apply these useful tips to help you better navigate the site, play and design games, and interact with other users.

Always keep these important pieces of information in mind. If you skim certain chapters in this book, be on the lookout for this icon.

The technical information marked by this icon is entirely optional, though you may find it interesting or helpful.

Look out! These warnings tell you how to avoid common or major mistakes.

Beyond the Book

To supplement the content in this book, you can find extra content online. Go online to find the following items:

- **Cheat Sheet:** You can view the Cheat Sheet for this book online, where you'll find a summary of its important concepts and ideas. The Cheat Sheet is a useful companion to the book because you get to know the Gamestar Mechanic site. Remember to keep the Cheat Sheet handy to refer to repeatedly, or to refer to quickly and easily when the book isn't nearby. To view the Cheat Sheet online, see

  www.dummies.com/cheatsheet/gamestarmechanic

- **Dummies.com online articles:** To help you get more from this book, a number of online articles expand on its most important subjects. These articles, which can help you extend and implement the information in this book, include links to interesting examples that you can further explore. The articles appear on the book's Extras page, at

  www.dummies.com/extras/gamestarmechanic

- **Updates:** Occasionally, Wiley's technology books are updated. If this book has technical updates, they'll be posted on the book's Extras page at

  www.dummies.com/extras/gamestarmechanic

Where to Go from Here

Though you may be well served by reading the chapters in this book in order, you may instead want to focus on certain sections if you're looking for specific information.

If you're just starting out with the Gamestar Mechanic site, I highly recommend Parts I and II for introducing you to the site. The other parts can be read in any order you like. If you're interested in the more interpersonal components of Gamestar Mechanic, see Part III. If you want to gain a deeper understanding of game design, focus on Part IV. If you're looking for a more interesting experience, try Part V. Lastly, Part VI contains other helpful pieces of information that you might find interesting.

Part I
Introducing the Gamestar Mechanic World

getting started

with

Gamestar
Mechanic

In this part . . .

- ✔ Find out what you can do with Gamestar Mechanic.
- ✔ Get to know the main areas of the site: the Quest, the Workshop, and Game Alley.
- ✔ Set up a Gamestar Mechanic account.
- ✔ Navigate the website.

1

What Is Gamestar Mechanic?

*T*he website *Gamestar Mechanic*, created by E-Line Media and the Institute of Play, lets you create and play action games in which the player can navigate, shoot enemies, collect coins, and solve labyrinths. You can easily build your own games and publish them for other users to play and review, providing feedback on what you did well and what could be improved.

The concept of a *level editor* is prominent in a number of games, enabling you to arrange the components of the game in a unique way. Gamestar Mechanic goes the extra mile, using its official levels to teach you the elements of a fun game. Having a community of people who design, play, and review games allows you to step into the world of the game designer, the play-tester, and the critic, having fun every step of the way.

This chapter gives you an overview of what you can do with Gamestar Mechanic and introduces the main areas of the site.

Gamestar Mechanic: An Introduction

Most video game design platforms, as with all programming languages, can be intimidating to beginners — your imagination is often limited by your programming ability. In Gamestar Mechanic, you don't need to know a programming language to create a game. You're provided with *sprites* (the components used to build a game), and the goal is to apply them in a fun and innovative arrangement.

In Gamestar Mechanic, you play *quests* (games created by the Gamestar team) that teach you the core concepts of game design, build your own games in the *Workshop,* and play a nearly limitless arcade of other people's games in

Game Alley. While playing, you grasp new concepts and apply them to your own games. After you design a game, you can immediately publish it so that it shows up in Game Alley, sharing the game with other players.

Gamestar Mechanic is a safe environment for sharing and discussing and is a useful resource for all ages. Figure 1-1 shows the first page you see when you log in to the site.

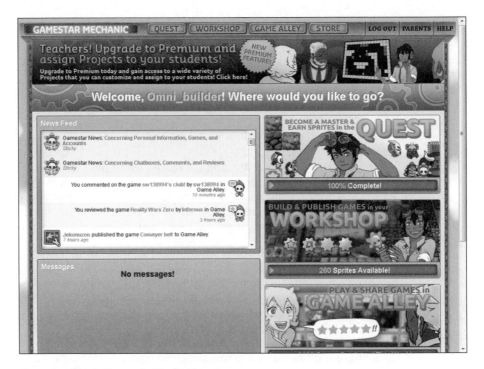

Figure 1-1: This is Gamestar Mechanic.

In the following sections, I discuss the three main areas of Gamestar Mechanic and what you can do there:

- The Quest
- The Workshop
- The Game Alley

The Quest

The *Quest* is a combination of interesting games and interactive comics that follow the training of game designer Addison Cypher. Each quest involves tutorials and advice that teach you the concepts of game design, allowing you to learn from experience by playing games, repairing broken games, and designing your own games. You must complete the first quest in order to *publish* games for other users to play, because these quests contain valuable information about how games are made. (See Chapter 4 for more on quest missions.)

The free quests introduce you to the essential concepts of game design via active play and interaction, whereas the premium quests define more advanced concepts that are weaved into a more intense storyline. (I discuss premium accounts in Chapter 14.) Whether you're a new game designer or you have experience in other programming languages, the Quest is a good place to start introducing yourself to the site.

The Workshop

The *Workshop,* shown in Figure 1-2, is your turf. You can see your rank, achievements, games, challenges, and more. The Workshop is also where you begin designing new games and where teachers manage their classes (see Chapter 16 for more on classes).

The *toolbox* is a subsection of the Workshop. You're given an array of all your *sprites* (the objects that comprise games, as described in Chapter 5), a grid to place them on, and a few tools. In this robust environment, you can build games quickly and thoughtfully, in any way you can think of. The toolbox is the heart and soul of the Gamestar Mechanic interface, the canvas on which you put into practice the concepts you've absorbed elsewhere on the site.

When you first sign up for Gamestar Mechanic, you receive a default set of sprites in your toolbox. As you proceed through the Quest, you earn additional sprites that you can use to build more elaborate games.

Understanding terms used in this book

This book often refers to the terms *games, levels,* and *sprites.* In the context of Gamestar Mechanic, a *game* is a complete, playable work to be published on the site. Every game is divided into separate *levels,* which are rooms that are cleared in sequence while playing the game. Lastly, levels are created by arranging (on a grid) little creatures or objects — known as *sprites* — that contribute different functions to the game.

I also talk about games in terms of designers, players, and reviewers on Gamestar Mechanic.

A *designer* is a user who designs games; a *player* is someone who plays games; and a *reviewer* is a player who gives feedback in the form of reviews on the site. You may read phrases such as *gaining players* or *gaining reviewers,* which simply refer to attracting people to play and review your games. This book shows you how to do all three jobs for the full Gamestar Mechanic experience — as a designer, a player, and a reviewer.

Figure 1-2: Your workshop displays your profile, as well as the tools for changing it.

Game Alley

Designing games is fun, but games are meant to be played. Game Alley is the place where you can share games with friends and acquaintances, by way of a safe and private system. You can surf Game Alley and play some of the hundreds of thousands of user-created games or publish your own games for the community to try out. The reviewing system for games (discussed in Chapter 7) lets you review other users' games, and they can review yours, in a safe environment.

Depending on your preferences, designing a game can take anywhere from five minutes to days on end. No matter how you design it, though, your game will be playable by a community of thousands who can review and comment on it. Even if you only occasionally check the site to play or design games, you can immediately find new ways to enjoy and understand game design.

The Gamestar Mechanic community includes a database of over 500,000 games, all of which have been created by its huge community of users. Thousands of games are published every week, and users have played these games more than 15 million times in the history of the website. In addition, more than 6,000 schools use Gamestar Mechanic to teach a number of different subjects. On this site, you'll never find a shortage of players, designers, reviewers, or mentors.

Exploring What You Can Do on the Site

Gamestar Mechanic contains a number of intuitive interfaces, which you can quickly pick up and then master over time. The following sections introduce you to the interfaces for playing, designing, and reviewing games.

Playing games

The games designed in Gamestar Mechanic all follow the same general system: A single avatar sprite is placed in a level, and the avatar responds to the commands that the player enters from the keyboard. The player controls the movements of the avatar with the keyboard.

Game *levels* are a series of independent challenges that lead players through the game. Each level has a *perspective,* which determines how sprites function within the world. Here is a quick rundown of the two perspectives in Gamestar Mechanic (which are covered in more detail in Chapter 2):

- In a **top-down** game, the player looks down on the level from above, and sprites can move up, down, left, or right.
- In a **platformer** game, the player has a side view: Sprites can move only left or right, but they can also jump into the air or fall down because of gravity.

Games can take on many different forms, depending on the kinds of sprites you use to build them. You can design your own goals by adjusting sprites' settings and properties and adding parameters (in the form of *system sprites*) for completing the level. You are provided with lots of different sprites that have different abilities and behaviors. You can place various sprites in each level of your game and adjust their settings to decide what they do. A little creativity can unfold into millions of ideas, concepts, innovations, and patterns. For more on the five categories of sprites (avatar, enemy, block, item, and system), check out Chapter 5.

Designing games

The interface for designing games is simple: The levels are split into square grids, and designers can drop sprites from the library onto the grid to use. The simple click-and-drop interface, combined with four tools for manipulating sprites and patterns, provides an intuitive experience (see Figure 1-3).

Designers often test their levels multiple times during the design process. The Edit/Play button in the upper-left corner of the toolbox allows you to quickly switch between editing and playing, enabling you to revise and expand on levels.

You can save or publish a game with the click of a button. As long as you've beaten all the levels you've created, you can publish the game immediately to be played by others. (See Chapter 5 for details on designing and publishing a game.)

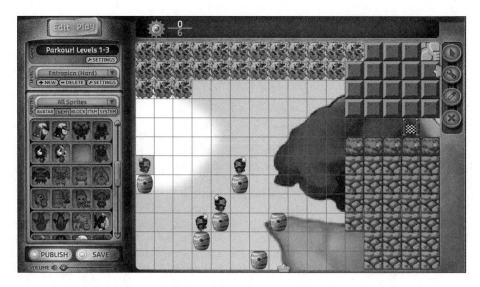

Figure 1-3: Gamestar Mechanic's design interface, the toolbox, is easy to use.

The interface for designing, testing, and publishing games not only requires no knowledge of programming or marketing but also eliminates the tedious bits, allowing you to focus on the design and how the elements of your game system come together. In this way, Gamestar Mechanic provides a useful training ground for future game designers.

Reviewing games

You primarily communicate with other users by way of reviews and comments. Every game page has a list of reviews and comments from other users saying how they felt about the game. (The lower-right corner of Figure 1-4 shows the fields you fill out to submit a review.) The Mechanic Rank system rewards users for playing, designing, and following the Quest, but it also rewards good reviews and *digital citizenship,* the process of being polite and well-adjusted in your interactions with the online community.

Reviews and comments are updated as players try out the game and submit their feedback, with the most recent comments appearing at the top. The more reviews a game accumulates, the more precise the average rating becomes. This safe, friendly system provides a way for users to indirectly discuss game design. (See Chapter 7 for more on reviewing games.)

Figure 1-4: When you're done playing a game, you can review it to tell the designer what you thought of it.

The time commitments of Gamestar Mechanic

In short, Gamestar Mechanic has no time commitments. While working on a game, you can save it as a draft and easily return to it later. You can stop using the site for months and then go back whenever you have a new idea. Even if you're out of ideas or motivation, you can still visit the site and play some games for inspiration. Designing games in Gamestar Mechanic is similar to riding a bike: Even after a long break, you can jump right back in.

Remember: Don't use the site to the point that it interferes with your work. Limit your time, and use Gamestar Mechanic as a reward for completing other work. You can even use Gamestar Mechanic as a supplement to a job or class, by designing games based on the subject you have to work on. Of all the time-consuming activities available, Gamestar Mechanic is a constructive choice.

Teaching and Learning via Gamestar Mechanic

Gamestar Mechanic is built around the idea that designing a video game can be a positive and constructive learning experience. Thus, the program is useful for not only budding designers but also teachers and the parents of young users.

Developing skills through game design

Gamestar Mechanic is an effective way to learn game design, allowing you to build games right away and learn from both professionals and other users. You discover how to build balanced and detailed games, and capture the elusive element of fun in an activity. Moreover, the field of game design contributes to development in other areas, such as science and processes, programming, creative composure, art, and critical analysis.

As Gamestar Mechanic shows, game design teaches the four major components shown in the inner ring of Figure 1-5, which lead to mastery of the subjects shown in the outer ring.

Courtesy of E-Line Media

Figure 1-5: The positive effects of game design.

The following list describes some of the skills that you can develop by designing games:

> ✔ **Critical thinking:** Critical thinking is the process of breaking down and analyzing something (such as text, an argument, or a game) and understanding it at a deep level. Making a game that's fun to play isn't easy, and you can discover a lot of critical-thinking principles while trying to complete your game. Because no formula exists for creating

and measuring fun, you must critically analyze your game to determine what's working and what isn't. Chapter 11 details how you can evaluate and improve your game.

- **Systems thinking:** Systems thinking is the thought process that deals with *systems* — objects composed of several interlocking functions, such as environments or computer programs. Games are composed of challenges that players must solve in order to win; each of these challenges is a system in itself.

  A game is an interesting type of system: Its components are tuned to challenge users and reward them for their input, creating an engaging, intriguing, and enjoyable experience. To make a game fun, you (the designer) must therefore understand how to build robust and interesting systems. You can learn this skill through practice with the website and game design in general, as well as the Quest and this book. Video games are excellent examples of applied systems, and the process of creating such systems is a vital skill in process-oriented careers.

- **Media literacy:** As a game designer, you have to keep up with the media in order to make your games successful. In Gamestar Mechanic, this *media* is represented by the huge community of players and reviewers roaming the website. Game Alley, where you publish your games for other users to play and review, is a training ground for *media literacy*. Media literacy refers to understanding the particular parameters, constraints, challenges, and components of various media (for example, film, music, art, literature, and in this case, games) and how you can use and relate to them.

  Game Alley provides a preparatory environment for the many careers involving digital citizenship. Lots of jobs require people to communicate online or use social media programs, whether to collaborate with coworkers or reach an audience, so Gamestar Mechanic is a great resource for getting started in a safe environment.

- **Creative skills:** Being able to apply creativity to practical goals is a helpful skill throughout life. For a game to be truly successful, it must be innovative in some way. Designing video games is an extremely creative process, with many ways to succeed and many ways to learn from failure.

Gamestar Mechanic can be used as a supplemental resource to other subjects of learning. For example, the annual STEM Video Game Challenge (www.stemchallenge.org) supports Gamestar Mechanic, giving you the challenge of creating a game that reflects an academic subject in a fun and engaging way. (See Chapter 15 for more on contests and challenges.)

Designing games can give you a great sense of pride and self-accomplishment. As a designer, you can produce lots of creative content quickly, making a big impact in a short time. Whether you're creating a level, reading a positive review, or beating a difficult game, Gamestar Mechanic excels at making you (rightfully) feel good about yourself.

Examining the role of teachers

Because students don't always have the drive to teach themselves, Gamestar Mechanic offers the Teacher system. Teachers can lead classes ranging from small groups to school-wide activities.

When a class is created, the teacher can

- ✔ View the statistics and progression of students.
- ✔ Customize and assign projects for students.
- ✔ Leave feedback on students' games and projects.

Teachers may have as many or as few class meetings as they want, online or offline, but always provide hands-on work for students, enabling classes to provide a combination of fun and education.

 Gamestar Mechanic offers extensive resources for active teaching and lesson plans at https://gamestarmechanic.com/teachers. For more on how teachers can create classes and projects, see Chapter 16.

2

Getting Up and Running

In This Chapter

▶ Setting up an account

▶ Finding your way around the site

▶ Exploring the lobby and the Workshop

▶ Getting started with the Quest

▶ Finding games to play in Game Alley

▶ Producing a mechanic bio

*C*reating an account on Gamestar Mechanic is easy — and completely free — so you can try out the program to see whether it's right for you. This chapter explains how to create an account, navigate the main areas of the site, and begin your journey as a mechanic. You can start with the Quest, the Workshop, or Game Alley, each of which has its own, introductory advantages. This chapter tells you how and why to get started on each one.

Users on the website are often referred to as *mechanics,* whether they are acting as designers, players, or reviewers.

Creating an Account

After taking a few simple actions, you'll be ready to design some games. First, you need to create an account by following these steps:

1. **In your favorite browser, go to the Gamestar Mechanic home page at** www.gamestarmechanic.com.

2. **Click the orange Get Started button on the right side of the screen.**

   As long as you aren't logged in as someone else, clicking this button takes you to the Step 1 page for becoming a mechanic, as shown in Figure 2-1.

3. **In the Username text box, enter the name that you want to appear on your games, reviews, and comments.**

   It can be a simple name, such as Isometrus, or a more technical name, such as GamingMasterJC109.

GAMESTAR MECHANIC   PARENTS HELP

Get started with Gamestar Mechanic!

Step 1: Create your new account

Already have an account? Click here to log in!

Username: [   ]

Password: [   ]

Confirm Password: [   ]

Birthday: Month ▾   Day ▾   Year ▾   ?

☑ I have read and agree to the Gamestar Mechanic Terms of Service.

Register!

Figure 2-1: Fill out these fields to create an account.

Make sure your username properly reflects yourself. Also try to avoid egocentric names such as Best_Designer_In_World_999.

4. In the Password text box, enter your preferred password.

Create a strong password. Try using numbers and other non-letter symbols that are difficult to guess. Also you might choose words and abbreviations that are meaningful only to you so that you can remember your password easily. Most importantly, never give your password to anyone, including people claiming to be Gamestar Mechanic administrators (the real administrators will never ask for your password).

5. Confirm your password by entering it again in the Confirm Password text box.

This step checks for typos.

6. Select your birthdate from the Month, Day, and Year drop-down lists.

Because the program is intended for all ages, certain age-restricted features that are supported by the site have to know the user's exact age.

7. Scroll down to the text that reads I have read and agree to the Gamestar Mechanic Terms of Service **and click the Gamestar Mechanic Terms of Service link. When you're finished reading this document, return to the previous page.**

This online document outlines the rules of the website.

8. Select the check box to confirm that you have read, and agree to, this document.

9. Click the large orange Register button.

10. **Follow the rest of the instructions.**

    You're asked some multiple-choice questions about topics such as your favorite animal, school subject, and color. The site asks you these questions twice, to confirm that you remember them, and again if you want to recover your password. Write down and save your answers in case your preferences change.

    After you've confirmed your answers, you see the Get Started page, which offers several ways for you to start your Gamestar Mechanic journey:

    - Start your free adventure with the Addison Joins the League quest.

    - Buy a premium account ($19.95 at the time of this writing) that includes lifetime access to Addison's Complete Quest, including Addison Joins the Rogue and Dungeon of the Rogue. (If you want to find out more about the premium account options, flip ahead to Chapter 14.)

    - Enroll in an online learning course ($249 at the time of this writing), where you learn how to design games from professional designers.

11. **For now, you can start with the free version. Click the orange Get Started button to start poking around.**

When you first create your account, you are automatically logged in. If you want to log in to the site in the future, go to the home page (www.gamestarmechanic.com) and click the orange Log In button, which appears under the larger Get Started button. The login page opens, where you enter your username and password in the appropriate text boxes and click the Play Now button to access the site.

If you're logging in from your own computer (rather than a shared computer), or if you visit the Gamestar Mechanic website often, select the Remember My User Name check box. This action automatically fills in your username when you log in, enabling you to more quickly enter the site.

If you're inactive for too long (about an hour), then your session will expire. If you try to load a new page or level, Gamestar Mechanic will prompt you to log in again. Don't worry about losing your progress; if you were in the middle of playing or designing, the login screen appears on the game screen, and you can return as soon as you enter your username and password.

Navigating the Website

After you've created an account, as described in preceding section, you can access the Gamestar Mechanic website. At the top of every Gamestar Mechanic web page (except for the home page and the pages at http://gamestarmechanic.com/teachers), you see the two toolbars shown in Figure 2-2. These toolbars let you navigate the major sections of the website.

Header toolbar

Footer toolbar

Figure 2-2: Navigate Gamestar Mechanic with ease using the toolbars.

Exploring the header toolbar

Here's a description of the different buttons on the header toolbar and where they take you:

- ✔ **Gamestar Mechanic:** Takes you to the lobby or, if you aren't logged in, to the home page. (I describe the lobby later in this chapter.)

- ✔ **Quest:** Takes you to the Quest, where you can play games that nurture your design ability. You must complete the first free quest before you can publish your games. By completing missions in each quest, you unlock new sprites to use in your games. Quests can be replayed at any time, but if it's your first time playing, you have to complete most of the content in order. (For more on quests, see the later section "Starting Off on the Quest," as well as Chapter 4.)

✓ **Workshop:** Leads you to the Workshop, where you can see your achievements, games, and challenges, as described in the "Exploring the Workshop" section, later in this chapter. You can personalize this page, because it contains your Mechanic Bio, Showcase Game, and Favorite Games. The Workshop is also the gateway to the toolbox, where you design your own games, as explained in Chapter 5.

✓ **Game Alley:** Takes you to Game Alley, where you play and review other people's games. This is the Gamestar Mechanic arcade, which continually updates as you or others add games to it, as described in the section "Finding Games to Play in Game Alley," later in this chapter.

✓ **Store:** Directs you to the Gamestar Mechanic store. You may not want to visit this page unless you have some experience with the site and you're relatively sure that you want to spend money on it. The store includes all the extra content you can buy, as discussed in Chapter 14.

✓ **Log Out:** Closes your current session on Gamestar Mechanic and returns you to the Log In page. This button is useful if you're sharing a computer with another Gamestar Mechanic user. By logging out when you're done playing or designing, the other user will have to log in with his information to start a new session — and you can both be sure you're working in the right account.

✓ **Parents:** Provides a wealth of information for the parents of Gamestar Mechanic users, including how the program is educational and why it's safe.

✓ **Help:** Opens the Help page, where you can try to solve any problems you might have. The text at the top of the page contains a link to the Frequently Asked Questions (FAQ) document, which you should look at first. If you can't find the answer to your problem, or it's too big for you to solve on your own, clearly state the issue in the large Problem text box and click the orange Submit Report button.

Examining the footer toolbar

In addition to the header toolbar, there is a toolbar at the bottom of each page (refer to Figure 2-2). This toolbar contains additional links to areas of the site, as described in the following list:

✓ **Manage Account:** Lets you control the features of your account. Clicking this button takes you to the Manage Your Account page where you can modify your account in a variety of ways, delete your account, change how messages are sent to you, and link to the store. The Edit My Account Settings button on this page reveals a number of features, as explained in the next section.

✔ **FAQ:** Takes you to Gamestar Mechanic's Frequently Asked Questions. Here, you see a number of questions about the site (preceded by *Q:*), followed by the answers (preceded by *A:*). Click the buttons labeled FAQ Topics, or click the Previous and Next buttons at the end of the FAQ list, to see questions about different topics. This section helps you solve any problems you might have by explaining issues that users have commonly experienced.

✔ **Parents:** Shows information for parents about the learning value and safety of the site.

✔ **Teachers:** Directs you to the Teachers' section, which looks substantially different from the rest of the site. This section is for teachers who want to teach by way of Gamestar Mechanic, containing information, sample games, and a store for educational resources. You may return to the main site via the buttons in the upper-right corner. (I cover the Teachers' section in detail in Chapter 16.)

✔ **Credits:** Lists the people who designed the Gamestar Mechanic site and software.

✔ **Privacy Policy, Terms of Service, and Rules of Conduct:** Lead you to documents about etiquette and the proper use of the Gamestar Mechanic program. It's a good idea to read these documents yourself and pass them on to an adult if you're under 18.

Editing Your Account Settings

If you click the Manage Account link in the footer toolbar (as mentioned in the preceding section), the Manage Your Account page appears. Next, click the Edit My Account Settings link to go to the Manage Account/Settings page (http://gamestarmechanic.com/account/settings), where you can modify your account in a variety of different ways.

The options provided are as follows:

✔ **Account Information:** This section shows your username and the e-mail address associated with it. To change your e-mail address, type it in both text boxes and click the Save button.

✔ **Change Password:** This section allows you to change the password you use to enter the site. To do so, enter your current password in the top text box, and the new one you want in the other two text boxes. Then click the Save button.

✔ **Social Media and Networks:** This section contains check boxes representing various forms of social media. When a check box for a social network is activated, the Share function allows you to share games over that network. You may see check boxes corresponding to Facebook, Twitter, Edmodo, and others, depending on your e-mail's associations.

- ✔ **User Generated Content:** This option allows you to decide whether you want to use custom content on the site. At the time of this writing, this option doesn't seem to have an effect.

- ✔ **Mozilla Persona Integration:** In this section, you can enter your Mozilla Persona Email to link it to your Gamestar Mechanic account, enabling you to easily share your World Badges (see Chapter 8).

- ✔ **Security Code:** This section contains the Change Security Code Answers button. Clicking this button allows you to retake the survey you completed when you created your account. If your favorite subject, animal, color, or activity changes, you should change your Security Code accordingly.

Getting to Know the Main Page: The Lobby

The first screen you see after you log in to your account is the *lobby,* which is the hub for Gamestar Mechanic users (see Figure 2-3).

News feed

Message box   Unread message

Figure 2-3: The lobby screen you see when you log in to the site.

On the right side of the screen, you'll notice three large buttons: Quest, Workshop, and Game Alley. Immediately below each button, you can see the following notifications:

- ✔ The Quest button tells you the percentage of missions you've completed.

- ✔ The Workshop button displays the number of sprites you have (or unread messages, if you have any).

- ✔ The Game Alley button shows how many games have been published in the past week.

There are two additional areas on the left side of the lobby: the news feed and the message box, which I describe next.

Understanding the news feed

The upper-left corner of the lobby contains the news feed, which provides news about the Gamestar Mechanic community (refer to Figure 2-3). Each entry includes an icon and a couple lines of text.

Here's how the news feed works:

- ✔ **It connects you with the dynamics of the website.** The news feed tells you all about what's going on with you as well as the mechanics you're following. (I explain how to follow other mechanics in Chapter 9.) If the icon for a post is to the right of the text, the post is about something you've done recently. If the icon is on the left, someone whom you're following has done something interesting.

- ✔ **It's interactive.** All users, news articles, and games mentioned in the feed are highlighted in blue, allowing you to click them to view the relevant pages.

- ✔ **It's quick and easy to use.** You don't need to regularly watch and respond to the news feed — it's simply there. The news feed provides a constant stream of helpful information, so you can glance at it whenever you pass through the lobby.

You can recognize the content of each post at a glance by looking at the icons and the keywords highlighted in blue. The following list shows you what the icons in the news feed correspond to:

- ✔ **News:** Refers to *sticky posts,* the news items occasionally posted by the Gamestar Mechanic administrators. Shown over a yellow background, a sticky post adheres to the top of the news feed, becoming the center of attention until the next important news post replaces it.

✔ **Publication:** Indicates that you — or someone you're following — has published a new game. Click the name of the game to play it.

 ✔ **Edit:** Signifies that a game has been edited and republished, which means that it has been updated, improved, expanded, or otherwise changed in some way.

 ✔ **Review:** Signals that either you reviewed a game or someone you're following reviewed one of your games.

 ✔ **Comment:** Similar to the icon in the preceding bullet, refers to a comment from you or someone you're following.

 ✔ **Following:** Suggests that either you're following someone new or someone you're already following has decided to follow you.

 ✔ **Badge:** Refers to an achievement obtained by you or someone you're following. The badge obtained through the achievement is used as the icon.

 ✔ **Recommendation:** Implies that someone you're following has recommended a game that you might like. This icon also appears whenever you recommend a game to someone.

 Whenever you log in to the site, the lobby updates you on activities on the website.

Reading the message box

The lower-left corner of the lobby contains a message box, which lists all the messages you've received (refer to Figure 2-3). These messages can include notifications of new reviews and comments, news about the site, and other notes, depending on your account settings. Unread messages appear in bold text with a yellow background. Simply click on a message to read it, and then if you want to delete the open message, click the Delete Message button.

The message box can display only six messages at a time, so you'll need to delete messages to see the others. Here's how to delete messages from the message box:

✔ **To delete a single message from the message box,** click the check box to the left of the message and click the Delete Selected button.

✔ **To delete all the messages shown in the message box,** click the check box in the upper-left corner of the message box and then click the Delete Selected button.

 Check your message box for notifications about new reviews and comments so that you don't have to check each of your games individually. The message box is especially useful for staying informed about feedback on your games.

Any message titled New Review or New Comment contains blue text that links to your game so that you can read feedback. If you have several messages titled New Review or New Comment regarding your various games, and your computer is fast enough, you can open each link in a new browser tab and read the reviews quickly. To open a link in a new tab, right-click the link and select the option to open it in a new tab, or middle-click the link. (Press down on the scroll wheel, if your mouse allows it.)

Starting Off on the Quest

After you have set up your account on Gamestar Mechanic and are familiar with the layout of the site, you're ready to start playing games. If this is your first time playing a Gamestar Mechanic game, the Quest is a good place to start. Following a smooth difficulty curve, quest missions are helpful for gaining practice with the controls and the general technique of playing Gamestar Mechanic games. And as you work your way through its missions, you can see how the play and design processes work.

These games, which are set to a recurring storyline, introduce you to the elements of game design. By completing these quests, you unlock new sprites and options for designing games.

The introductory free quest, Addison Joins the League, is a perfect tutorial for the elements of play and design, as well as a useful supplement to this book. After you've set up your account, as described earlier in this chapter, follow these steps to start this quest:

1. **Go to the Quest page.**

   To get to this area, click the Quest box on the lobby page, or the Quest button at the top of any page.

   The first time you load the Quest, you see the introduction scene, shown in Figure 2-4. This type of scene is in the form of an animated graphic novel, so you can look through the scene at your own pace.

2. **Read the introduction. Advance to the next page by clicking the screen or using the buttons in the lower-left corner.**

   The Quest page may take longer to load than other pages because all its content has to be loaded into a Flash player, like individual games on the site.

   You can always view the introduction again if you want.

Figure 2-4: The quest begins.

3. **When you see the screen asking whether you want to play as the Male Addison or Female Addison, make your selection and then click Continue.**

4. **Proceed through the rest of the introduction.**

   When you're finished, you see the Episode 1: Journey to Factory 7 page, listing all the story missions.

You're now ready to start your missions. See Chapter 4 for all the details about completing quest missions — and a pacing guide.

 Don't try to rush through the Quest — it's there to introduce you to the techniques of playing and designing. Explore the levels, analyze the sprites, and build the best games you can within the templates. In this way, you enter the Workshop and Game Alley well-experienced.

Exploring the Workshop

One of the site's more complex pages, the *Workshop* displays a large amount of information about you and your games, as shown in Figure 2-5. You can build your own games from this page as well.

Figure 2-5: The top of the Workshop, displaying general information about you as a designer.

The Workshop is also vital to teachers, who manage their classes on this page. Teachers can track students' progress and manage class projects alongside their normal challenges. You can find more information about the Teachers' system in Chapter 16.

The content of the Workshop is split into a number of parts, as described in the following sections.

The Build a New Game button

The greatest teacher of game design is your own imagination — if you want to design to the best of your ability, you have to practice. To start designing a game, click the Build a New Game button at the top right of the Workshop (refer to Figure 2-5), which opens the toolbox. From here, you use the toolbox to design your game, as described in detail in Chapter 5. Also, check out Part IV, which goes deeper into the techniques of game design.

As you design and create games, keep the following tips in mind:

✔ **Make draft games.** Design games without worrying about publishing them. Try out ideas and concepts. As long as you keep your imagination active, designing games is similar to riding a bike: After you gain some practice and understanding, you never forget it.

✓ **Examine the Template Games.** The Template games in your workshop are useful because they're simple, editable, and useful to analyze. The Pinwheel and Dragons templates use only four sprites, which happens to be your starting set.

Mechanic profile

The *mechanic profile* is basic information about you as a user. The following list describes the sections you can find on your profile, from top to bottom:

✓ **Username:** Your username is displayed at the top of the page, along with some information about your progress on the site.

✓ **Rank:** Next to your username, you can find your rank on the site. (You can find more information about ranks in Chapter 8.)

✓ **Following/Followed By:** Below your rank and next to your username is a line of blue text containing two numbers. The first number represents how many other mechanics you're *following,* a feature explained in Chapter 9. The second number shows how many mechanics are following you. You can click these numbers to see your followers as well as the mechanics you're following. Click the red X next to any user you're following to stop following them.

✓ **Gamestar Badges:** Displays the six most recent badges you've obtained. Click the View All Badges button to see the rest, including those you haven't yet obtained. (Badges are discussed in detail in Chapter 8.)

✓ **World Badges:** Monitors each world badge and your progress in completing it. Incomplete badges have a button that lets you continue your progression of them. (World badges are described in Chapter 8.)

✓ **Mechanic Bio:** Contains personal information that you write about yourself (as described later in the chapter). It includes two small chunks of text describing who you are and specifying which games you like.

✓ **Showcase Game:** You can set one of your published games as a showcase game, as described in Chapter 5. Other users who visit your workshop see this game immediately, along with its rating and popularity.

✓ **Classes:** This section (shown in Figure 2-6) appears if you're in an official Gamestar Mechanic class, either as a student or teacher. Only you can see this section in your workshop. The Classes section contains links that allow you to view or control aspects of your class. (I describe classes in detail in Chapter 16.)

Figure 2-6: The middle part of the Workshop, showing your classes and games.

Exploring the rest of the Workshop

The following sections describe the remaining sections of the Workshop.

My Draft Games

The My Draft Games section (refer to Figure 2-6) contains all the games you have saved but not published. Each game listed includes two buttons:

- **Edit:** Lets you continue working on the game
- **Delete:** Removes the game

A deleted game is gone forever, whether it's a draft game or a published game. Don't delete a game unless you're absolutely sure you want to.

If you have more than five draft games, these additional buttons appear in the upper-right corner:

- **Previous, Next:** Scroll through your games.
- **See All:** Display a special page with your draft games displayed on a grid.

Alternatively, you can click the orange Make a New Game button in the My Draft Games section to begin work on a new game.

Pending Games

This section appears in your workshop only if you've published a game that hasn't yet been added to Game Alley. Games in the Pending Games section are ready to be published, but they contain custom backgrounds that haven't yet been approved by the website moderators. If you create a new, custom background for your game, as described in Chapter 14, your game may remain in this section for a few days before it's published.

My Published Games

The My Published Games section (refer to Figure 2-6) displays your six most recent games. Each game contains a rating and these four buttons:

- ✔ **Edit Game:** Make changes.
- ✔ **Share Game:** Open a menu for publicizing your game.
- ✔ **View Stats:** See your level-by-level statistics.
- ✔ **Delete Game:** Remove the game.

You (and anyone viewing your workshop) can see all of your published games by clicking the buttons in the upper-right corner of this section. (I give you more information about publishing games in Chapter 5.)

Challenges & Contests

The Challenges & Contests section, shown in Figure 2-7, contains a number of challenges, either for earning more sprites or winning national acclaim. You can click them for more information. Use the buttons in the upper-right corner of the section to scroll through them. (I give you more information about contests and challenges in Chapters 8 and 15.)

Projects

The Projects section, which appears only if you're leading or attending a class, contains challenges just as in the Challenges & Contests section, but they're personalized and sometimes required by your instructor (unless you're an instructor yourself). You may click them for more information.

Submitted Games

The Submitted Games section lists all the games you have submitted for contests or special quest missions. You cannot edit these games, but you can click the Get a Copy button to edit and publish a copy of the game. The challenge or quest corresponding to each game is printed under the title of your game, and can be clicked to view the page describing the challenge.

Figure 2-7: Additional sections of the Workshop.

Template Games

Games in the Template Games section can be copied into your workshop, containing pre-created arrangements that you can edit any way you like. At the time of this writing, if you build a game from a template, you cannot publish it to Game Alley.

My Favorite Games

The My Favorite Games section shows games you have marked as favorites. Other users can see and link to your favorite games, and you can scroll through them with the buttons in the upper-right corner of the section.

Finding Games to Play in Game Alley

You can play games in both the Quest and Game Alley. Because the Quest has only a limited selection, most users spend their time searching for games in Game Alley. But keep in mind that the Quest contains very good games that are worth replaying every once in a while.

After you find a game you want to play, be sure to check out Chapter 3, which explains how to control your avatar, navigate a level, and interpret the goals and rules of the game.

Exploring Game Alley

Game Alley is where all user-created games end up, as shown in Figure 2-8. It begins with a few options under the Game Alley Guide section. The features provided are as follows:

- **Left sidebar:** The sidebar is where you can search for games. You can use the Search text box to search for specific games or users. Or you can click one of the buttons for accessing other sections of Game Alley, as well as explore channels containing interesting example games.

- **Gamestar Mechanic Store:** This box provides news regarding the Gamestar Mechanic Store.

- **Gamestar News:** Here you can see news posts uploaded by the Gamestar team. The See All News button takes you to a page where you can browse all posts.

Figure 2-8: Surfing Game Alley.

Below the Game Alley Guide section, you find various sections containing lists of games. To ensure that everyone's games can be noticed and played, Game Alley continually updates these sections to show you a different group of games each time.

Here's a rundown of the various sections:

- **Featured Games:** Games selected by the Gamestar team. These games stay on the front page until a new set of featured games is selected and used. Usually consisting of six to eight games, the Featured Games are placed in random order every time the page is loaded so that you see a different set of games each time you visit.

- **Challenge Winners:** For people who have won national contests on the Gamestar Mechanic platform. This section rarely changes, but it contains especially noteworthy games.

- **Fresh Games:** For games that have been available for a while but have received only a few plays. It encourages users to play games that may have been missed by the community.

- **Up and Coming Games:** Games that are going strong in the community, receiving good reviews within a short time after being released. Many interesting games are posted there every day.

- **Games from Online Learning Program Students:** A special section for games that were created in the Online Learning Program, which I discuss in Chapter 16.

- **Classic Games:** For games that were published a long time ago (months or even years) and were well received. This section reintroduces games and allows players to discover old gems, or rediscover familiar ones.

- **New Games:** Freshly published, sometimes seconds before you found them. Whenever a game is first published, it makes the top of the New Games section.

- **Top Rated Games:** A selection of highly acclaimed games. Coming from a number of different periods, these games are often recorded as having perfect 5-star ratings, a feat that requires an average rating of at least 4¾ stars.

- **Class-Specific Games:** If you join a class, as described in Chapter 16, this section appears in your Game Alley. It works similarly to the New Games section, showing the latest games created by users in the same class. The name of the section is the same as the name of your class. Similarly, one of these sections appears in your Game Alley if you complete the Mentor Badge. (See Chapter 8 for more on badges.)

You can scroll through all the games in a section of Game Alley by using the Previous and Next buttons.

Every game on this page displays a rating given by other users, and you can click the image to play the game. Move the mouse over a game title to display the following information:

- ✔ The number of people who have played the game
- ✔ The number of times the game has been played
- ✔ The number of reviews the game has received
- ✔ How long ago the game was published

I explain these statistics in more detail in the "Interpreting a game's rating and stats" section, later in this chapter.

Searching for games

You can search for games that aren't listed on the main Game Alley page. Here are a few ways you can find and play specific games or groups of games:

- ✔ **Use the Search box.** In the upper-left corner of Game Alley is a Search text box (refer to Figure 2-8). To search for a specific game, enter the title or part of the title and click the Find It button. If you want to find a particular user, first click the Users radio button above the search box and then type the name of the user you want to find. The results show everyone whose name or mechanic bio contains the search term.

    If the Find It button is unresponsive, reload the page.

- ✔ **Click one of the Categories buttons.** You can also find five white Categories buttons in the left sidebar that link to subsections of Game Alley. If you're looking for practice in Game Alley, always check the Featured and Top Rated categories, though all games are useful for mastering basic gameplay. *Featured* games are selected by the administrators as examples of good experiences, and *Top Rated* games are very popular among other users.

You can also find games directly from game pages. If a user publishes a game you like, try seeing what else that person has worked on. When you're playing a game, a random selection of five other games by the same user is displayed in the lower-right corner for you to try (see Figure 2-9). Alternatively, click the creator's username (on the right side of the screen, under the title of the game or in the box titled The Designer) to see that person's workshop. Then you can see the user's Showcase game, a list of the user's games, and a number of the user's favorite games that the user thinks you might enjoy.

Other games by this designer

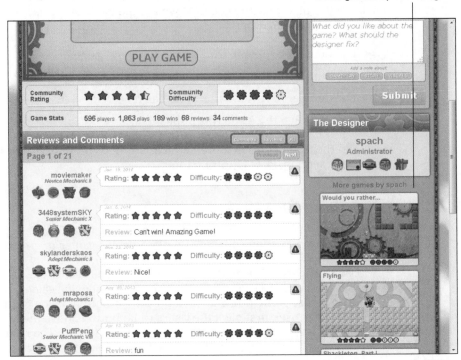

Figure 2-9: Find additional games by the designer in the lower-right corner of a game page.

If you find a game you like, add it to your Favorites list. (Click the heart-shaped button in the upper-right corner of the page for the game.) The game is stored in your workshop so that you can play it again later — and recommend it to others who view your workshop.

Interpreting a game's rating and stats

To find a fun game with a difficulty level that's right for you, examine the game's rating and statistics, as shown in Figure 2-10. You generally want to look for games with a large number of stars — you can also check the number of wins to see if the game is particularly easy or hard.

If you're a beginner, try finding games with almost as many wins as plays. You can also look for games with a difficulty rating of 3 or less, though this rating is sometimes misleading.

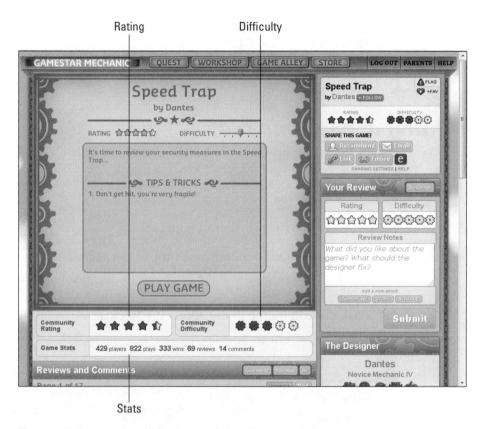

Figure 2-10: A game page displaying a rating and some statistics.

The game in Figure 2-10 has been played 822 times by 429 users, and 333 of those plays ended in victory. The game received 69 reviews averaging four and a half stars, and was generally referred to as a game of medium difficulty. Here are some ways you can interpret this game's statistics to determine whether it's a good challenge for you:

- **It's a well-received game.** Four and a half stars is a good rating, often indicating clever gameplay and well-balanced components. This game has 69 reviews, which is more than enough to provide a trustworthy verdict. Games with at least a few reviews generally produce meaningful star ratings.

- **It's a moderately difficult game.** Because this game had 822 plays and 333 wins, every attempt at playing it had about a 40 percent chance of being successful. Also, because the game has a difficulty rating of 3 gears out of 5, it's probably a moderate challenge: You may win, or you may not. Whether or not you're successful at playing a particular game, you can always learn from the experience.

> ✔ **Most players tried the game more than once.** A total of 429 players attempted the game 822 times, so the average player made about 2 attempts at the game. Examining these two numbers is useful for understanding how most players play this game.

Writing a Mechanic Bio

If you're just starting out on the Gamestar Mechanic site, you should compose a mechanic biography, or, officially, a *mechanic bio*. This biography is visible to everyone who views your workshop, so take a little time to describe who you are.

Follow these steps to begin writing your bio:

1. **Click the Workshop button at the top of the page.**

   The Workshop appears. In the Mechanic Profile box, you'll see a section labeled Mechanic Bio.

2. **Click the Edit button under About the Mechanic.**

   The Edit Profile page appears, as shown in Figure 2-11.

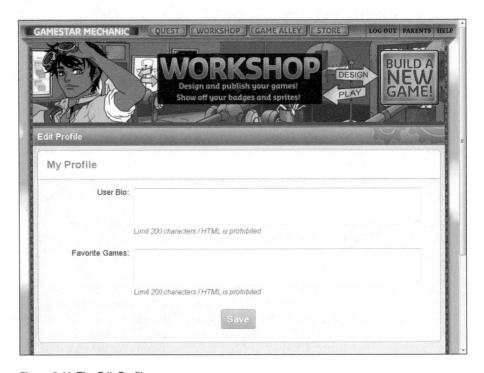

Figure 2-11: The Edit Profile page.

3. Type your user bio and favorite games in the appropriate text boxes.

Because your bio is your face online, be sure to make it as interesting as possible. Here are a few things to consider:

- *You're briefly defining yourself.* Both fields must be, at most, 200 characters — the length of this bullet point. This is your face online; write something that gives users a good idea of who you are.

- *You're among game designers.* Saying that you're interested in game design isn't exactly interesting here. Be more specific, or describe your other interests.

- *You're in a safe environment.* Gamestar Mechanic is for all ages — express your interests freely, but also respect the expressions of others.

- *You may find others with similar interests.* The Favorite Earth Games section of your Mechanic Bio is a good way to connect with people who have similar interests in gaming.

- *The style of your writing translates to that of your character.* Many people like to post enthusiastic biographies with lots of exclamation points, or apathetic biographies consisting of single unpunctuated words. Your writing style can say a lot about whether you're cheerful, blunt, or formal, for example. Define yourself the way *you* want to be defined. Avoid poor grammar, which can sabotage your portrait.

4. Click the Save button.

You can always edit your bio later if you want to make changes.

Part II
Playing and Designing Games

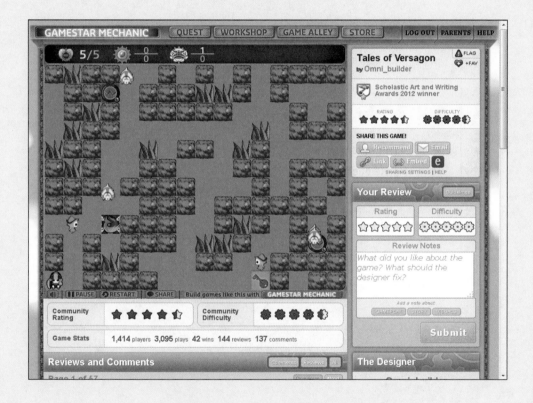

Find out how to design levels from scratch in Gamestar Mechanic at www.dummies.com/extras/gamestarmechanic.

In this part . . .

- ✔ Find games to play in Game Alley.
- ✔ Complete quest missions.
- ✔ Understand what sprites are.
- ✔ Explore the five elements of game design.
- ✔ Examine the tools for designing your own games.
- ✔ Create your first game in the Workshop.

3

The Basics of Playing a Game

▶ Controlling your avatar

▶ Understanding player techniques

▶ Taking a look at goals and rules

*T*o design good games, and to understand how a Gamestar Mechanic game is composed, you must first play some games. Whether completing the Quest or surfing Game Alley, playing games is a great way to understand what is fun and what is not, as well as what the Gamestar Mechanic platform is capable of. This chapter shows you how to play the two types of games on the site — top-down and platformer — and how to operate various controls.

Understanding How to Control Your Avatar

Every game contains exactly one *avatar,* a little sprite that forms the connection between your commands and the gaming world. You use the game controls to make the avatar move around and perform various actions. If you aren't sure which sprite is the avatar, don't worry: At the beginning of the level, or after you pause and unpause the game, a spinning red arrow points out the avatar for a few seconds, as shown in Figure 3-1.

Gamestar Mechanic offers two types of games, each with a different set of controls:

▸ **Top-down:** You're looking at the board from above — the *bird's-eye view* (see Figure 3-1). The principle of gravity doesn't apply, so everything appears flat, and all movable sprites can move up, down, left, or right.

▸ **Platformer:** You're looking at the board from the side, as shown in Figure 3-2. Sprites stand on platforms on which they move left or right or jump into the air.

The following section explains how to use the controls for both types of games.

Spinning red arrow   Goal block

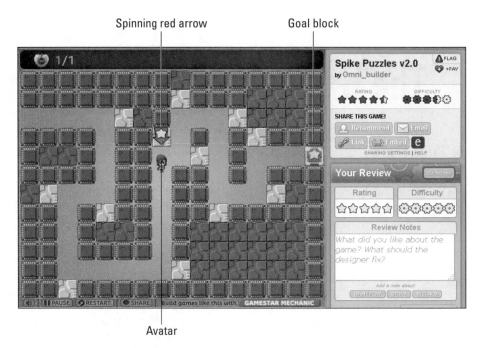

Avatar

Figure 3-1: A top-down game with an avatar and a goal block.

Figure 3-2: A classic platformer game.

Top-down controls

The top-down controls, shown in Figure 3-3, allow for several different configurations, and you can play using any configuration you choose.

Figure 3-3: Top-down controls.

Table 3-1 lists the standard top-down controls. To use them, place the three middle fingers of your left hand (the ring finger, middle finger, and index finger) on the letters A, W, and D — and then place your thumb on the spacebar. This arrangement lets you control the avatar with one hand and manipulate the mouse cursor and other keys with the other hand. The arrow keys on many keyboards can be small and cumbersome to use, so this arrangement doesn't require you to use them.

Table 3-1	Standard Top-Down Controls	
Command	*Key*	*Finger to Use*
Move Up	W	Left hand, middle finger
Move Down	S	Left hand, middle finger
Move Left	A	Left hand, ring finger
Move Right	D	Left hand, index finger
Attack	Spacebar (not shown in Figure 3-3, but it works well). B and C also work.	Left thumb for spacebar; right hand index finger for B; left hand thumb or index finger for C

(continued)

Table 3-1 *(continued)*

Command	Key	Finger to Use
Action	Z (or M)	Left hand, ring finger for Z; right hand, ring finger for M
Inventory	I	Right hand, any finger
Pause	P (or click outside the screen)	Right hand, any finger

Though you sometimes need to move your fingers to different keys, remember the A-W-D-spacebar position for your hand so that your fingers always return there afterward.

Table 3-2 lists an alternative system in which you move by using your right hand and operate the other controls with your left hand. Place the three middle fingers of your right hand on the left-, up-, and right-arrow keys, and then position your left hand so that your index ("pointer") finger is on M and your ring finger is on B. Then you can use the Pause and Inventory buttons more easily — and feel more connected by using both hands at one time.

Table 3-2 Alternative Top-Down Controls

Command	Key	Finger to Use
Move Up	Up arrow	Right hand, middle finger
Move Down	Down arrow	Right hand, middle finger
Move Left	Left arrow	Right hand, index finger
Move Right	Right arrow	Right hand, ring finger
Attack	B (or C)	Left hand, any finger
Action	M (or Z)	Left hand, any finger
Inventory	I	Left hand, any finger
Pause	P	Left hand, any finger

Platformer controls

Though the platformer controls (shown in Figure 3-4) are similar to the top-down controls, they work on a different perspective. Instead of moving up or down, the platformer controls allow you to jump. The standard platformer controls use the same keys as the standard controls for a top-down game, as described in Table 3-3.

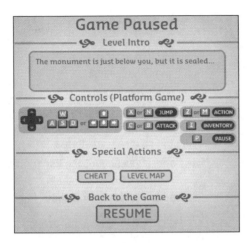

Figure 3-4: Platformer controls.

Table 3-3		Standard Platformer Controls
Command	*Key*	*Finger to Use*
Move Left	A	Left hand, ring finger
Move Right	D	Left hand, index finger
Jump	W (or X or N)	Left hand, middle finger (right hand, middle finger for the N key)
Attack	Spacebar (or C or B)	Left thumb (right hand, index finger for the B key)
Action	Z or M	Left hand, ring finger. For the M key, use the right index finger or the right ring finger, depending on the other controls you use.
Inventory	I	Right hand, any finger
Pause	P	Right hand, any finger

Table 3-3 does not list the Move Up and Move Down keys, because they don't do anything in platformer games. The W key for Jump and the spacebar for Attack do not appear in the figure, but they still work.

Similarly, the alternative platformer controls use the same positions as the alternative top-down controls, using both hands instead of one, as described in Table 3-4.

Table 3-4		Alternative Platformer Controls
Command	*Key*	*Finger to Use*
Move Left	Left arrow	Right hand, index finger
Move Right	Right arrow	Right hand, ring finger
Jump	Up arrow (or X or N)	Right hand, middle finger (left hand, middle finger for X or N; use the ring finger if you're using the spacebar to attack)
Attack	Spacebar, C or B	Left hand, index finger (ring finger for B)
Action	Z or M	Left hand, ring finger for Z; index finger for M
Inventory	I	Left hand, any finger
Pause	P	Left hand, any finger

Playing quest missions is a helpful way to become familiar with the controls without having to learn by playing games that are too difficult.

Effectively Navigating a Level

When navigating a game level, you should not only understand the essential controls and components but also have an intuitive sense of the game's "feel." As you gain experience playing games, your movements will become more seamless, and you'll become more adept with the controls. This section introduces some combination commands to make your gameplaying experience feel smoother.

Whether you're playing a top-down game or a platformer game, follow these tips, ranging from basic to advanced, to play more effectively:

✔ **Test combinations of short-term and long-term thinking.** When playing a game, you can think about the level in two ways:

- *Short-term:* Deal with each obstacle and goal as it appears.

- *Long-term:* Consider the whole game, figuring out the route to take to victory.

To beat a difficult level, you may need a combination of short-term and long-term thinking. If you're having trouble, try a different strategy.

✔ **Recognize cues from the environment.** If you're unsure how to solve a level, look for any important messages you may have missed. Examine the system sprites at the beginning of every level, to understand the goals and rules of the game. (I discuss system sprites in "Understanding the Goals and Rules of a Game," later in this chapter.)

Well-balanced games always contain clues to guide you through the level. These clues may not be explicitly stated, but the level should be designed so that you know in general where to head.

✔ **Take advantage of projectile collisions.** An interesting gameplay element in Gamestar Mechanic is that "good" projectiles (fired by your avatar) can collide with "bad" projectiles (fired by enemies). When two opposing projectiles collide, they cancel each other out. You can often use this situation to your advantage, by blocking enemy attacks with your own and overrunning them with a superior fire rate. Most projectiles also sport a small *hitbox,* the area around them that justifies a collision. With careful movement, you can avoid this type of collision and hit enemies tactically.

The following sections offer additional tips for navigating the two types of games.

Navigating a top-down game

Top-down games are relatively easy to understand because the avatar can generally use only one motion at a time (with the exception of blasting). Follow these movement guidelines in top-down games:

✔ **Dodge in straight lines.** Never turn while avoiding danger, if you can help it. Taking straightforward routes gives you quicker passage and easier planning — and a better chance at gaining the upper hand in a fight. Exceptions to this method are the Naviron lancer and Naviron sentry sprites, enemies with spears and shields that require you to make serpentine motions to force them into revealing their blind sides. (See Chapter 6 for more on these sprites.).

✔ **Don't stop to turn.** If you hold down two movement keys simultaneously, your avatar moves in the direction you pressed most recently. If you're moving and you want to change direction, therefore, you can press another direction key and release the first key afterward. This action allows your avatar to stay in motion while you're navigating the levels.

✔ **Cut corners of blocks.** When your avatar runs into the corner of a block, it can shuffle around the corner and continue on its way. This makes the interface much smoother when moving through mazes and tight levels.

Navigating a platformer game

Platformer games are significantly more difficult to master because you need to use your intuition to make their controls work well. Follow these common techniques to navigate a platform level:

- ✔ **Run and jump.** The controls for moving in a platformer game are designed so that you can easily hold down a jump key and a movement key at the same time, to jump onto ledges or avoid obstacles. This type of jump is the most common one you'll use.

- ✔ **Control yourself while airborne.** While your avatar is off the ground, you can still move it left and right however you want. Be sure to control your airborne movement to hit platforms and avoid obstacles. You can also do a hook-jump or boomerang-jump — jump in one direction, and then turn back partway through the jump — to jump onto a platform directly above you or to hit targets off the edge of a platform. Design or play games with a low gravity setting to get a feel for the controls. (See Chapter 5 for more on gravity settings.)

- ✔ **Make small jumps.** Though you can hold down the Jump key to help your avatar jump as high as it can, sometimes it's better to tap the Jump key briefly, to cause your avatar to make a smaller jump. The strength of the avatar's jump is proportional to the length of time you hold down the Jump key, so practice jumping at different heights (though jumping to a precise point is extremely difficult).

Big jumps normally work well, though small jumps allow you to hit the ground faster and avoid potential obstacles above you. Smaller jumps are also useful when you have a blaster; when your avatar's vertical speed decreases, it can fire more shots in a concentrated area.

Understanding the Goals and Rules of a Game

Your objective in every game is to navigate your avatar to complete every goal. Usually, this objective is to navigate your way to the *goal block,* which is a golden, starred block at the end of the level (refer to Figure 3-1).

However, the designer may sometimes put in secondary goals, which make the goal block untouchable until all other goals are completed. These objectives are provided in the Goals & Rules section of the level's intro screen (refer to Figure 3-3), and are represented as icons, or *system sprites,* at the top of the screen during the level (see Figure 3-5). These secondary goals can change the overall structure of the game, so watch out for them.

If a game has secondary goals but no goal block, you win the level as soon as you complete all the secondary goals.

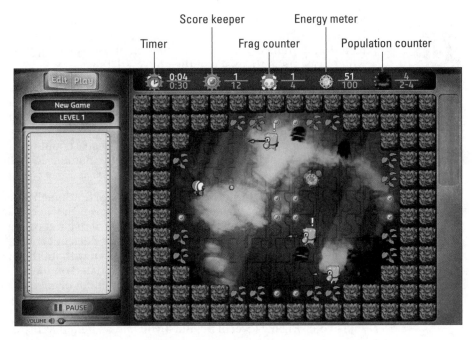

Figure 3-5: Five extra goals are created by system sprites.

Introducing system sprites

System sprites (shown in Figure 3-5) add conditions to the game that players must pay attention to in order to win the level. The six system sprites are described in this list:

- ✔ **Timer:** This sprite has an alarm clock icon. It can have one of these two forms:

  - • *Time limit:* This one shows a white digital clock that's constantly counting down. If the clock reaches 0:00, the level is lost, so complete your objectives quickly!

  - • *Survival timer:* Quite different from the time limit, the survival timer contains a white clock that counts up and a blue stationary clock (as shown in Figure 3-5). You can't win the level until the time on the white clock reaches the time on the blue one. For example, if the timer says 0:00/1:30, you have to survive for 90 seconds before you can win the level.

- ✔ **Score keeper:** This sprite is represented by a yellow and blue coin. It contains a white number representing your score. Your score starts at 0, and you increase it by moving your avatar over items such as coins, apples, or gold nuggets. You complete the objective when the white number matches or exceeds the blue number beneath it. Often, you need to find and collect every point in a level to win, so look for anything obtainable and grab it.

Sometimes, designers do tricky things such as hide points behind blocks to ensure that players go where directed. You know when you've collected something if you see an animation of two spinning yellow rings, which appears in the place of the collected item.

✔ **Frag counter:** Bearing a mechanical skull and crossbones icon, this sprite counts the number of enemy sprites you've destroyed — or, in gamer-speak, the number of *frags* (fragmentations) you've caused. Every time your avatar directly defeats an enemy, the counter increases by one. Damaging destructibles such as glass doesn't count toward your frag score. The objective is complete when the number in white matches or exceeds the number in blue.

✔ **Health meter:** This sprite simply informs you of how much health your avatar has, so it's not included in Figure 3-5. However, you can see this sprite in many games — it has a metallic heart with a red core as its icon. The health meter is the only system sprite that does not add extra goals or rules, because the avatar can lose health even without the health meter. Its primary use is keeping the player updated on the avatar's status. The number in white represents the number of *hit points* the avatar has; this is how much damage your avatar can take before fragging. The number in white turns red if your health is low. The number in blue represents your original level of health. If you find an item that restores health, remember that the white number cannot exceed the number in blue.

If the health meter is missing, your avatar can still lose health and be destroyed. If your avatar is damaged and ends up reduced to a single point of health, you hear an urgent whirring noise instead of the normal damage sound effect.

✔ **Energy meter:** The energy meter is yet another way your avatar can be destroyed. This sprite consists of a continually decreasing number in white above a stationary number in blue. The number in white, which represents the avatar's energy, turns red when your energy is running low and frags your avatar when your energy is fully depleted.

Energy is different from *health* in that it can be set to extremely high values (and cannot be directly depleted by enemies), but its value is reduced every second, so you have to move quickly and eat to survive. You can replenish your energy level with items such as water, bread, batteries, and candy corn (some dinosaur avatars can even eat certain enemies to gain energy). You cannot increase your energy level above the value of the number in blue, however.

✔ **Population counter:** This sprite's icon takes the form of an enemy sprite in the game. The first number (in white) represents how many enemies of the type shown are in the level, and the second number (in blue) specifies how many such enemies you need to win the level. If the second number is 3, the level must contain exactly three enemies matching the sprite shown on the counter; if the second number is a range such as 2–4, there must be between two and four of them. You can have multiple population counters in a game at one time. You may win the game only when all population counters are satisfied at once.

Understanding the system sprites in a game

Look at the level shown in the game in Figure 3-6. Despite being a big level with lots of room to explore, it contains only three system sprites, as well as a goal block in the final dungeon (not shown in the figure).

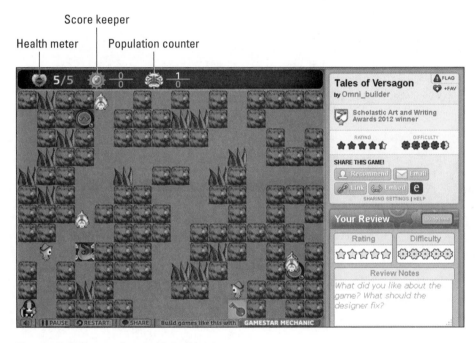

Figure 3-6: This game has multiple objectives.

The use of the system sprites along the top of Figure 3-6 are described in the following list:

- ✔ **Health meter:** This sprite lets you see the level of your health at a glance. In this level, you have to conserve your health, so the meter helps you keep track of it. In the game shown in Figure 3-6, you start the game with 5 hit points. Many users place the health meter close to the left side of the screen; because system sprites are added from left to right, players often keep the closest eye on the leftmost ones.

- ✔ **Score keeper:** This sprite tracks the number of points you've collected. When the bottom number is 0, as shown in the figure, the objective is always complete. In this case, collecting points is therefore an optional objective: You can ignore them, if you want, or accept the personal challenge of collecting as many points as possible.

✔ **Population counter:** This sprite indicates the number of enemies of a certain type in the level. When the bottom number is 0, as shown in the figure, the player's goal is to frag all such enemies in the level. In the figure, the counter shows that the level has one sprite matching the given picture. If you want to unlock the goal, you have to frag this enemy.

4

Completing Quest Missions

In This Chapter

▶ Examining the "story" and how it relates to game design

▶ Taking a look at the three quests

▶ Exploring the tricks and rewards you earn for individual missions

*T*he *Quest* is an interactive graphic novel and game in which you play as Addison, a mechanic-in-training whose journey guides you through the components of game design. Completing quest missions is vital because you can then earn new sprites that you use to build more complex games.

The quests in Gamestar Mechanic follow a closely related "story," so this chapter provides an overview of the story and what it tells you about game design. You can also find information about how to complete the quests, as well as a pacing guide for the quests' challenges and rewards.

Introducing the "Story" Told through the Quest

In the Quest, you follow the adventures of Addison Cypher, a citizen of Factory 2 who leaves to study game design at Factory 7. When you begin the Quest, as described in Chapter 2, you're allowed to select Addison's gender, changing the character's appearance on the site and allowing you to identify easily with the character.

While learning how to design games from instructor Jhansi and Gamestar Mechanic Samson, Addison faces the mysterious Rogue, a masked vigilante by the name of Rodney Gil. Rodney steals sprites from other mechanics as he causes trouble in the factory. As you progress through the Quest, you help Addison improve as a game designer by completing missions that deal with the qualities of game design, and eventually face the Rogue and his minions. The Quest is told by way of a motion comic graphic novel that tells the story and introduces the concepts, as shown in Figure 4-1.

Figure 4-1: This animated comic appears at the beginning of the first quest.

In premium quests (discussed in Chapter 14), the story becomes more complex as Addison progresses through a series of conflicts with the Rogue. In addition, you see a number of different ways to create games as you trek through four schools of game design, meeting the master mechanics of each school along the way — all of which grants you a deeper experience in game design as you follow the Rogue.

Addison's story parallels your own as you discover and master new sprites and methods. In contrast, Rodney is a less-than-perfect designer who often serves to elaborate on poor design concepts. By the end of the Quest, he begins to improve, showing methods for repairing and improving games. The world of Gamestar Mechanic is a tapestry of the elements of a game designer's life, from skill to social connection to teaching and learning.

Exploring the Three Quests

The story is divided into multiple Quests — however, if you don't have a Premium account, you will be automatically directed to the first one. (If you're just starting out on the site, see Chapter 2 for details on getting started with the first quest.)

At the time of this writing, these three quests are available:

- Addison Joins the League
- Addison Joins the Rogue
- Dungeon of the Rogue

Quests are divided into *episodes,* collections of games that tell a story in each location. The episodes themselves consist of several *missions* that split the story into large components.

After you complete the first episode of Addison Joins the League, you're given a map that appears whenever you enter a quest, as shown in Figure 4-2. The map contains numbered notes representing each episode, pinned wherever the episode takes place.

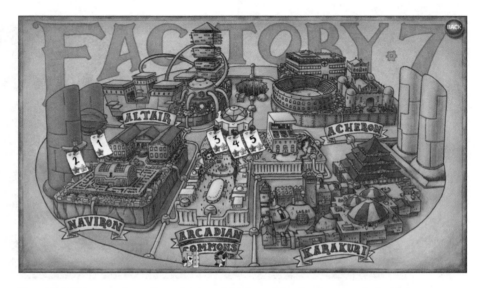

Figure 4-2: This map shows the episodes of Addison Joins the League, all of which are completed.

Scroll over a note to see a pop-up description of the episode, followed by two rows of beige rectangles: The rectangles in the top row represent missions, and those in the bottom row represent bonus missions. You see blue check marks over every mission you've completed, as well as some text in the bottom-right corner telling you what percentage of the episode you've finished.

Click a note to play the episode. If you complete an episode, the next episode becomes available.

Most missions are games, which you must win in order to access the next missions. Other missions require you to build or repair games with certain restrictions, and publish them (though the result does not go on Game Alley) to continue. Between the missions are *cut-scenes,* which are animated comics that fill out the story between challenges. You may see these cut-scenes labeled as *intro, intermission,* or *outro,* depending on where they are in the episode. Every episode begins with an intro and an outro.

When you select an episode, the missions are laid out in two rows on the screen, as shown in Figure 4-3:

- ✔ **Story Missions:** At the top; required in order to complete the episode

- ✔ **Bonus Missions:** (Optional) At the bottom; give neat rewards, including sprites, backgrounds, and music not found in the story missions. You can access and complete a series of bonus missions at any time, but they are not required to complete the quest.

Figure 4-3: An example of quest story missions.

After you complete a mission, a star appears over it: Story missions have bronze stars, and bonus missions have silver ones. If you complete all of the story missions or bonus missions on an episode, the corresponding note on the main map has similar stars printed on it to acknowledge your completion of the episode.

It isn't always possible to earn a silver star. Don't worry if you have only a bronze star on an episode — it may have no bonus missions.

Some missions may be grayed out on the screen, indicating you can't play them unless you've completed the previous missions. Other missions are marked with stars, indicating that you have completed them — though you're always allowed to play them again.

In the lower-right corner of every mission in the episode is an icon indicating the type of mission, as described in this list:

✔ **Play:** Win the game to complete the mission. Be sure to analyze the design concept that's being taught — pay attention to the cut-scenes and in-game message to understand what the program wants you to learn.

✔ **Repair:** Play a game, find out what's wrong with it, and fix the problem. You are given a limited number of sprites, and some design functions are locked (such as Edit or Clone). In addition, some of the sprites in the level are faded out while editing; these sprites cannot be moved or edited, so you have to build the game around them. (See Chapter 6 for more on sprites.)

✔ **Design:** Design a game from scratch, using the available tools. The game must fit certain requirements, prompting you to learn about the corresponding element of game design.

You can find tutorials for designing games by clicking either the Tutorials button on the Pause menu or the question-mark (?) button in the lower-right corner. These buttons appear only on Repair or Design levels.

To succeed in the story missions, you should understand what the designers want you to gain from the experience. For example, some missions use trails of items to guide you through certain movements, and others give you games to repair with particular focuses such as gravity and space. The story missions are meant to teach you the necessary concepts of game design, so be sure you learn these topics in order to understand the purpose of the Quest and gain a better understanding of the program in general.

The Pacing of the Quest

The tables in this section describe the individual missions and their tricks and rewards. If you get stuck at any point in the Quest, read this section to get back on track. Table 4-1 lists the missions in Addison Joins the League; Table 4-2 describes the missions in Addison Joins the Rogue; and Table 4-3 describes the missions in Dungeon of the Rogue.

Table 4-1		Missions in Addison Joins the League	
Mission Name	*Episode*	*Rewards*	*Advice*
Naviron Adventure	1	Naviron scout	Watch how enemies move, and then navigate around them. Some enemies walk back and forth, whereas others can turn left or right.
Altair Journey	1	Altair jumper	Practice moving and jumping at the same time. You don't need all the points in the last level.
Acheron Gauntlet	1	Acheron marksman	Dodge enemies until you're in a good position to shoot. Watch for patterns.
Karakuri Mindbender	1	Karakuri chaser	Run off the edge of the screen to reappear on the other side. Figure out mazes by tracing a path backward from the goal to the avatar.
Naviron Elevator	2	Point	Wait for ghosts to disappear before passing. Use the blaster on Level 2 to find hidden items.
Naviron Elevator EDIT	2	Bonus point	Use reduced gravity to control your jumping. The goal block is in the upper-right corner — stay high in the sky for as long as possible.
Elevator Elevation	2 (bonus)	Train tracks 2 background	There are many health packs in this level. Move through the level quickly to regain your health faster than you lose it. You can wait on platforms without worrying about shooters.
Security System Goals	3	Frag counter, score keeper	Keep an eye on the goal of each level. Some points and goals are impossible to reach, so don't let them distract you.
Goal Repair	3	White block, black block appearance	Move blocks to clear a path from the avatar to a goal.
Security System Space	3	Orange block appearance	Find places to hide to avoid chasers on Levels 2 and 3.

Mission Name	Episode	Rewards	Advice
Space Repair	3	Red block appearance	Move blocks to clear a path for your avatar.
Security System Rules	3	Health meter	Hide in the spaces between corridors, and run when enemies move out of the way.
Rule Repair	3	Timer	Use the Wrench tool on the health meter and timer at the top of the screen to increase your health and time limits. You can also edit the score keeper to require fewer points.
Timer Dash	3 (bonus)	Green fog background	Plan your route, and leave the points near the goal block for last.
Safe Spots	3 (bonus)	Orange flare background	Advance carefully, and stay ahead of predictable enemies. Find places to hide so that you can retreat when you need to.
Perspective Theater	4	Grass block, dirt block	Move carefully, and get a feel for the interface before starting. All enemies have the same script. Save health bonuses for times when you need them.
Is it the Shoes?	4	League jumper	Go to the level settings (described in Chapter 5), and set the gravity level to 1. Watch out — enemies are hacked and can jump, even though such sprites can't jump under normal circumstances.
Component Theater	4	League pacer	Run and jump at the same time to clear gaps. Jump over pacers while they're walking toward you.
Raining Pacers?	4	Cloud block	Build a path to the goal block using as few blocks as possible. Because pacers never leave the platform, you can place blocks under them to keep them away from the avatar.

(continued)

Table 4-1 *(continued)*

Mission Name	Episode	Rewards	Advice
Top-Down?	4 (bonus)	League pouncer	Go to the level settings, set the game to Platformer, and then wait for enemies to drain into the pits before you advance. If you can't make it, try changing the gravity level.
Platforming?	4 (bonus)	League marksman	Go to the level settings, and set the game to Top-Down. Shoot through enemy routes until you can safely cross.
Walk and Chew Gum	5	League sniper	Be careful to shoot enemies while putting yourself in only minimal danger. Keep an eye on the objectives.
Harmony of Health and Time	5	Dark blue block appearance	Every level has three paths. Take the one colored blue.
Stabilized Space	5	League of Mechanics music	Use safe spots to maneuver past back-and-forth enemies. When confronted with enemies running around in a loop, follow them until you reach your stop.
Crazed Marching	5	Blue block appearance	Edit the enemies so that their motion paths don't inhibit the avatar.
Clean Slate	5	Gold block (also allows you to publish games)	Build a point-collecting game in any way you want. Publish the game to win — you can always delete or edit your game later.
A Real Hero	5 (bonus)	Beautiful day background	Shoot dangerous enemies and watch out for enemies that shoot back. Also watch out for jumping pacers. Remember to collect the underground point in the lower-right corner.

Table 4-2		Missions in Addison Joins the Rogue (Premium)	
Mission Name	*Episode*	*Rewards*	*Advice*
Blocked Tunnel	1	Altair scout	Hold down the right-arrow key, pressing the up- and down-arrow keys to dodge obstacles.
Spiked Tunnel	1	Damage block	Avoid the damage blocks before they get close, and aim for thick routes that leave room for error.
Commuter Tunnel	1	Altair sniper	Be careful, and give other commuters a wide berth. When you reach a crossing, wait for a noticeable path to open, and then charge through it.
Traffic Jam	1	Altair chaser	Move the enemies into manageable columns, packing them into the upper and lower gaps for extra space.
Where Sprites Fear to Tread	1 (bonus)	Purple fog background	On Level 1, move off the top of the screen and run with the chasers to circumvent most of the level. On Level 2, run off the left side of the screen to appear close to the goal block. On Level 3, be careful: Make most of your movement upward or downward because the Altair scout is tall but thin.
Wrong Side of the Tracks	1 (bonus)	Train tracks 1 background	Time your movement to proceed past enemies. You may have to sacrifice a hit point at the end of Level 4.
Guide to Jumping	2	Floating islands background	Pay attention to the techniques that you're taught. Make jumps multiple times if you miss some points.
Cavern Jumps	2	Yellow fog background	Pay attention to the text, and apply the techniques on Level 4.
Jump and Blast	2	Altair hero	Whenever possible, shoot at the top of a jump for better accuracy.

(continued)

Table 4-2 *(continued)*

Mission Name	Episode	Rewards	Advice
Tackling the Nemesis	2	Altair nemesis	Shoot early to make up for imperfect reflexes. Bullets cancel each other out, so when facing nemeses, attack immediately after they do.
Planetary Platforming	2	Altair pouncer	Size up the gravity of each level before playing, and plan your route carefully.
Gravity Lever	2	Floating dirt appearance, Altair jig music	Several gravity settings work on this level, each producing a different kind of game. Try a few of them.
Expert's Guide to Jumping	2 (bonus)	Blue flare background	On each level, you must be able to change direction while jumping. Practice the technique, and then try it.
Blast Hopping	2 (bonus)	League hero	Tap the Jump key, pulling up your wrist as you press the key, to make a small jump. You don't need to jump over the first gap of Level 2 — just run off the ledge onto the platform.
The Ascent	3	Outside the Factory 2 background	Carefully control your horizontal motion while jumping. The hard-to-achieve time bonuses award 10 seconds, whereas most others award 5.
Iron Boots	3	Timer bonus	You can complete each level in several ways, so try a different one if you get stuck. On Level 3, you cannot obtain the goal block on the left without first stocking up on the time bonuses to the right.
Rooftop Flight	3	Altair pacer	When you make big jumps, try jumping whenever you hit a point.

Mission Name	Episode	Rewards	Advice
Rooftop Repairs	3	Blue fog background	Build a path to the goal block with, at most, 50 clouds. To do this, use a series of platforms and block off dangerous spikes with more clouds.
The Empty City	3	Nighttime streets of Factory 7 background	Build a game in which an avatar must collect points within a time limit. You can always delete or edit this game later.
Low Gravity, High Pressure	3 (bonus)	League nemesis	On Levels 1 and 3, remember that you don't need to collect points. On Level 2, you're forced to jump on damage blocks to reach points, so save health packs for times when you need them.
Rooftop Running	3 (bonus)	Altair marksman	When you have to choose between health and time, pick the one that you think you'll need more. This level may require several tries before you find the route that works best for you. You don't need to frag enemies.
Flanking Maneuvers	4	Acheron sniper	Duck behind walls, and shoot enemies from the side whenever possible. Find the least dangerous route to win, and neutralize enemy bullets with your own.
Barricades	4	Purple flare background, Acheron beat music	Block enemy weapons with blocks, allowing you to frag them from the side.
Evasive Maneuvers	4	Glass block	On Levels 1 and 2, shoot carefully to preserve the glass that locks in enemies. On Level 3, break the lower-left glass and then — quickly — the lower-right glass, to divide enemies into avoidable groups.

(continued)

Table 4-2 *(continued)*

Mission Name	*Episode*	*Rewards*	*Advice*
Just the Right Blast	4	Acheron pacer	Destroy glass to cause the enemies to fall. White-headed sprites happily walk off edges, but purple-headed sprites are smarter — you have to knock the ground from under their feet. Be sure not to destroy glass if it causes the level to become unwinnable.
Fragile Fragging	4	Acheron pouncer	Your avatar must reach the top of the level in order to activate all enemies. Use glass platforms to reach the top, and use more glass to keep enemies under control.
The Spawning Source	4	Acheron chaser	Destroy spawner blocks as soon as possible so that you have fewer enemies to deal with.
Frozen Survival	4 (bonus)	Frozen tundra 1 background	On Levels 1 and 3, fire at tactical choke points to frag large waves of enemies, and *be near the goal block* as time runs out. On Level 2, spawned enemies have only one hit point, so turn and frag them as they draw close.
Spawning Blueprints	4 (bonus)	Enemy spawn point	Create a game where a player has to survive a constant onslaught of enemies. You can always delete or edit this game later.
Never Go Down	5	Acheron nemesis	Avoiding damage is impossible, so you have to continuously collect health pack items. Use health packs to heal yourself faster than enemies can hurt you.

Mission Name	Episode	Rewards	Advice
Heal Stations	5	Health pack	Place health packs wherever you're having trouble, making the game easier. You can still beat the game using no health packs.
Dash and Blast	5	Acheron scout	Blasters last only for a short time in this game, so make the most of each one before picking up another.
Three's the Magic Number	5	Blaster	Place blasters throughout the stage to allow your avatar to frag enemies. To solve the mazes in the top and middle sections, use a trail of blasters to mark the best route.
Big Bad Boss Battle	5	Acheron hero	The better you fare against the minions, the more prepared you are for the boss. Bosses are big.targets, so find places where you can catch them moving predictably and cause a lot of damage.
The Showdown	5	Acheron megachaser	You're given a limited number of 2-point health packs and 10-second blasters. Space items carefully so that you don't pick up several at a time. To win within the time limit, attack the enemy close up, retreating to a health pack whenever necessary.
Getting Even	5 (bonus)	Acheron jumper	The first few levels are quite difficult, so practice some well-timed jumps until you find the "sweet spot" of each system. Release your frustration by using the blaster on Levels 4 and 5.

Table 4-3		Missions in Dungeon of the Rogue (Premium)	
Mission Name	**Episode**	**Rewards**	**Advice**
The Bounding Room	1	Karakuri sniper	On Levels 1 and 2, think short-term thoughts to survive, and convert to long-term planning whenever you can. On Level 3, keep track of your avatar, and run against walls from outside to catch a glimpse of its position. On Level 4, place the platform at the center of the screen to land on it.
Ghostly Games	1	Karakuri ghost	Wait next to the nearest ghosts, and run through them when they disappear.
Red Light, Green Light	1	Karakuri scout	Use the Ghost avatar, and run only when enemies are invisible, turning invisible yourself before they reappear.
Vanished	1	Karakuri jumper	Vanish immediately before you're hit, and reappear immediately afterward.
The Invisible Hero	1	Karakuri hero	Move close to enemies on Level 1 to defeat them. Enemy bullets fire at a constant rhythm, so you can win with some well-timed vanishing. Vanish before you hit a ceiling to drop.
Hidden Agendas	1	Karakuri marksman	Run into walls to check them for hidden goals. Sometimes, vanishing is easier than shooting.
Specters, Shades, Sprites	1 (bonus)	League ghost, Altair ghost, Acheron ghost	Both Levels 1 and 3 have an element of flow, a procession of ghosts that you must follow correctly whenever they reappear. Though Level 2 is straightforward, it requires good reflexes.
Find the Goal!	1 (bonus)	Hidden goal	Build a game in which the goal is not apparently visible. You can always edit or delete this game later.
Is This Magic?	2	Red flare background	Use the teleporters whenever you can. On the last level, figure out what kind of momentum you need in order to exit the portal at the right angle.

Mission Name	Episode	Rewards	Advice
Hub and Spokes	2	Karakuri pacer	Save health packs for times when you need them, and retreat to the hub whenever necessary. On Level 1, you can vanish. On Level 2, collect keys and then the blaster, and then quickly clear a difficult room by fragging enemies.
Danger on All Sides	2	Karakuri megasniper	On Level 1, continue moving with the flow. On Level 2, run fast and collect health packs on the way. On Level 3, rather than attack bosses directly, shoot into portals to control the board with your own attacks.
Teleporter Mechanic	2	Karakuri pouncer	Build a system of teleporters that leads you to all the coins. A pit is at the bottom to contain enemies; have a portal lead to the platform just above it, filtering enemies into the pit.
Warp Overload	2	Karakuri nemesis	Think fast whenever you emerge from a portal. On Level 1, try portals only if you have to. On Level 3, portals are proportional to the rooms. For example, entering the lower-right portal in a square takes you to the lower-right room.
Unknown Destination	2	Teleport origin	Build a game with the template, in which the avatar must enter the room via a teleporter. You can always edit or delete this game later.
Choose Your Own Adventure	2 (bonus)	Karakuri megachaser	Many different paths are available to you, so pick a different one if you get stuck on a particular sequence.
Fiddling with Riddles	3	Moss skin, question/ book/sign message block skins, text message block	On Level 1, take the seventh route from the left. On Level 2, dodge enemies by finding hidden goals. On Level 3, follow hints to find the hidden goals, and try guessing if you get stuck.

(continued)

Table 4-3 (continued)

Mission Name	Episode	Rewards	Advice
Puzzling Platforms	3	Naviron informer (female and male), legacy treasure appearance	On Level 1, talk to librarians for clues. On Level 2, solve the riddle or use trial and error — think about why the chaser in the middle *must* be the liar. On Level 3, zigzag through the treasure, as hinted by the sign. You need to open only some of the chests to win.
The Impervious Defender	3	Naviron defender	Use a control scheme that allows you to use your shield and to move with different hands. Because you can turn on a dime while shielding, try to block and turn rather than turn and block.
Sentry Smashathon	3	Population counter	Use a population counter for sentries, setting the minimum count value to 0 and the maximum count value to 56. Then use your shield to cause mayhem in their ranks.
The Cave Prison	3	Naviron guardian, cobblestone skin	On Level 2, the giant cobblestone arrows tell you how to navigate the room on the right. By reading them from left to right and from top to bottom, you can find the route by which you must zigzag across the platforms. On Levels 1 and 3, listen to the dialogue for help.
Too Few Keys	3 (bonus)	Blue key, blue lock	Each door can be approached from the bottom or the top; move bottom-bottom-top to use the right sequence of keys. Then add more locks to deflect the enemies into manageable patterns, allowing you to get the other keys.
Touch of Danger	3 (bonus)	Green key, green lock	Contain as many enemies as you can, and quickly collect health packs as you search for points.

Mission Name	Episode	Rewards	Advice
The Emerald Knight	4	Naviron knight	Trick enemies into turning so that you can attack them from the side. The slower the enemy, the more difficult it is to defeat from the front.
Soaring Swordsman	4	Naviron hero	Your sword can block bullets as well.
Close Encounters	4	Naviron sentry	Lure sentries into positions where you can attack them from the side. They stop moving when they're confused, so try to outwit them.
Facing On Foes	4	Steel skin, stone skin, wood	Attack pouncers immediately after they jump so that they can't evade you. Attack nemeses from behind.
Spear Sidestepping	4	Brick skin, green block skin	Use bricks to prevent enemies, especially lancers, from seeing you. Try building a path along the bottom of the screen.
Vacant Sentinels	4 (bonus)	Hedge skin	Build a Naviron game in the template. You can always edit or delete this game later.
Vault Clearing	4 (bonus)	Naviron lancer	To fight a lancer head-on, attack immediately before it reaches you, because your sword is longer than the spear.
Rise of the Phoenix	5	Rodney scout	Levels 1–3 in this mission are designed to give examples of poor techniques, so always look for the easy way out. At the end of Level 2, the portal in the lower-left corner of the maze takes you all the way to the end. Level 4 requires some thought, so advance carefully.
Phoenix Nest	5	Phoenix block	Increase the duration of the phoenix blocks to ten apiece, and then frag enemies and collect points while the blocks are regenerating.
Unstable Ground	5	Rodney jumper	Take note of poor designs, but focus on clearing the true challenges.
Make Your Own Way	5	Moving block, Minion Altair jumper	Use motion blocks to clear a path to the exit. The easiest way to do this is via a series of fast elevators.

(continued)

Table 4-3 *(continued)*

Mission Name	Episode	Rewards	Advice
One Cool Blaster	5	Minion Acheron hero	Freeze enemies to make temporary platforms for you to jump on, allowing you to reach ledges and avoid damage blocks.
A Freezing Fix	5	Freeze blaster	Add a permanent freeze blaster for your avatar to collect, as well as some enemies to use as platforms. Because some of your bullets inflict damage, give enemies a lot of health.
A Very Important Mission	5	Naviron VIP	Stay close to the VIP during dangerous parts so that it doesn't follow you into danger.
Blocker Bodyguard	5	Minion Naviron VIP, Minion Naviron scout	Use blasters to help your avatar clear a path, and use cobblestone to block off enemies when possible.
Puzzle Garden of DOOM!	6	Emile scout	Move quickly, and use your items whenever your energy level reaches 50 or lower.
Puzzle Garden of DOOM Fix	6	Emile jumper	Use a message block to provide the answer to the first challenge, add informer sprites to lead you through the maze, and perform any other edits necessary to make the game work.
Informants	6	Backpack	Give yourself enough information to take the correct paths. You can see the whole map while editing.
Armordillo	6	Amstrad scout	Run quickly through challenges, picking up all armor packs. At the end, don't try to reach the goal blocks at the bottom — instead, find the goal in the gift on the left.
Armordillo Fix	6	Amstrad jumper	Place armor packs so that you can win the game with only four. Rearrange certain rooms to make them more original.

Mission Name	Episode	Rewards	Advice
Crowded Cave	6	Armor pack	Rearrange enemies and armor to fit the level. Be sure to place enemies near the blasters, because each blaster gives you only ten seconds.
KaraCHAOS!	6	Naja scout	Avoid the second half of the level by taking the first teleporter you find.
KaraCHAOS! Fix	6	Naja jumper	Remove some of each enemy to make the level more manageable.
The Boss of Who	6	Phasing	Add power-ups before each battle, and place blocks to hinder enemies. You can also move some red blocks.
Double the Air	6	Aran scout	Take the lower route and double-jump if you start to fall.
Double the Air Fix	6	Aran jumper	Take the upper route, adding clouds to build a path to the goal block in the upper-right corner.
Up, Down, In, Out	6	Double jump boots	Remove unnecessary points and give the avatar double-jump boots. Add any other sprites that you think would make the game better. You can edit messages and keys, if you want.
Forging the Way	6	Addison scout, Addison jumper	Build a game with whatever sprites you want. Most of the template can be edited. You can always edit or delete this game later.
Mega Trouble	6 (bonus)	Jhansi scout, Jhansi jumper, league megachaser	Advance through Levels 1 and 2 carefully. Move quickly in Level 3, before the megachaser can block the exit.
Mega? More Like Ultra!	6 (bonus)	Samson scout, Samson jumper, league mega-sniper, Altair megasniper, Acheron megasniper	Watch the enemies' patterns, and keep a safe distance from them.

The only quest available for free is Addison Joins the League. You must have a premium account to access the information in Tables 4-2 and 4-3. (See Chapter 14 for more on premium accounts.)

If a mission has you stumped, here are some suggestions for how to complete the mission: Try different methods; ask a friend for help; reread the text in the mission (message sprites, instructions, and so on) to ensure that you know what's going on; or stop playing for a while and come back later. Also, check the tables in this chapter to see which rewards are important to you. Bonus missions are often difficult, so don't worry if you don't complete them.

5

Designing and Publishing
Your First Game

*T*o become an outstanding game designer, you must practice designing games. You can't simply read a list of tips and immediately know exactly how a game that's fun functions — you have to try, fail (sorry about that), and try again. Gamestar Mechanic gives you the tools to obtain this practice. In this chapter, I explain how a game is created in Gamestar Mechanic and how to get started in the designer's seat.

Understanding Sprites — the Building Blocks of a Game

To understand how a game is composed, you must first understand how sprites work. Sprites are the building blocks of any game, and the objects in which most of the code exists. The sample game shown in Figure 5-1 uses four different sprites: one controlled by the player (league scout), numerous enemies controlled by the game (league chasers), several blocks of concrete, and a goal. Games often require a number of sprites to be complete; keep the overall structure of your game in mind so that you aren't overwhelmed trying to position individual sprites.

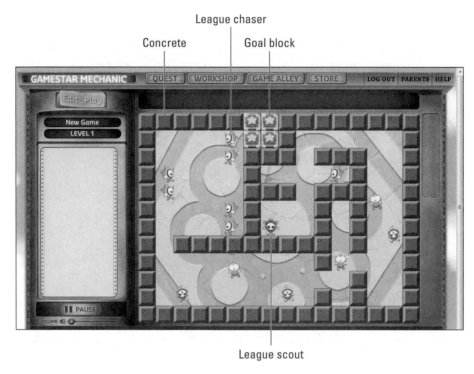

Figure 5-1: A simple game with four different sprites. The enemies in this game are all the same sprite, but use different programming.

Sprites fall into one of these five categories (shown in Figure 5-2):

- An **avatar sprite** is controlled by the player. Its controls depend on whether the game is top-down or platformer (as detailed in Chapter 3). Every game must have exactly one avatar that the player controls. An avatar can have many abilities based on which one the designer chooses for the level, from shooting to invisibility and varying degrees of strength and speed. Many avatars have no abilities. Most players can determine the avatar's abilities on sight, or they can simply test the Attack and Action keys to understand what sort of abilities the avatar has.

- **Enemy sprites** are often the primary obstacle in a game and cannot be controlled by the player. Players try to avoid or frag these enemies, most of which deal damage to the avatar on contact. Enemies that do not deal damage are sometimes called *non-player characters,* or *NPCs;* they can act as characters that tell the player useful information, or they can simply exist to add atmosphere to the level. Enemies are often the most versatile sprites, and their characteristics are determined by the game designer.

- **Block sprites** define various kinds of walls, floors, and ceilings in the game. With the exception of a few avatars and enemies, a block is the only sprite that produces collisions, stopping other sprites from passing through it. Most blocks are used as platforms, bunkers, or restrictions for players, sometimes carrying special properties: Some blocks can be destroyed, some display messages, and some damage the player on contact, for example. Meanwhile, other blocks don't collide with anything, staying in the background and containing abilities such as the creation of sprites and the teleportation of avatars.

- **Item sprites** don't interact with any other sprite except the avatar. When the avatar touches an item, such as a point or a blaster, the avatar is improved in some way, by obtaining points or health or various *power-ups* (armor, weapons, extra abilities, and so on). An item has the powerful effect of being able to change the game, by revealing goal blocks, extending the avatar's limits, or providing abilities that open up new interactions with the level. Even simple-looking item sprites can be used to add new elements of complexity to the game.

- **System sprites** appear on the blue bar just above the game, as described in Chapter 3. You can add as many as five system sprites to a single level, and each system sprite (such as the health meter shown in Figure 5-2) consists of an icon and some text to keep track of variables such as the avatar's health, score, and energy.

  Most system sprites also add new rules to the game. For example, population counters make the level unwinnable unless a certain number of a specific enemy appears in the level, and the timer destroys the avatar if time runs out. Every system sprite can drastically change your game by adding new goals and rules, and thus changing the process players must take to win.

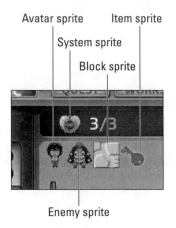

Figure 5-2: The five kinds of sprites used to create a top-down game.

Taking a Look at the Structure of a Game

Every game on this site is a collection of elements (one of which is controlled by the player) that function together in a system — you can use a nearly infinite level of creativity when creating and arranging these elements. Games consist of a number of sprites, as described in the preceding section. These sprites are initially laid out in the spaces of a grid by the designer (as described later in this chapter), and from there, they can move or act or be created or destroyed.

It's your job as the designer to arrange sprites in a fun, engaging way. The visual style of a game is determined by the kinds of sprites and backgrounds you use, and the gameplay is defined by how you position these components.

Figure 5-3 shows an example of a simple game that uses only a few sprites with rudimentary abilities. As a player, you control the little blue avatar in the lower-left corner, using your keyboard to make the avatar move up, down, left, or right (flip back to Chapter 3 for a refresher on keyboard commands). The goal is to navigate your avatar to the *goal block,* which is the yellow block enclosing a gold star. Touching this block allows you to win the game, but it's being guarded by several white sprites that pace around and destroy the avatar on contact. If the avatar is destroyed, you must restart the level.

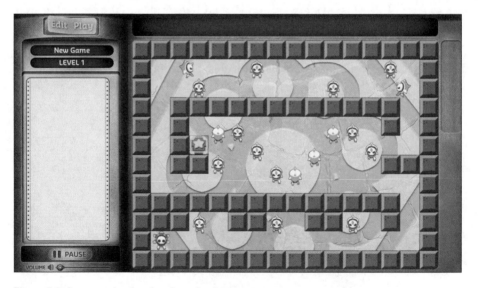

Figure 5-3: An example of sprites in a simple game.

You should recognize several important characteristics about a game such as this one:

- **It's top-down.** Essentially, the player is looking down on the sprites from above, watching them move around a two-dimensional landscape. From a designer's perspective, you must understand the benefits and restrictions of a top-down game, as explained in Chapter 3.

- **It's navigational.** Navigational games are the simplest to design and play in Gamestar Mechanic, because you just have to reach one or more objectives while avoiding enemy sprites. Other games may require you to frag the enemies, survive by way of skill and reflexes, or satisfy various other goals and rules.

- **You already have all the sprites you need to build this game.** When you first join the Gamestar Mechanic website, you're given only four sprites to design with:

  - League scout (an avatar type)

  - League chaser (an enemy type)

  - Concrete (a block type)

  - Goal block (a block type)

These sprites are the only ones that appear in the game in Figure 5-3. No matter how long you've been on Gamestar Mechanic, you have all the resources you need to make this game right now.

Introducing the Five Elements of Game Design

The preceding section analyzes the basics of a simple game. This section moves to a more general topic: the structure and qualities of games in general. In Gamestar Mechanic, you can analyze a game's qualities by looking at these five elements:

- Space
- Rules
- Goals
- Components
- Mechanics

These terms are often used when describing games and the design process, because a good game should be balanced in all five of these elements, which are described in detail in the following sections.

As you design your first few games, work on committing these five elements to memory. To do this, you can try building games around elements that you want to practice. For example, build a game while focusing on the space you want to create, or design a game around an interesting mechanic. Alternatively, when you play or design a game, try taking some time to do a mental exercise: Figure out how each of the five elements appears in the game, and what it adds to the experience.

The five elements of game design are necessary, but not sufficient on their own to create a game that's fun to play. Don't be discouraged if you can't find the elusive element of fun — later chapters in this book give you tools to help you look.

Space

Space (sometimes referred to as *game space*) is the environment where the game takes place. Your use of space determines your game design — how the game looks as well as progresses.

If you're lost for ideas, think about the space you want to design: Do you want your game to feel open or tight? Do you want to design an arena, a dungeon, or a progression of rooms full of enemies? Also consider how much of your space you need to use, as well as how much you can reserve for visual elements (collections of sprites, usually blocks, that build the visual style of your level).

As you gain experience, you may start designing the game space at the same time you're focusing on other components, to ensure that the game space is a good fit for your ideas. However, dividing the game space into manageable sections, such as rooms or paths, is a helpful way for both beginners and veterans to build fun, well-rounded games.

An open space has the power to give a wide, expansive feel to a game, though wastefulness isn't recommended. The game should include enough detail to justify the quantity of space, and players should be able to find and reach objectives quickly.

Rules

In physical games such as sports or board games, *rules* are written restrictions that define what players can and cannot do in a game. In a video game, you define the rules via your design of the game: The abilities of the avatar and the restrictions on the player's actions form the rules of your game. Rules make the actions of players meaningful by providing the guidelines for what they can and should do in the game.

When designing the rules of your game, think about how you want the player to play. System sprites are excellent for easily designing rules. For example, add a health meter to make the player try to survive, add a timer to keep the avatar running, or add a population counter to limit the destruction of certain enemies. You may also implement rules using the properties of sprites — to grant certain consistent abilities to the avatar, enemies, blocks, and items — by combining the element of rules with the element of components, as explained later in this chapter.

Because all Gamestar Mechanic games work within the same engine (the grid of sprites), a few universal rules must apply in any game, as described in this list:

- **The avatar cannot pass through solid blocks.** In this way, every collection of solid blocks is a rule in itself — you can use walls and platforms to restrict where the player is allowed to go. The less common nonsolid blocks, such as item generators, have different properties.

- **The avatar is destructible.** Whether you add a health meter or not, harmful sprites may damage and frag the avatar. This rule can be bypassed with the *phoenix block,* a sprite with the ability to make other sprites regenerate (as described in Chapter 6).

- **Every sprite has a limited set of actions.** This important rule is affected by the perspective of the level (top-down or platform), the properties of the sprite, and in the case of avatars, the items available to the sprite.

- **A sprite must obey the rules of the level.** The rules include gravity and *edge bounding* (whether or not sprites can move off the screen).

When designing a good game, you should not only work within the rules of your system but also use rules to your advantage, by placing the right restrictions on the player so that the player feels challenged and inspired.

Some rules are easy to implement: If you want to create a shooter-style game, for example, use an avatar with a blaster. Gameplay is often based around rules, from collisions to timers to *screen-wrapping* (a level setting that lets sprites move instantly from one side of the screen to the other). Thus, if you're having trouble with this component, build your game around one or more rules that you find interesting. Consider a rule, and then consider the kinds of games that the rule might expand to.

Goals

Whereas rules add new restrictions to a game, goals give the game purpose. *Goals* are the conditions that the player must satisfy to beat the level. Unlike with rules, you can design only a limited number of goals, as described in this list:

- **Reach the goal block.** As long as at least one goal block (or the variation sprite *hidden goal,* described in Chapter 6) is in the level, the component is added as a goal. The player may touch the goal block after all other goals are complete, making that block the end point of the level.

✔ **Collect points.** By adding a *score keeper* system sprite to the game (as explained in Chapter 3), you give the player the incentive to collect items that grant points. Though you can set the score keeper to require any number of points from the player, it's most often used to make the player collect every point in the level. This tool is useful because it requires the player to complete several tasks that aren't necessarily *linear* (completed in a certain order).

Use points to lead the player through an adventure. Placing points at key locations is a good way to ensure that the player moves to them.

✔ **Interact with enemies.** The *frag counter* and the *population counter* system sprites (described in Chapter 3) require the player to have a deeper interaction with the game, by either fragging them or keeping a specific number of an enemy in the level.

To get creative with goals, look for interesting ways to apply the goals you can use. System sprites can be used in several different ways — for example, the score keeper can compel the player to explore a level, find secret areas, or make choices that grant various degrees of reward. Keep your goals in mind when designing a game, and remember that you can add multiple goals at a time.

Some games use optional goals for a more dynamic experience: By adding a score keeper or a frag counter sprite that requires 0 points or 0 frags, you can prompt players to record their scores and share them with others. You can also do this with a timer sprite that gives the player lots of time; because all system sprites are visible during the Level Win screen, the player can see how fast the level was beaten. Certain players may then become more inclined to review your games in order to post their scores.

Components

Components are the raw materials of a game, such as well-placed sprites or a group of sprites that fit into the rules and goals of the level. For example, a gauntlet of pacing enemies is a good component in a navigational game, but more aggressive foes may be a better fit in a shooter game.

Whether they're a progression of platforms, a fleet of enemies, a scattering of health packs throughout the level, or an element of your own design, components are the essential ingredients of a game — you should practice using them in order to come up with new and better ideas.

Choosing what components to use in your game can be difficult, because you have so many options. Fortunately, you can add, remove, or change components however you want, and other players have lots of components for you to incorporate and adapt to your own ideas.

Because components are the building blocks of your game, you must make sure that they fit well with the other elements of game design. Components often emerge from forming a good idea of the game's space, rules, goals, and mechanics. However, if you think of an interesting component, you can use it to start off your game and derive other elements from there.

Mechanics

The *mechanics* of a game are important because they define the actions you take as a player — from simple actions, such as jumping and collecting points, to procedural ones, such as solving puzzles and racing to complete a level in time. Mechanics are central to the communication between designer and player — the way the game works depends on the actions the player needs to take.

Mechanics can be as simple or complex as you want, from running and jumping to solving a logic puzzle. Many complex games use multiple mechanics that are connected. For example, the mechanics can cause players to frag enemies within a time limit or complete multiple levels in which the only transportation is a dangerous elevator. Usually, all mechanics are in orbit around a single *core mechanic*, which the player applies more than all others. For example, the core mechanic of a racing game is almost always the player's speed and agility, while the core mechanic of a level of locks and keys would probably be the puzzle-solving mechanic.

Mechanics are often the most difficult element for designers to implement in their games, because you not only have to provide possible actions to your players, but also give them challenges that call upon these actions. To give a fundamental example, suppose you give an avatar the ability to jump — you want to make the player jump across gaps just challenging enough to make the jumping mechanic interesting, or add a timer if you think the average player's method isn't urgent enough.

To get the full value out of your mechanics, you should practice playing games to understand the ways a player can be challenged. Even simple mechanics such as shooting can be used in many different ways, from battles to puzzles to games that test the player's reflexes. After you have a solid understanding of Gamestar Mechanic games, you may want to design games that showcase your own, unique take on a mechanic.

Academic or leisurely pursuits often inspire new ideas for game mechanics. If you're stuck, you can always combine in an interesting way some mechanics that you already know.

Defining the Gameplay

Creating a game may seem intimidating at first because you have many combinations of sprites and options available to you and only a few examples of working models. To make a truly fun game, you must understand how sprites function together to form comprehensive systems.

Learning by example is often the best way to start, though you should understand how to make not only a certain game but also a certain *type of* game. The following sections describe a few examples of games to practice with.

Building a top-down navigation game

The simplest type of top-down navigation game is to complete objectives while dodging enemies (refer to Figure 5-3).

The first quest missions contain a lot of top-down navigation games that you can try. If you're a Premium user, you can go to the Naviron DX channel (on the left sidebar of Game Alley) for a wider selection.

Here are some ways you can incorporate the elements of game design (described in the preceding section) to create an efficient and sufficiently challenging top-down game:

- **Space:** Define the game space for each challenge. The dimensions of a room, for example, determine the function of the challenges within. You can design a space linearly, connecting a number of rooms in a chain, or find ways to mix and branch out challenges. Figure 5-4 shows a game split into spaces of three different sizes.

- **Rules:** A top-down navigation game often has simple rules: The player cannot be hit by enemies too many times, and must progress through the rooms as led by the designer. Though you may stick with this outline, you can use a number of other rules to give players a unique experience. For example, you might add a timer for an element of urgency or make enemies follow careful patterns that prevent the avatar from standing still, keeping it in constant danger to make for a more interesting challenge. Well-placed blasters or power-ups also add depth to the game, using a single space with different sets of rules.

- **Goals:** The primary goal of a top-down game is navigation — advancing past enemies to reach the goal block. The primary purpose of adding goals to this type of game is to provide extra elements to guide the player. For example, a series of points can guide the player through every corner of your design.

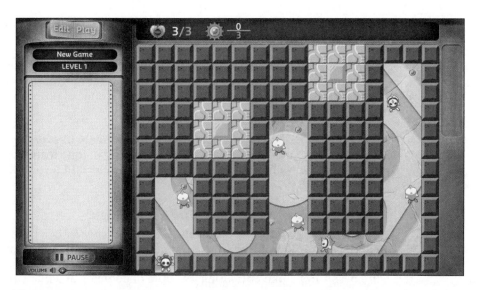

Figure 5-4: The spaces in this game are made more intricate by the enemy at the bottom of the screen, which runs through all three portions of the level.

✔ **Components:** In a simple game, you need only an avatar, a block, a goal, and one or two types of enemies. However, remember that enemy paths, the routes that sprites take to challenge the avatar, count as components. Orchestrate patterns of enemies that cause interesting complications for the player (without being too frustrating), and apply the elements of space and rules to figure out how the other components fit together. After you gain experience, you can implement more detailed visual elements and enemy patterns.

To design original components for a top-down game, try to keep track of which squares in your level can be accessed by at least one enemy. When an avatar is on one of these squares, the player must be alert, because an enemy will be coming along soon to attack. Stationary shooters can threaten only straight lines; moving enemies can be adapted to threaten many tiles by running in more intricate patterns. If you want to keep the player on guard, get some enemies to run through the unthreatened squares; don't let the player rest during any challenge that values urgency. This method lets you see your components at a deeper level and gives you a rough idea of which parts aren't quite challenging enough. However, you can always leave some squares unthreatened so that the player can catch a break before continuing the level.

>
>
> ✔ **Mechanics:** In a navigation game, the core mechanic is mostly laid out for you: Players must find their way through a series of dynamic levels, running through the level while avoiding damage and possibly a time limit. However, the game still has lots of room for ingenuity: Innovative mechanics add flavor and depth to basic navigation games. For example, players can enjoy solving puzzles and finding special power-ups to help them during the journey.

You don't have to add new mechanics and components to every game you make. Even if you can't come up with an especially unique feature (though you may later), a well-formatted but classic game can still be outstanding.

Arranging a platformer-shooter game

A popular and adventurous genre, the *platformer-shooter* is a type of game in which the avatar jumps and frags opponents. This game type is interesting because it can simulate intense battles with simple arrangements of sprites. Figure 5-5 shows a player fighting a couple of enemies in a platformer-shooter game.

Figure 5-5: The player can only deal damage while the shielded enemy is facing away.

Here are some ways to incorporate the elements of game design to build an effective platformer-shooter game:

> ✔ **Space:** A platformer-shooter game generally requires some flat sections where enemies can maneuver more easily. You can simply have a single route through which the player advances, fragging enemies along the way.

But you may also want to add intricate buildings and tactical landscapes to put some useful innovation into each space.

Consider both your avatar and its enemies in your design so that all the sprites are well-suited for the environment.

- ✓ **Rules:** The universal rules of the platformer-shooter game include gravity, fragging, and projectile collisions. Though these concepts are fairly simple, they should define the components and mechanics of your game. Other rules, such as timers, can help. A particularly interesting one is the population counter: If this rule is used well, you can add a new element of difficulty by limiting the fragging of certain enemies.

- ✓ **Goals:** A platformer-shooter game can have many different goal combinations. Points and goal blocks lead the player through the level, and frag counters and population counters add more focus on the shooter concept. A frag counter can make for a fun, simple game, and removing the frag counter can give the player a choice: Rush through the level or defeat all the enemies.

- ✓ **Components:** Adding components in a platformer-shooter game is, in many ways, much easier than in other games. All you have to do to implement challenge is to place enemies — or groups of enemies — in strategic places throughout the level, editing their attributes to produce a balanced difficulty level. You can add components such as items and block-based obstacles for more uniqueness.

Keep enemies in certain places to spread them throughout the level without clumping them or leaving sections empty. You can keep enemies in place by either making them stationary or having them patrol over a selected area. (I discuss how to edit sprite settings later in this chapter.)

- ✓ **Mechanics:** The avatar can jump and shoot, so the core mechanics of this game are defined by your arrangement of platforms and enemies. Set up your level to inspire particular actions from the player. For example, if you have an enemy walk back and forth along an isolated platform, the player must jump around to avoid it while shooting the enemy whenever possible.

Sprites such as bosses, enemy generators, and phoenix blocks can inspire interesting mechanics, especially for a platformer-shooter game. Chapter 13 helps you understand how to build interesting systems.

Constructing a racing game

The *racing game* is a more specific category of game than the ones I just described, but designers have found a lot of ways to apply and improve on the genre. Racing games require the player to navigate a course quickly, reaching a finish line before time runs out. It takes some skill to keep a racing game interesting, because the avatar must rush through many obstacles before reaching the goal.

Figure 5-6 shows a top-down racing game driven by two threatening system sprites: The energy meter makes the player race between pit stops (spots where energy is refilled), whereas the timer requires the player to complete the whole course in time.

Figure 5-6: The pit stops in this game act as mini-goals, each of which is a race in itself.

Whether you make your racing game top-down or platformer, experiment with these methods:

- **Space:** The space in a racing game is the track, the routes by which the avatar completes the level. The track's shape, size, and thickness all contribute to the feel of the game — keep the components of your game in mind, and design your game's space to fit.

- **Rules:** Use blocks, enemies, timers, and whatever else you can think of to efficiently enforce the rules of your game: no leaving the track and no running out of time. The element of rules isn't quite as important unless you want to add special rules. You can define the rule set for a racing game in many ways, but even a simple, balanced timer can produce a well-defined racing game.

- **Goals:** The goal of most racing games is to reach a certain point (the finish line). Closely connected to a rule, the goal is the simplest part of a race. However, you can always add your own innovations by having the player run multiple laps, for example, or frag enemies along the way.

- **Components:** The base components of a race are the player, the track, and the finish line. Sometimes these components are sufficient if you fill out the track with frequent challenges and points of interest. Other components — from damage to pit stops to other racers — can make for a more interesting experience, but these additions require you to implement new mechanics, which can affect the structure of your level.

✓ **Mechanics:** The core mechanic of a racing game is the player's racing mindset: The player must reach the goal as fast as possible and act with urgency and agility. To improve on this core mechanic, try adding enemies and other hazards to test the player's reflexes along the way, or add other mechanics such as point-collecting and energy-gathering, which encourage the player to think fast.

Touring the Toolbox Interface

To start designing your own games, go to the Workshop and click the large, orange Build a New Game button in the upper-right corner. The toolbox opens, where you can design and publish your games.

The toolbox contains all the tools you need to add, arrange, and edit sprites to design a game and then test the game to ensure that it's ready to be published. Figure 5-7 shows what the game in Figure 5-3 (earlier in the chapter) looks like from the designer's perspective.

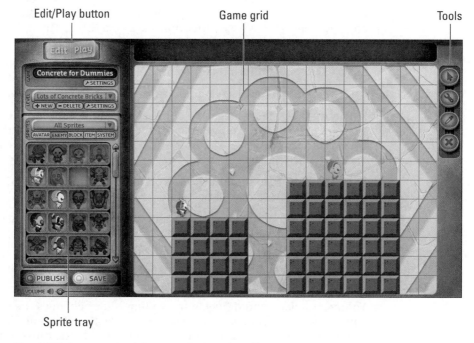

Edit/Play button   Game grid   Tools

Sprite tray

Figure 5-7: An example of the game designer's toolbox.

When you open the toolbox to create a new game, the grid in the center (where your game is displayed) is empty, and the background is black by default. The interface is relatively simple: You're given a list of the sprites that you can move onto the grid, and a set of tools for editing them. In the following sections, you find out how to use the various components of the toolbox.

Exploring the sidebar

On the left side of the toolbox, you see a sidebar that contains a number of editing options, as described in this list, from top to bottom (see Figure 5-8):

- ✏ **Edit/Play button:** At the top of the sidebar is a gray, two-position switch with the sides labeled Edit and Play. The flattened side, which is Edit by default, is the side that's selected. Click the Edit or Play side of this button to *toggle* (switch) between editing a level and playing it.

  If you click the Edit side of the button while testing a level, you must restart the level the next time you test it.

- ✏ **Game:** This section contains the name of the game and a Settings button. I describe this vital button later in this chapter.

- ✏ **Level:** This section lists the name of the level you're currently viewing. Click the drop-down menu to see a list of all levels in the game, allowing you to switch between them or even to click and drag the levels to change their order. Three other buttons are in this section:

  - *+ New:* Creates a new level
  - *– Delete:* Removes the current level
  - *Settings:* Manages level options, as described later in this chapter

- ✏ **Sprite tray:** The largest section of the sidebar, the sprite tray contains a grid of every sprite you've collected. You can place sprites from the sprite tray onto the grid, as described in "Building a Game in the Toolbox," later in this chapter.

- ✏ **Save/Publish:** This section allows you to record your game privately or publicly, by using a pair of buttons:

  - Click the *Save* button at any time to save an unfinished game in the Workshop for only you to play and edit.
  - Click the *Publish* button to officially release your game, if it's ready, to Game Alley. I explain the restrictions for publishing later in this chapter, in the section "Saving and Publishing a Game."

- ✏ **Volume:** Clicking and dragging the volume slider changes the volume of sound effects and music while designing or testing the game. The left side of the slider mutes the volume, and the right side turns it up.

Figure 5-8: The Toolbox sidebar provides a quick glance at the tools you can use to build your game.

Examining the tools

You can find four round buttons on the right side of the toolbox. Exactly one of these buttons is selected at all times, and it determines the way you edit your game. You often have to switch tools many times to design a level in its entirety. The four tools, shown in Figure 5-9, function as follows (from top to bottom):

- ✔ **Move:** This tool is selected by default. When selected, you can move the sprites you've placed by clicking and dragging them.

- ✔ **Edit:** When this tool is selected, you can click on a sprite you've placed to pull up a menu, where you can edit the sprite's settings.

- ✔ **Clone:** This tool allows you to copy a sprite and paste it elsewhere in the level, with all its settings intact. When this tool is selected, click on a sprite to copy it and then click where you want to paste it (or click and drag over multiple squares to paste several copies).

- ✔ **Delete:** When this tool is selected, you can click over sprites to delete them from the level.

  Be careful with this tool so that you don't delete the wrong sprites by mistake.

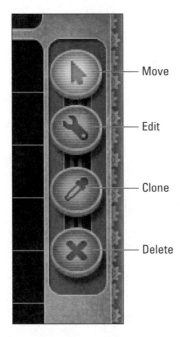

Figure 5-9: The mechanic's tools are on the right sidebar.

Building a Game in the Toolbox

The toolbox is a game design engine that allows you to build great games quickly. After you become familiar with its simple format, you can immediately start designing your own games. This section helps you understand the functionality of the toolbox.

Adding sprites

To place a sprite from the sprite tray onto your game, follow these steps in the toolbox:

1. **Click on a sprite in the sprite tray on the left.**

   After you obtain a large number of sprites, finding the one you want may be difficult. As shown in Figure 5-10, you can sort your sprites for easy use:

   • The orange drop-down menu allows you to select sprites of a certain genre.

Sorting controls   Currently selected sprite

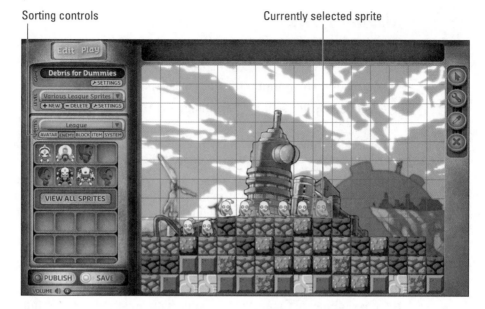

Figure 5-10: Use the buttons and drop-down menu to find sprites easily.

- The five buttons labeled Avatar, Enemy, Block, Item, and System allow you to look at sprites with a particular purpose.
- Use the gray View All Sprites button to close all filters.

2. **On the grid, click the square where you want the sprite to go.**

   As shown in the figure, the square glows green if available; a red square means another sprite is in the way.

3. **Place more sprites on the grid if you want.**

   You can repeat Step 2 to place multiple sprites, or simply click and drag over many squares to place the same sprite in all those squares.

4. **Put the sprite away by clicking in an empty spot on the sprite tray.**

   The sprite disappears from your cursor when you click its place in the sprite library.

By placing many sprites on the field, you can design rooms, mazes, gauntlets of villainous sprites, and any sort of challenge you can think of.

If the name of a sprite in your library appears grayed out, the sprite has a *bad sprite perspective;* see Chapter 6 for details.

Moving sprites

If you've misplaced a sprite or simply want to move it to a new location, follow these steps:

1. **Click the Move tool if it's not already selected.**

   See the earlier section "Examining the tools," for more on the different tools in the toolbox.

2. **Click and drag a previously placed sprite to a new square and then release the mouse button to drop it there.**

   The sprite stays on your cursor as long as you hold the mouse button. Releasing the mouse button drops the sprite if the square is unoccupied. If you try to drop a sprite on an occupied square, the sprite returns to its original position.

Editing sprites

Placing sprites on a grid can allow you to be creative, but to truly discover the possibilities of Gamestar Mechanic, you must look deeper into the properties of sprites. All sprites, particularly enemies and avatars, can be edited to change their characteristics and behaviors.

Follow these steps to edit a sprite's properties:

1. **Select the Edit tool.**

   This button has a wrench icon, second from the top (refer to Figure 5-8).

2. **On the grid, click on the sprite you want to edit.**

   A dialog box opens, containing a number of sliders, buttons, and text boxes, depending on the type of sprite it is (see Figure 5-11).

   If a dialog box has no options (such as the one for the goal block, shown in Figure 5-12), the sprite cannot be edited.

   Sometimes, you unlock new *skins* for your sprites, allowing you to change the look of the sprite. You obtain skins just as you do sprites: from completing quests or various challenges. Keep an eye out for these skins because acquiring one might mean that you can edit previously uneditable sprites, such as concrete.

3. **Adjust the options.**

   For enemies, you can change their health, damage, motion paths, and more. Avatars and other sprites give different options, which are detailed later in this chapter.

4. **Click the Save button to save your changes.**

   Or click the Cancel button to return to the game without implementing your changes.

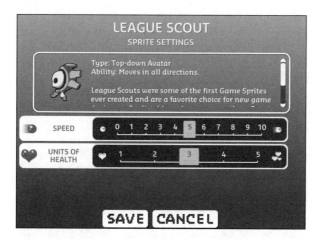

Figure 5-11: The League Scout, a basic avatar, has two editable attributes.

Figure 5-12: No matter which game you play, the goal block always functions the same way.

Cloning sprites

As a designer, sometimes you may want to use a large number of the same sprite to create a line of turrets or a maze of blocks or whatever else. Simply placing the sprites in the right pattern is rarely enough detail for a well-structured game — you have to edit each of them with the Wrench tool, performing the same operation over and over for each sprite. Fortunately, Gamestar Mechanic has a simple and elegant tool for fixing this: the Clone tool.

The Clone tool allows you to copy a sprite from one place to another, keeping all its settings and allowing you to place as many identical sprites as you want. To clone a sprite, follow these steps:

1. **Add a single sprite and edit it to your liking.**

   You may want to test the game at this point to make sure that your sprite is functioning properly before you clone it.

2. **Select the Clone tool.**

   It looks like an eye dropper (refer to Figure 5-8).

3. **Click the sprite from Step 1.**

   The sprite appears on the cursor as though you've taken it from the sprite tray.

4. **Select the square or squares you want to clone the sprite to.**

   By clicking, or clicking and dragging, you can place clones of your sprite on different squares. If you want a line of pacing enemies, for example, copy the first one and drag it along the line.

5. **Put away the sprite by selecting a new tool or placing the sprite back in the sprite tray.**

If you've finished the steps and realize you made a mistake, that mistake has been copied to all your sprites. Rather than use the Edit tool to fix each one, use a similar cloning approach: Delete all but one sprite, edit the remaining sprite, and clone the sprite again with the change.

If the sprites you're placing are similar, but different in some way (such as facing in different directions), the Cloning method still applies. Create one sprite and edit it, and then clone it. Because the cloned sprites are halfway edited already, refining their behavior is much quicker and more efficient.

Deleting sprites

Removing sprites is relatively easy, compared to the other options in the toolbox. To delete sprites, click the lowermost tool, with an X printed on it (refer to Figure 5-8), and then click or click and drag over the sprites you want to delete.

If you delete a sprite, you cannot undo that action! Be careful about which sprites you delete. If you delete something really important, refresh the page to reload your game from the last time you saved it.

Editing universal game features

If you want to change options that affect the entire game, click the Settings button under the name of your game, at the top of the sidebar. The button opens the Game Settings dialog box, shown in Figure 5-13.

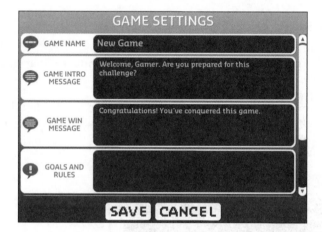

Figure 5-13: The first three settings are filled in by default, but I recommend that you change these messages.

Here's a rundown of these options:

- **Game Name:** This is the name of the game, of course. Always change this name to personalize the default name, New Game. This name is the one that players see in Game Alley and on the player page. The name can be no longer than 25 characters.

- **Game Intro Message:** This message explains the game or introduces a storyline. This message, displayed at the beginning of the game, has a maximum size of 500 characters.

- **Game Win Message:** This message is displayed on the You Win screen, after the player beats the game. It must also be 500 characters or fewer.

- **Goals and Rules:** This is a special section of the Game Intro Message in which you can describe the elements of the game to players. This section is optional and doesn't show in your game if you enter nothing. It can hold 150 characters.

✓ **Tips and Tricks:** You can use the five text boxes to add tips to help players beat the game. You can fill in none, some, or all of the text boxes, and they're printed accordingly. Each tip holds 150 characters.

At the bottom of the dialog box, click Save to update your game settings or click Cancel to undo your changes.

If you have a lot to write about, you can do so through special sprites such as the text message block, described in Chapter 6. Just use the Game Settings to introduce and wrap up the game, and leave the rest to your levels.

Editing levels

By placing, editing, cloning, and removing sprites, you can build the heart and soul of your game. However, you usually have to make some changes to the level as a whole.

As discussed earlier, you can access the level settings by clicking the Settings button on the left sidebar of the toolbox. You see a dialog box with a number of useful options, as shown in Figure 5-14.

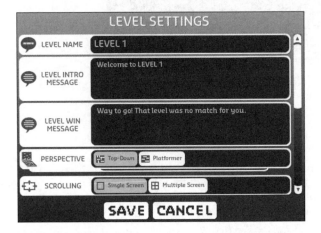

Figure 5-14: The default level settings are set for a small top-down game.

Here's a description of the options in this dialog box:

✓ **Level Name:** This is the name of the level, which players see onscreen when the level begins. The default name is LEVEL 1 for the first level, followed by LEVEL 2, and so on. It's often a good idea to change the name of every level in your game, to show that you've added sufficient detail.

✔ **Level Intro Message:** This message is displayed to players who start the level. The default message is

```
Welcome to <level name>
```

though you can change it to include hints, advice, or encouragement — or even pieces of the storyline. The message cannot exceed 100 characters.

✔ **Level Win Message:** This message is displayed whenever a player successfully completes a level. You should change the default message — Way to go! That level was no match for you. — so that you convey originality. The message must be no more than 100 characters long.

✔ **Perspective:** This setting is the current perspective of the level. You can choose from two options to change the perspective: Top-Down and Platformer. (See Chapter 3 for more on these options.) The default setting is Top-Down, so *remember to change it* if you need to.

✔ **Gravity:** This option appears only if you've selected Platformer in the Perspective section. By moving the slider to any value from 1 to 6, you can change the gravity of the game and, consequently, the height and speed at which sprites jump and fall. A higher number indicates higher gravity, making sprites jump lower and fall faster. As you move the gravity slider from 1 to 6, you allow sprites to rise 10, 6, 4, 3, 2, or 1 blocks, respectively, with a single jump.

✔ **Scrolling:** This option is useful in levels that have expansive landscapes or challenges. You can choose from two options: Single Screen (the default) and Multiple Screen. Selecting Multiple Screen allows for levels with larger dimensions, making the levels bigger than what is shown in the toolbox grid and allowing the avatar to scroll through them.

✔ **Wrap Around:** This option, when set to On, lets the avatar walk off the side of the screen and reappear on the other side, reminiscent of games such as Pac-Man. This option appears only in single screen games.

✔ **Level Width / Level Height:** These sliders let you change the size of a level, allowing you to scroll around the level in the toolbox and access more space for the level. The level size is measured in screens, and each screen is 12 blocks tall and 16 blocks wide. You can view the exact size in the toolbox. By adjusting the sliders, you can make a level as large as ten screens wide and ten screens high. This option appears only in multiple screen games.

Never use more space than you need. The camera through which the player sees your game always follows the avatar until it hits the edge of the level; if the level is too large, players will easily notice.

If you're unsure how much space you need, start building in the upper-left corner of the grid. If you decide to shrink your level, the screens are removed from the bottom and right sides, so your work in the upper-left screens isn't erased.

✔ **Edge Bounding:** You select from these four options to change the behaviors of the edges of the level. A *bounded edge* of the level prevents all sprites from passing through it, and an *unbounded edge* lets sprites walk right out of the level. The Edge Bounding options allow you to bound all edges, no edges, vertical edges, or horizontal edges. It's usually best to bound all four edges so that avatars can't get lost off-screen; however, unbounded levels have their own virtues: Enemies can be given the ability to leave the level if required, and platformer games cause avatars to be destroyed if they fall off the bottom of the screen.

Enemies are destroyed if they walk off-screen. If an enemy moves through an unbounded edge, it won't come back.

✔ **Background:** This setting contains two options: No Background or Choose a Quest Background. Clicking the Choose a Quest Background option opens a new menu that displays all the backgrounds you've earned. Click a background and then the Choose option to set the background for your level, or click Cancel to return.

If you completed the Custom Backgrounds Challenge, as described in Chapter 8, a third option appears: Choose a Custom Background. This option allows you to build your own collection of backgrounds, as described in Chapter 13. Play around with different backgrounds so you get a feel for what fits with your game.

✔ **Background Style:** This setting has no effect unless you're making a multiple screen game, or you have a custom background. All quest backgrounds are the size of a single screen, but sometimes the background size doesn't match the level size. These are your Background Style options:

  • *Fill* (the default setting) stretches the background to completely fill the level, without stretching one dimension more than another. Though this method is often preferable, it can crop part of the image off the edge of the level.

  • *Stretch* stretches the background to the exact dimensions of the level; if a level is wider than it is tall, or vice versa, the background is warped accordingly.

  • *Tile* doesn't change the background, but instead *repeats* it until it fills the level.

✔ **Background Scrolling:** This option, which has no effect unless you're making a multiple screen game, determines how fast the background moves when the camera scrolls through the level. A slow-moving background causes the background to seem far away from the player, giving a feeling of vastness; a fast-moving background is more close-up and apparent to the player. Moving the slider to the right increases the speed of the background, from None (the background doesn't move at all) to Locked (the background moves with the avatar, which is good for top-down games).

✓ **Music:** This setting allows you to set the music that plays along with your level. It contains options for every soundtrack you've unlocked, plus one labeled No Music. Typically, players won't mind a game with music as long as your use of music is consistent. In other words, if you put music in one level, be sure to put it in every other appropriate level.

Your game can have as many levels as you want. As detailed earlier in this chapter, you can add or delete levels with the New and Delete buttons, to the left of the Settings button on the left menu.

Saving and Publishing a Game

When you're finished working on your game, you can either save it or publish it by using the Save and Publish buttons in the lower-left corner of the toolbox.

Save

As you're creating your game, click the Save button frequently because it saves your game in a Draft Games section of the Workshop that only you can access and edit. If you're developing a large game, click the Save button when you need take a break from designing. You should also save your game after making significant changes because technical problems (accidentally closing the window, crashing your web browser, and so on) can set back your hard work.

If you see a login screen when you click Save, you were inactive for too long; just log back in to save your game. Saving can take a long time, depending on how big your game is. It's a good idea to save your game every time you put in a lot of work or make a significant change.

You can find your saved games in the My Draft Games folder of the Workshop. From there, you can use the Edit button to edit one of your games, or the Delete button to remove your save.

Publish

The Publish button saves your game to Game Alley, where others can play and review it. Usually, you click this button only after your game is complete. However, note that the Publish button has a light on the left side — this light tells you whether your game is publishable or not.

A game is publishable if the following restrictions are satisfied:

- ✔ You have earned publishing rights for your account by completing the first quest.
- ✔ Every level has an avatar.
- ✔ You've beaten every level during testing.
- ✔ The game has a title.
- ✔ The game has a game intro. (See the earlier section "Editing universal game fields.")
- ✔ The game has a win message. (See the earlier section "Editing universal game fields.")

Clicking the Publish button while the light is red tells you which levels you still have to test or which fields you still have to change.

When you publish a game, it goes in either the Pending Games folder or the My Published Games folder in your workshop, depending on whether the game has an unapproved custom background (see Chapter 13). Pending games become published if the Gamestar Mechanic administrators approve the backgrounds you used. However, whether a game is pending or published, you can still edit or delete it.

Use the Save button while editing a published or pending game to cause it to become a draft again. If the game was published, it's removed from Game Alley. When you publish the game again, all its statistics and reviews return to the way they were when the game was unpublished.

Analyzing Your Game's Reception

By selecting your game from the My Published Games section of your workshop, you can see the player page for your game. This is exactly like the player page detailed in Chapter 2: You can see reviews and comments on your game, the average rating of your game, basic statistics, and a collection of buttons for sharing or recommending the game. Here, you can play your game from a player's perspective and read what others have to say about it. Learning from feedback and revising your games is vital to the design process and essential when learning how to master your skills; see Chapters 12 and 13 for more information about editing and improving your games.

It's bad form to review or favorite your own games, even if you try to be honest. You can sometimes comment on your own games if you think people are going to read the comment on your player page, but be sure that you're complying with the rules of conduct (there's a link to these rules in the footer toolbar).

Reviews and ratings for your game

Every game has an easily accessible rating that's displayed below or next to the game everywhere it appears. The rating consists of one to five stars representing the quality of the game, and one to five gears representing the difficulty. These ratings are obtained by averaging the reviews of players and rounding to the nearest half-star or half-gear. The gear rating doesn't have much to do with the quality of your game, so you don't have to worry about it much. A game with a low difficulty rating is well-suited for inexperienced players, and a game with a high difficulty rating is intriguing to skilled players. The star ratings are what you should pay the most attention to. The following helps you interpret star ratings:

- ✔ **1 to 2½ stars:** Don't be discouraged by this rating! No one can create ideas in Gamestar Mechanic that are always popular. Try to figure out why some people disliked your game, and improve it. However, you might also get this rating by simple bad luck — certain people rate every game they see as 1 star (without providing good reasons), and it's your job not to let these ratings bother you. If one or two of those people get to your game first, don't worry — and remember that higher ratings often follow.

- ✔ **3 to 3½ stars:** This often means you made a good game, but can still improve. Read your reviews to find constructive criticism that might help you pinpoint where you can make your game better.

- ✔ **4 to 4½ stars:** This is a game well worthy of praise! In addition to improving via your reviews, try to see what players liked about this game and apply those concepts to future projects.

- ✔ **5 stars:** Five-star games are the most likely to hit the Top Rated section of Game Alley. With an average rating of at least 4.75, these games are the best you can get; to further improve, try getting a 5-star game with as many reviews as possible.

Game statistics

When you view the My Published Games page in your workshop, you see that each game has a View Stats button to its right. Click the button to load a funnel chart showing how players progressed in your game as a whole (see Figure 5-15). The vertical axis corresponds to the levels of your game, and the width of the funnel at each level describes the percentage of players who have reached that level. This graph is useful for seeing how many players beat each level of your game and which levels create choke points in the graph where players give up.

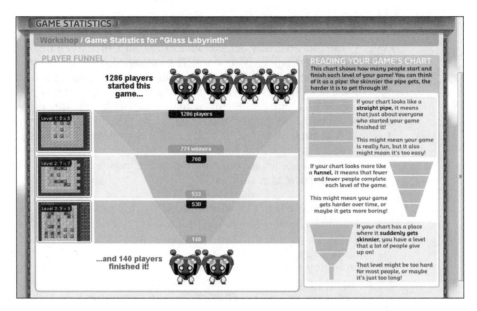

Figure 5-15: Game statistics over three levels.

6

Understanding Sprites

*T*he fundamental concept behind Gamestar Mechanic is the form and function of its sprites. A *sprite* is a basic object — an avatar, an enemy, a block, an item, or a system sprite — that can be used to form a simple component of a game. Games are composed of many sprites, locked together and edited to form a well-functioning machine.

To produce a working game, you must understand the purpose and possibilities of the sprites you use. This chapter lists the types and properties of the pre-created Gamestar Mechanic sprites and explains the different ways you can adjust their abilities.

Introducing the Properties of Sprites

All sprites follow patterns that affect how they act and interact. To maintain a consistent and easy-to-learn system for designing games, all sprites are made to be somewhat similar, except for certain special abilities that make them unique.

Before delving into the individual properties of sprites, I want to explain the mechanics that most (or all) sprites use to function within a game. As you gain experience, applying these mechanics should become second nature to you — though this chapter serves as a reference in case you're unfamiliar with some of them.

Perspective: Defines how sprites interact with the level

The *perspective* of a game (top-down or platformer, as described in Chapter 5) is the function that defines how sprites interact with the level itself. Understanding perspective is essential because it defines the space of the level and determines the motion of sprites.

Most avatars and enemies — as well as certain other sprites — are specific to a particular perspective:

- **Top-down sprites:** When someone is playing a top-down level, the level is treated as a flat game board on which various sprites are placed. The sprites may therefore be at rest anywhere in the level, and may have the ability to move anywhere in the plane of the game space.

- **Platformer sprites:** Platformer levels are much different from top-down levels, simpler in some regards and more complex in others. In plat-former mode, the level is treated as a backdrop for sprites, which exist in a world of horizontal (left and right) and vertical (toward the sky or the ground) dimensions. In this mode, the element of gravity is pulling down on all sprites at all times (blocks and items are exempt), and ava-tars can move only left or right, often with the capability to jump some distance upward before falling down again.

If you try to use a sprite meant for platformer games in a top-down game, or vice versa, the sprite has a *bad sprite perspective,* and it's grayed out in the list of sprites in the toolbox. If you want to use one of these sprites, clicking it causes the `Bad Sprite Perspective` message to appear. Click the Use Anyway button to bypass the message.

Using a sprite with a bad sprite perspective can lead to certain anomalies:

- **A top-down enemy in a platformer game** can fall without producing a "falling" animation. It gets stuck when trying to move up or down. It can fight or move with gravity a little bit, but a random motion setting is the only choice to prevent vertical enemies from getting stuck on the ground.

- **A top-down avatar in a platformer game** can fall without producing a "falling" animation and has the ability to overpower gravity. Its up-and-down motions allow for a strangely configured power of flight: It cannot move horizontally while accelerating vertically, giving it powerful but clumsy mobility.

- **A platformer enemy or avatar in a top-down game** only moves left or right, and cannot jump. It cannot move up or down without being pushed.

If you avoid these anomalies, sprites with "bad perspective" can actually be useful in a game. For example, the League Sniper can be used as a pacing or stationary turret in a platformer game, if you want a less humanoid-looking shooter.

If you want to include sprites with bad sprite perspective in your game, you should understand how they function in that perspective. I describe the rec-ommended perspectives for avatars and enemies in Tables 6-1 and 6-2, later in this chapter.

Practice using perspectives before you attempt to break the pattern. Always use sprites that fit the perspective, when you can, unless you truly want a particular image or ability.

Collisions: Interactions between sprites

Collisions, which are caused by contact between different sprites, form the basis of interactions between the components of your game. Because most sprites are *nonsolid,* they can pass through each other. If an avatar and an enemy collide, for example, their motion paths don't change, though the avatar may take damage. You can find more information about the different types of sprites in Chapter 5.

Most blocks and certain enemies cause *solid collisions,* stopping the other sprite. These types of sprites are necessary when defining your game space through walls and platforms. You can also create solid collisions with the walls of a bounded level, as described in Chapter 5.

With nonsolid collisions, sprites interact without bumping into each other, causing effects such as damage. For example, when an avatar and an enemy collide, they continue moving without bumping into each other, but the avatar takes damage. Similarly, a large swarm of enemies usually moves around with no interaction between the enemies because they don't affect each other. With the exception of special sprites that I discuss in the following list, nonsolid collisions occur between the following types of sprites:

- ✔ **Avatars and enemies:** Usually, the result of this encounter is the avatar taking damage. The amount of damage is determined in the enemy settings, which you set with the Edit tool, as described in Chapter 5. Exceptions include the Naviron chomper and Naviron omnivore (avatars that can damage the Naviron grazer enemies through nonsolid collisions), and enemies such as the Naviron informer (which displays messages when colliding with the avatar).

- ✔ **Avatar bullets and enemies:** Some avatars can shoot projectiles. When a projectile hits an enemy, the projectile is destroyed, and some effect takes place, depending on the type of projectile. Projectiles can freeze, damage, or *transmogrify* (change into another sprite) the target. (I describe the transmogrifier, whose projectiles act as avatar bullets, in Table 6-5, later in this chapter.) The most common projectile is a blue orb that deals 1 point of damage to its target.

- ✔ **Enemy bullets and avatars:** Some enemies can also shoot projectiles. Whenever a projectile hits an avatar, the projectile is destroyed and causes the projectile's effect: projectiles can freeze or damage the avatar, depending on the enemy. The most common projectile is a red orb that deals damage — almost all damage-inflicting enemy projectiles deal 1 point of damage, with the exception of certain megasniper sprites (described in Table 6-3, later in this chapter).

✔ **Avatar bullets and enemy bullets:** When two opposing bullets collide, as shown in Figure 6-1, they cancel each other out. Thus, when an avatar and its enemies are firing at each other, the sprites take damage only if one side starts firing more bullets than the other side. This concept adds an interesting element to blaster fights, giving an advantage to the highest fire rate and allowing for more strategy-oriented action. It's also an effective player technique because avatars typically fire much faster than enemies.

After a sprite takes damage, it flashes red briefly. During this time, it does not participate in damage-inflicting nonsolid collisions. This is because there is a limit to how rapidly a sprite can take damage, and while a solid collision only deals damage briefly, nonsolid collisions cause damage as long as the two sprites occupy the same space. This technical feature has various consequences that you should be aware of. For example, if you fire a blaster with a high fire rate at a stationary enemy, every other bullet will pass through the enemy without colliding.

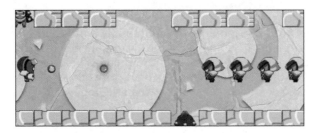

Figure 6-1: The blue and red bullets are about to collide.

✔ **Avatars and items:** An avatar collects an item, such as a point, health pack, or blaster, by colliding with it. This removes the item and grants the player some bonus — such as points, health, extra abilities, and so on. An item has no function except to be collected by the avatar in this way, making it rely on non-solid collisions. Enemies such as the Naviron grazer are exceptions to this concept: Grazers can eat plant items and recover energy just like the avatar.

Examining the Characteristics of Individual Sprites

To master the technique behind a game, you need to develop a firm understanding of the sprites that compose it. When you obtain a new sprite to use in your games, a combination of analysis and practice can greatly help you understand and optimize the sprite's possibilities. The following sections describe the qualities and properties of each sprite and give you tips for using them.

Discovering avatars and their functions

The avatar you use in each level is crucial in a game because you can have only one per level. Gamestar Mechanic offers many different avatars, and they don't have quite as many possible settings as their enemies do. When you add an avatar to your game, the most important choice is the sprite itself, followed by the settings within that sprite.

Avatars can have various abilities; blaster and phasing are the two most common. The *blaster* lets the avatar shoot when the player presses the Attack button, and *phasing* lets the avatar disappear and hide in place when the player holds the Action key. Several other abilities are available, as described in Tables 6-1 and 6-2.

Many of these sprites must be unlocked in quests or challenges, and some of them require premium membership. See Chapter 4 to find out which sprites the Quest rewards, and see Chapter 15 for details on rewards you can earn from challenges.

You can always change the health and speed of an avatar with the Edit tool, as discussed in Chapter 5. Tables 6-1 and 6-2 give you the *maximum* possible value. All avatars have a minimum health of 1 and a minimum speed of 0.

Table 6-1			Platformer Avatars	
Sprite	**Name**	**Max Health, Speed**	**Abilities**	**Notes**
	Acheron hero	8, 6	Blaster (fast fire rate)	A slow, hard-hitting hero
	Acheron jumper	8, 6	None	A durable jumper sprite
	Addison jumper	5, 10	None	A sprite version of Addison
	Altair freezer	5, 15	Freeze blaster	A jumping variant of the Altair iceman, which freezes enemies (with ice that lasts from 2 to 10 seconds, depending on the avatar's settings)
	Altair hero	5, 15	Blaster (slow fire rate)	A fast-moving but slow-shooting hero

(continued)

Table 6-1 *(continued)*

Sprite	Name	Max Health, Speed	Abilities	Notes
	Altair jumper	5, 15	None	A jumper with a high capacity for speed
	Amstrad jumper	8, 6	None	A sprite version of amstrad
	Aran jumper	5, 15	None	A sprite version of aran
	Bee hero	5, 10	Gliding, Blaster (medium fire rate)	A sprite that can glide horizontally for a short time when the Jump key (see Chapter 3) is pressed and held down, when a player is otherwise unable to jump. Can also shoot stingers (which are equivalent to blaster charges) at foes
	Bee jumper	5, 10	Gliding	Has the same gliding ability as the bee hero, but can't shoot
	Calamari jumper	5, 10	None	A basic underwater jumper
	Cowboy hero	8, 6	Blaster (fast fire rate)	The Western equivalent of the Acheron hero
	Emile jumper	5, 10	None	A sprite version of Emile
	Fitness jumper*	5, 10	None	A jogger sprite
	Flame mage	5, 10	Blaster (medium fire rate)	An avatar that shoots fireballs with the same effect as blaster charges
	Frost mage	5, 10	Freeze blaster (medium fire rate)	An avatar that shoots ice bolts to freeze enemies for 2 to 10 seconds, depending on avatar settings

Sprite	Name	Max Health, Speed	Abilities	Notes
	Jhansi jumper	5, 10	None	A sprite version of Jhansi
	Karakuri hero	4, 9	Blaster (medium fire rate), phasing	A hero that can shoot, jump, and disappear
	Karakuri jumper	4, 9	Phasing	A jumper with reduced abilities but with the added benefit of phasing; it can freeze in place and avoid damage while holding the Action key
	League hero	5, 10	Blaster (medium fire rate)	An avatar that can both jump and shoot
	League jumper	5, 10	None	A basic platformer sprite
	Minion Acheron hero	8, 6	None	A variant of the Acheron hero, with a metallic color scheme and a Rogue mask
	Minion Altair jumper	5, 15	None	A variant of the Altair jumper, with a metallic color scheme and a Rogue mask
	Naja jumper	4, 9	None	A sprite version of naja
	Naviron guardian	5, 10	Shield	An avatar that uses its shield (the Action key) in conjunction with its ability to jump
	Naviron hero	5, 10	Sword, Shield	A knight with a sword, a shield, and jumping ability
	Pengo jumper	5, 15	None	A penguin jumper that can move as fast as the Altair avatars

(continued)

Table 6-1 *(continued)*

Sprite	Name	Max Health, Speed	Abilities	Notes
	Rodney jumper	5, 10	None	A sprite version of Rodney
	Samson jumper	5, 10	None	A sprite version of Samson
	Seahorse hero	5, 10	Blaster (medium fire rate)	The underwater hero sprite; resembles the Calamari Jumper
	Witchy jumper	5, 15	None	A Halloween-themed jumper that can move as fast as the Altair

* To get this sprite, go to http://gamestarmechanic.com/landing/redeem, enter the code **Newgrounds***, and click the Validate button.*

Table 6-2   Top-Down Avatars

Sprite	Name	Max Health, Speed	Abilities	Notes
	Acheron marksman	8, 6	Blaster (fast fire rate)	A powerful shooter and a figurehead of the marksman type
	Acheron scout	8, 6	None	A scout that can survive numerous hits before being fragged
	Addison scout	5, 10	None	A sprite version of Addison
	Altair iceman	5, 15	Freeze blaster	An avatar that uses its blaster to freeze enemies (with ice that lasts from 2 to 10 seconds, depending on the avatar's settings)
	Altair marksman	5, 15	Blaster (slow fire rate)	A shooter that can be quite fast but fires slowly

Sprite	Name	Max Health, Speed	Abilities	Notes
	Altair scout	5, 15	None	A navigator with a high capacity for speed
	Amstrad scout	8, 6	None	A sprite version of Amstrad
	Aran scout	5, 15	None	A sprite version of Aran
	Cowboy marksman	8, 6	Blaster (fast fire rate)	The Western equivalent of the Acheron marksman
	Emile scout	5, 10	None	A sprite version of Emile
	Fitness scout*	5, 10	None	A jogger sprite
	Flame wizard	5, 10	Blaster (medium fire rate)	The top-down variant of the flame mage
	Frost wizard	5, 10	Freeze blaster (medium fire rate)	The top-down variant of the frost mage
	Fox scout	5, 10	None	A scout sprite resembling a blue fox
	Husky scout	5, 10	None	A variant of the fox scout, resembling a Siberian husky
	Jhansi scout	5, 10	None	A sprite version of Jhansi
	Karakuri marksman	4, 9	Blaster (medium fire rate), Phasing	A shooter that can disappear when needed
	Karakuri scout	4, 9	Phasing	A ghostlike sprite with the power to disappear
	League marksman	5, 10	Blaster (medium fire rate)	A basic top-down shooter

(continued)

Table 6-2 *(continued)*				
Sprite	**Name**	**Max Health, Speed**	**Abilities**	**Notes**
	League scout	5, 10	None	The first avatar in the game
	Minion Naviron scout	5, 10	None	A variant of the Naviron scout, with a black cloak and a rogue mask
	Naja scout	4, 9	None	A sprite version of Naja
	Naviron chomper	5, 10	Damages Naviron grazers on contact; gains 100 energy points by fragging grazers this way; cannot pick up energy items	One of only a few sprites that deals contact damage like an enemy; can deal various amounts of damage and is the only avatar that cannot eat energy items
	Naviron defender	5, 10	Shield	A sprite that can use its unbreakable shield by holding the Action button
	Naviron knight	5, 10	Sword, Shield	A powerful sprite with both a shield (the Action key) and a sword (the Attack key)
	Naviron nibbler	5, 10	Attracts nearby Naviron gnashers	A dinosaur-like sprite that's common in energy-based games
	Naviron omnivore	5, 10	Damages Naviron grazers on contact; gains 100 energy points by fragging grazers this way	The same as the Naviron chomper, but without the disadvantages

Sprite	Name	Max Health, Speed	Abilities	Notes
	Naviron scout	5, 10	None	The first Naviron avatar, and the only one with a counterpart in the other schools
	Rodney scout	5, 10	None	A sprite version of Rodney
	Samson scout	5, 10	None	A sprite version of Samson
	Seal marksman	5, 10	Blaster (medium fire rate)	A seal with a blaster mounted on its back
	Seal scout	5, 10	None	A simple underwater scout
	Turtle juggernaut	5, 10	Different control scheme, blaster (medium fire rate)	A blaster-wielding version of the turtle tank that can turn and shoot in any direction; helpful for picking off difficult opponents
	Turtle tank	5, 10	Different control scheme	A versatile avatar that rotates when you press the left- and right-arrow keys and moves forward and backward when you press the up- and down-arrow keys (respectively); can turn in any direction with this unique movement system
	Werewolf scout	5, 10	None	The basic Halloween-themed scout

* To get this sprite, go to `http://gamestarmechanic.com/landing/redeem`, enter the code **Newgrounds**, and click the Validate button.

TIP

The attributes of avatar sprites follow a few interesting patterns. To use avatars effectively without having to work from Tables 6-1 and 6-2, consider these general rules:

Avatar	Maximum Health	MaximumSpeed
Naviron, League	5	10
Acheron	8	6
Altair	5	15
Karakuri	4	9

There are also a couple of special qualities attributable to only certain sprite schools:

- ✔ Naviron avatars have no ranged attacks and are either dinosaurs or medieval characters.

- ✔ Karakuri sprites, with the exception of Naja, assume natural phasing ability.

Understanding enemies and their possibilities

Enemies are often the most complex sprites in the game because you (the designer) must edit them to function as effectively as possible, without the player's control. (The chapters in Part IV of this book detail the deeper strategies in game design.) Before examining Tables 6-3 and 6-4, you need to understand the qualities exhibited by enemies in general, as described in this list:

- ✔ **Only top-down enemies have the Turn Direction trait.** This trait lets you modify how the enemy reacts to a solid object. The Turn Direction trait always contains the Reverse, Left, and Right options, allowing the enemy to turn backward, left, or right (respectively) on contact. Some sprites have the Random option for this trait, so that they randomly select a direction when turning.

- ✔ **Most enemies have a set amount of health, damage dealt, and speed.** These three statistics define the power of the enemy; its movement pattern defines its style. Different enemies have different boundaries for these values.

- ✔ **All moving enemies have a Start Direction trait.** Top-down enemies can start the game facing Up, Down, Left, or Right. Platformer enemies can only start the game facing Left or Right.

- ✔ **Most enemies have a Movement Style trait.** You can choose from several options for an enemy's Movement Style; however, a single enemy generally has only two or three of these options available. You can find the movement styles available to each enemy in Tables 6-3 and 6-4. A few sprites, such as zombies or dinosaurs, may ignore their movement styles if they find something to follow.

At the time of this writing, here are the different movement styles, as follows:

- *Straight:* This is the default motion for all enemies, including those that do not have the Movement Style setting available. With this setting, the enemy moves in a straight line, changing direction only upon contact with solid objects.

- *Patrol:* Many enemies have this option available. When selected, the enemy sets boundaries for its own movement: one boundary in its starting space, and another boundary some distance away. You can choose this distance with a slider in the Enemy Settings, which appears when you select the Patrol style. The enemy then moves in a straight line, pacing back and forth between these two boundaries. This allows you to restrict enemy movement without solid objects, causing them to stay confined to a certain area or avoid walking off platforms. Note that the boundaries of a patrol are static, so if a patrolling enemy is jostled, it may start behaving oddly in order to stay within its bounds.

- *Random:* This movement style is a variation on Straight motion. If an enemy is set to this option, it changes direction (as if it hit a solid object) at random times. If you set the sprite's Turn Direction to Random as well, the enemy wanders aimlessly around the level.

- *Guard:* This movement style is reserved for Naviron lancers and Naviron sentries. They stay in one spot until they catch sight of the avatar, at which point they begin to chase it. However, they can be deceived: If you stay out of their line of sight for too long, they get confused and retreat to their starting space.

- *Follow:* This movement style is reserved for VIP sprites. Enemies with this option stay in place until the avatar approaches, at which point the enemy begins following the avatar around. There are other sprites that follow the avatar, such as zombies, but those sprites do not have the Follow option. This is because those enemies try to follow the avatar regardless of their settings and can break out of their normal movement styles if the avatar draws near.

The *start direction* determines which way the enemy is facing when it appears. The *movement style* allows the selection of certain specialized patterns, from straight lines to random motion to following and guarding. You can change both of these attributes with the Edit tool (see Chapter 5).

Tables 6-3 and 6-4 list all available enemy sprites and their attributes. They include the highest possible settings for each slider, and the enemy's available movement styles (excluding Straight, which is a possibility for all enemies).

Table 6-3			Platformer Enemies	
Sprite	**Name**	**Max Health, Damage, Speed**	**Special Movement Styles**	**Notes**
	Acheron nemesis	10, 7, 6	None	A powerful jumping foe that can blast at superfast speed; prone to falling off ledges because it has no special movement styles
	Acheron pacer	10, 7, 6	None	A powerful pacing sprite that reverses direction to avoid falling off ledges
	Acheron pouncer	10, 7, 6	Can patrol up to 10 blocks	A powerful jumping sprite
	Altair nemesis	5, 5, 15	Can move randomly or patrol up to 15 blocks	A jumping sprite that can manage only a medium fire rate, but makes up for it with speed and random movement
	Altair pacer	5, 5, 15	None	A fast enemy that reverses direction to avoid falling off ledges
	Altair pouncer	5, 5, 15	Can move randomly or patrol up to 15 blocks	A fast, jumping enemy
	Bandit nemesis	5, 5, 15	Can move randomly or patrol up to 15 blocks	A fast and versatile jumping enemy that can fire up to a medium rate
	Bunny pouncer	5, 3, 10	Can patrol up to 10 blocks	A giant rabbit that moves with hops at regular intervals
	Coach*	0, 0, 0	Cannot move	A coach that can't interact with the level (including gravity), but displays a message to the player on contact with the avatar

Sprite	Name	Max Health, Damage, Speed	Special Movement Styles	Notes
	Crabby nemesis	5, 3, 10	Can patrol up to 10 blocks	A powerful jumping crab that can shoot at a fast rate
	Cricket pouncer	5, 3, 10	Can patrol up to 10 blocks	A giant cricket that moves with hops at regular intervals
	Flame conjurer	5, 3, 10	Can patrol up to 10 blocks	A fire-wielding jumping sprite that can shoot fire-themed bullets at a fast rate
	Frost conjurer	5, 3, 10	Can patrol up to 10 blocks	An ice-wielding jumping sprite that can use a freeze blaster at a fast rate
	Fry pouncer*	5, 3, 10	Can patrol up to 10 blocks	A living, jumping box of French fries
	Hornet nemesis	5, 5, 9	Can patrol up to 10 blocks	A nemesis that can fire stinger-shaped bullets at a superfast rate; it can jump and briefly glide sideways before landing
	Hornet pouncer	5, 5, 9	Can patrol up to 10 blocks	An enemy that can jump and briefly glide sideways before landing
	Karakuri nemesis	5, 5, 9	Can only move straight	A powerful jumping sprite that can shoot at superfast speed, but lacks its fellow Karakuri sprites' ability to move randomly
	Karakuri pacer	5, 3, 10	Can only move straight	A basic enemy that reverses direction to avoid falling off ledges
	Karakuri pouncer	5, 5, 9	Can only move straight	A jumping sprite with a slightly lower capacity for speed
	League nemesis	5, 3, 10	Can patrol up to 10 blocks	A classic jumper-shooter that can shoot at a fast fire rate

(continued)

Table 6-3 *(continued)*

Sprite	Name	Max Health, Damage, Speed	Special Movement Styles	Notes
	League pacer	5, 3, 10	Can only move straight	A classic pacing enemy that reverses direction to avoid falling off ledges
	League pouncer	5, 3, 10	Can patrol up to 10 blocks	A classic jumping enemy
	Mummy pacer	10, 7, 6	Can only move straight	A mummy similar to the Acheron sprites; reverses direction to avoid falling off ledges
	Pengo pouncer	5, 3, 10	Can patrol up to 10 blocks	A spiny jumping penguin
	Piranha pacer	5, 3, 10	Can only move straight	A basic underwater pacer that reverses direction to avoid falling off ledges
	Piranha pouncer	5, 3, 10	Can patrol up to 10 blocks	A basic underwater jumping sprite
	Snowman	0, 0, 0	Cannot move	A snowman that can't interact with the level (including gravity), but displays a message to the player on contact with the avatar

* To get this sprite, go to `http://gamestarmechanic.com/landing/redeem`*, enter the code* **Newgrounds***, and click the Validate button.*

Table 6-4		Top-Down Enemies		
Sprite	Name	Max Health, Damage, Speed	Special Movement Styles	Notes
	Acheron chaser	10, 7, 6	Can move randomly or patrol up to 12 blocks, and can start in a random direction	A strong but slow sprite with a large patrol range

Sprite	Name	Max Health, Damage, Speed	Special Movement Styles	Notes
	Acheron ghost	10, 7, 6	Can move randomly or patrol up to 12 blocks, and can start in a random direction	A strong ghost with high health and strength, which can vanish up to a rate of Frequent
	Acheron megachaser	15, 10, 6	Can move randomly or patrol up to 12 blocks, and can start in a random direction	A classic Boss sprite with quadruple size and a high health capacity
	Acheron megasniper	15, 10, 6	Can move randomly or patrol up to 12 blocks, and can start in a random direction	An extremely powerful quadruple-size sprite, with a blaster that shoots three bullets up to superfast speed: one bullet straight ahead and one angled to either side
	Acheron sniper	10, 7, 6	Can move randomly or patrol up to 12 blocks, and can start in a random direction	A powerful shooting sprite that can fire up to superfast speed
	Altair chaser	5, 5, 15	Can move randomly or patrol up to 15 blocks	An extremely fast chaser
	Altair ghost	5, 5, 15	Can move randomly or patrol up to 15 blocks	A ghost with a high capacity for speed, able to vanish up to a rate of Often

(continued)

Table 6-4 *(continued)*

Sprite	Name	Max Health, Damage, Speed	Special Movement Styles	Notes
	Altair megachaser	12, 5, 15	Can move randomly or patrol up to 15 blocks	A quadruple-size, extremely fast chaser that must always start with at least 3 hit points
	Altair megasniper	12, 5, 15	Can move randomly or patrol up to 15 blocks	A quadruple-size shooter that moves fast and fires devastating triple-damage shots at up to a medium rate
	Altair sniper	5, 5, 15	Can move randomly or patrol up to 15 blocks	An extremely fast-moving shooter that can fire at a medium rate
	Bandit sniper	5, 5, 9	Can move randomly	A strong enemy shooter that can fire at superfast speed
	Coach*	0, 0, 0	Cannot move	A coach that cannot interact with the level (including gravity), but displays a message to the player on contact with the avatar
	Crocodile rover	5, 3, 10	Can patrol up to 10 blocks	A crocodile that, when turning, stops and rotates smoothly rather than turn instantly; at the time of this writing, available only for use in challenges with preselected sprite options

Sprite	Name	Max Health, Damage, Speed	Special Movement Styles	Notes
	Coyote chaser	5, 3, 10	Can patrol up to 10 blocks	A Western variant of the canine enemies
	Flame sorcerer	5, 3, 10	Can patrol up to 10 blocks	A sorcerer that can shoot fire-themed bullets at a fast rate
	Frost sorcerer	5, 3, 10	Can patrol up to 10 blocks	A sorcerer with a freeze blaster that can fire at a fast rate
	Fox chaser	5, 3, 10	Can patrol up to 10 blocks	A red-and-white fox
	Fry chaser*	5, 3, 10	Can patrol up to 10 blocks	A living box of French fries
	Ghastly phantom	0, 7, 6	Can move randomly or patrol up to 12 blocks, and can start in a random direction	A powerful sprite that chases down nearby avatars and turns transparent to pass through obstacles; can be fragged only by freezing it inside another sprite with a freeze blaster; its desire to chase the player is overridden by the Ignore Avatar setting, but nearby avatars always receive an extra 2 speed from the phantom's presence

(continued)

Table 6-4 *(continued)*

Sprite	Name	Max Health, Damage, Speed	Special Movement Styles	Notes
	Jackolantern chaser	5, 3, 10	Can patrol up to 10 blocks	A chaser that resembles a jack-o'-lantern pumpkin with legs
	Karakuri chaser	5, 5, 9	Can move randomly and start in a random direction	A chaser often associated with random motion
	Karakuri ghost	5, 5, 9	Can move randomly and start in a random direction	A ghost with the capacity for random movement; it can vanish up to a rate of Constant, but despite this terminology it cannot stay consistently hidden
	Karakuri megachaser	15, 8, 10	Can move randomly and start in a random direction	A quadruple-size, random sprite that always starts with at least 5 hit points
	Karakuri megasniper	15, 8, 10	Can move randomly and start in a random direction	A quadruple-size sniper that can shoot at a super-fast rate, and always starts with at least 5 hit points
	Karakuri sniper	5, 5, 9	Can move randomly and start in a random direction	An erratic sniper that can shoot at a superfast rate
	League chaser	5, 3, 10	Can patrol up to 10 blocks	The first enemy of Gamestar Mechanic

Sprite	Name	Max Health, Damage, Speed	Special Movement Styles	Notes
	League ghost	5, 3, 10	Can patrol up to 10 blocks	A classic ghost; it can vanish up to a rate of Constant, but despite this terminology it cannot stay consistently hidden
	League megachaser	16, 8, 10	Can patrol up to 10 blocks	A quadruple-size, chaser with a huge capacity for health, always starting with at least 6 hit points
	League megasniper	16, 8, 10	Can patrol up to 10 blocks	A quadruple-size sprite that can shoot at a fast rate; always starts with at least 6 hit points
	League sniper	5, 3, 10	Can patrol up to 10 blocks	A classic shooting enemy that can fire at a fast rate
	Lil foot	5, 0, 9	Can move randomly and start in a random direction	An unsettling but harmless sprite that runs away from nearby avatars, increasing its own speed by 2 when fleeing; has an obtainable lil yeti skin that changes its appearance from dark red to white

(continued)

Table 6-4 *(continued)*				
Sprite	*Name*	*Max Health, Damage, Speed*	*Special Movement Styles*	*Notes*
	Megadragon	15, 10, 6	Can move randomly or patrol up to 12 blocks, and can start in a random direction	A medieval variant of the quadruple-size Acheron mega-sniper; has a blaster that can shoot three fire-themed bullets at a superfast rate: one bullet straight ahead and one angled to either side
	Minion Naviron VIP	5, 0, 9	Can patrol up to 10 blocks or follow the avatar	A masked variant of the Naviron VIP that the player must protect at all costs: it can be damaged by enemies, and you fail the level if it's fragged
	Naviron gnasher	5, 5, 9	Can move randomly; ignores motion pattern to chase nearby Naviron grazers and Naviron nibblers	A dinosaur sprite that chases and frags herbivorous dinosaurs to keep its energy up; its energy settings can be modified, but it always gains 100 energy from eating a grazer

Sprite	Name	Max Health, Damage, Speed	Special Movement Styles	Notes
	Naviron grazer	5, 5, 9	Can move randomly; ignores motion pattern to flee nearby Naviron gnashers and obtain nearby energy	A dinosaur that eats plants (energy items with the Plant appearance) to stay alive. Can compete with the avatar during energy-based levels. It flees from Naviron gnashers and gains 2 speed while doing so; if not fleeing, it aims for nearby plants
	Naviron lancer	5, 3, 10	Can patrol up to 10 blocks or stand guard; waits in one place and looks straight ahead, chasing avatars when they're close enough to see; if confused, returns to its guard post	A strong guardian wielding a lance which occupies the space in front of it; the lance pushes the avatar, deals damage and blocks bullets
	Naviron informer	0, 0, 10	Can patrol up to 10 blocks	These enemies can't harm or be harmed by the avatar — on contact with the avatar, they give the player a piece of information written in the settings. It has 5 possible appearances, including a little blue fairy.

(continued)

Table 6-4 (continued)

Sprite	Name	Max Health, Damage, Speed	Special Movement Styles	Notes
	Naviron sentry	5, 3, 10	Can patrol up to 10 blocks, or guard; waits in one place and looks straight ahead, chasing avatars when they're close enough to see; if confused, returns to its guard post	A guard carrying a shield that pushes the avatar and blocks bullets; its shield frags the avatar by pushing it into a solid object; the sentry does damage but shield does not
	Naviron VIP	5, 0, 9	Can patrol up to 10 blocks, or follow the avatar	A harmless enemy that can only be damaged by other enemies, and must therefore be defended; players fail the level if any VIP is destroyed
	Polar bear	12, 5, 15	Can move randomly or patrol up to 15 blocks	A quadruple-size polar bear with the speed of Altair sprites; it can fire a freeze blaster at a medium rate; it always starts with at least 3 hit points
	Shark chaser	5, 3, 10	Can patrol up to 10 blocks	A simple underwater chaser

Sprite	Name	Max Health, Damage, Speed	Special Movement Styles	Notes
	Shark sniper	5, 3, 10	Can patrol up to 10 blocks	A shark with a blaster mounted on its head, which can fire at a fast rate
	Snowman	0, 0, 0	Cannot move	A snowman that cannot interact with the level (including gravity), but displays a message to the player on contact with the avatar
	Turkey megachaser	16, 8, 10	Can patrol up to 10 blocks	A quadruple-size turkey with extremely high power capacity; always starts with at least 6 hit points
	Undead chaser	10, 7, 6	Can move randomly or patrol up to 12 blocks, and start in a random direction	A zombie as strong as an Acheron sprite that follows the avatar when nearby; like the Ghastly Phantom, it can scare the avatar and increase its speed by 2
	Vampire chaser	5, 3, 10	Can patrol up to 10 blocks	A vampire-themed chaser
	Wolf chaser	5, 3, 10	Can patrol up to 10 blocks	A red-eyed wolf and the opposite of the Husky Scout

(continued)

Sprite	Name	Max Health, Damage, Speed	Special Movement Styles	Notes
Table 6-4 *(continued)*				
	Zombie chaser	10, 7, 6	Can move randomly or patrol up to 12 blocks, and start in a random direction	A green variant of the Undead Chaser, which follows the avatar and scares it (giving it an extra 2 speed); at the time of this writing, available for use only in challenges with pre-selected sprite options

* *To get this sprite, go to* http://gamestarmechanic.com/landing/redeem, *enter the code* **Newgrounds**, *and click the Validate button.*

Understanding general guidelines for enemies

Given the sheer number of enemies available to you, you should understand some of the patterns that different groups of enemies follow, as described in this list:

- **League enemies:** Have up to 5 health, 3 damage, and 10 speed.

  The same numbers apply to many sprites outside the main schools (Naviron, Altair, Acheron, and Karakuri), such as Underwater.

- **Acheron enemies:** Have up to 10 health, 7 damage, and 6 speed.

- **Altair enemies:** Have up to 5 health, 5 damage, and 15 speed.

- **Karakuri and Naviron enemies:** Have up to 5 health, 5 damage, and 9 speed.

  The Karakuri Pacer is an exception, having statistics equivalent to League enemies.

- **Karakuri and Acheron blasters:** Can fire up to superfast speed, whereas Altair can fire only at medium speed or lower.

- **Naviron enemies:** Are quite unconventional and have special abilities, geared for specific situations.

  These abilities are either energy-themed (consumption and hunger) or medieval-based (spears and shields).

Using enemy motion patterns

Earlier in this section, I describe the basics of how enemies are able to move. However, there are a lot more possibilities you can discover by tweaking the parameters of your enemy sprites. For example, if a sprite has a straight movement style but a random turn direction, the sprite moves in a straight line and turns in a random direction whenever it hits an obstacle. However, if the sprite has a random movement style and a turn direction of reverse, it shuffles back and forth erratically.

If a sprite has a patrol range and a random turn direction, it can lead to some strange behavior that you may not find very useful.

Examining blocks and their attributes

Blocks comprise the platforms, walls, and overall room design of your levels. They're solid (avatars and enemies cannot pass through them) unless stated otherwise in Table 6-5.

Table 6-5		Blocks	
Sprite	*Name*	*Abilities*	*Notes*
	Barrel block	Has 1 to 5 health, depending on settings	A destructible wooden barrel
	Blue gift (variants: green gift, legacy treasure gift, purple gift, red gift and yellow gift skins)	Turns into a block or item when touched	Modified by using the Pick Sprite button in the Edit menu to choose the surprise, and the Edit Settings button to customize the surprise's settings
	Brick (variants: cobblestone skin, snow brick)	None	A basic brick block with an interesting stone variant
	Cactus block	Deals 0 to 6 damage on contact with avatar, depending on settings	A cactus version of the damage block

(continued)

Table 6-5 (continued)

Sprite	Name	Abilities	Notes
	Checkpoint (variant: candy cane checkpoint)	Nonsolid; saves the avatar's progress on contact; reusable after a second checkpoint is reached	When the avatar is fragged after reaching a checkpoint, returns the game to the position it was in when that checkpoint had been reached (useful for breaking up long games)
	Cloud	None	A generic block with an airy texture
	Concrete (variants: moss skin, snow concrete, steel skin, stone skin)	None	A simple, versatile block
	Coral	Deals 0 to 6 damage on contact with avatar, depending on settings	An underwater version of the damage block
	Damage block (variant: holiday damage block)	Deals 0 to 6 damage on contact with avatar, depending on settings	A basic harmful block that's covered in spikes
	Dirt (variant: floating dirt skin)	None	A basic block resembling dirt
	Enemy generator	Has 1 to 5 health, depending on settings; spawns enemies	A block that can spawn enemies on adjacent squares. Edit the settings to change how rapidly enemies spawn (0 = none, 6 = fast) and to specify on which side of the block the enemies appear. The spawned enemy can be edited as well; use the Pick Sprite button to select the enemy you want to use and the Edit settings button to produce an enemy editing screen.

Sprite	Name	Abilities	Notes
	Enemy spawn point	Nonsolid; spawns enemies inside it	Creates a certain enemy, with the frequency determined in the settings; the spawned enemy can be edited as well — use the Pick Sprite button to select the enemy you want to use and the Edit Settings button to produce an enemy editing screen
	Energy generator	Nonsolid; spawns energy inside it	Creates the energy item (with the frequency determined in the settings), which can be modified with the Edit Settings button
	Glass block	Transparent; has 1 to 5 health, depending on settings	The simplest destructible block and one of the only transparent ones
	Goal block	Adds the Reach the Goal Block goal to the level; nonsolid until other goals are complete	Player is given the goal of reaching it (after completing other goals) as long as it's in play
	Gold block	None	A bright block marking the completion of Addison Joins the League
	Grass (variant: hedge skin)	None	A generic, plant-like block
	Hidden goal	Adds the Reach the Goal Block goal to the level; turns into a goal when touched; takes the appearance of another block; the avatar can jump off this block by holding the Jump key while landing, effectively making it a destructible platform	Used to provide variance and mystery to the goal block; disguise changes by using the Pick Sprite setting

(continued)

Table 6-5 *(continued)*

Sprite	Name	Abilities	Notes
	Ice damage block	Has 1 to 5 health, deals 0 to 6 damage to avatar on contact, depending on settings	A destructible damage block
	Item generator	Nonsolid; spawns items inside it	Creates a certain item, with the frequency determined in the settings; item can be selected with Pick Sprite and modified with Edit Settings
	Lock (red/blue/green)	Destroyed on contact if player has corresponding key; avatar can jump off it by holding the Jump key while landing, effectively making it a destructible platform	A colorful block that can be opened with the key item of the same color
	Moving block	Moves like an enemy, connects horizontally, defies gravity	A block that can take any nonrandom motion pattern with 1 to 10 speed, like an enemy sprite; when equivalent motion blocks are placed horizontally adjacent at the beginning of the level, functions as a single entity but becomes prone to glitches
	North flowers (variants: east flowers, south flowers, west flowers)	None	A flowery block with an open edge for connecting with vine blocks
	North vines (variant: east vines)	None	A block of vines that can be connected to flowers or vines on either side

Sprite	Name	Abilities	Notes
	Phoenix block	Has 1 to 5 health, depending on settings; causes a single destructible or consumable to regenerate	When it's placed, placement is completed by immediately clicking on another sprite; whenever linked sprite is destroyed (avatar, enemy, block) or collected (item), regenerates over time, taking 0 to 10 seconds depending on settings
	Sand	None	A basic sandy block
	Seaweed block (variants: bottom, horizontal, left, right, and vertical seaweed skin)	None	An underwater block that connects seamlessly with itself
	Snow block	None	A basic snowy block
	Soil block	None	A basic block of soil
	Teleport origin	Nonsolid; teleports the avatar to the corresponding destination	When this block is placed, placement is completed by immediately clicking on another space, creating a portal from the first space to the second; depending on settings, portal can be activated by pressing the Action key or on contact.
	Text message block (variants: book, question, sign, and tombstone message block skins)	Displays a message on contact with the avatar	A block that can be edited to create a message for the player that is split into a title (optional, visible at the top of the message) and a body (one or more pages of text, with a page four lines long)

(continued)

Table 6-5 *(continued)*

Sprite	Name	Abilities	Notes
	Transmogrifier (variants: transmogrifier boombox blue, boombox red, orange, tv red, tv yellow)	Has 1 to 5 health, depending on settings; fires bullets that convert enemies into other sprites; turned off and on at contact with avatar	Fires blue bullets in any direction, or in all directions, depending on settings; the fire rate of the bullets and the health of the block can be edited; by clicking the Edit Settings button, you can edit the bullet damage and the sprite that's created when the bullet frags an enemy; can create enemies or items out of its targets
	White block (variants: black, blue, dark blue, green, orange, and red block skins)	None	A useful, generic block with many variants
	Wood (variants: bark block, log skin, old bark block)	None	A basic wooden block
	Zombie crypt	Nonsolid; pawns zombies inside it	A specialized version of the enemy spawn point that spawns only zombies

Distinguishing items and their effects

Items are fairly basic sprites in that they serve only to grant effects on the avatar. At the time of this writing, the energy item is the only exception, because it can restore the energy of the Naviron grazer enemy. All items are nonsolid and are removed from play when collected (unless connected to a Phoenix block, as explained earlier in Table 6-5). In Table 6-6, you can find a list of all items, as well as the effects they provide the avatar.

Table 6-6		Items	
Sprite	*Name*	*Effect*	*Notes*
	Apple point*	Grants 1 to 10 points, depending on settings	An equivalent of the Point
	Armor point	Grants 1 to 5 armor, depending on settings	Gives the avatar armor, making the health meter turn gray and display an Armor value over it. Armor acts like extra health, preserving the avatar's hit points; an armor pack collected by an armored avatar replaces the old pack (as long as a higher Armor value results)
	Backpack	Gives the player an inventory	Somewhat of a meta-item; notifies the player when it is collected; when backpack is equipped, certain items (health packs, energy, blasters, double jump, and phasing) no longer activate when obtained. Instead, items are placed in the player's inventory and can be clicked on for use, giving the player more control over the use of items
	Bonus point	Grants 50, 100, 150, 200, 250, or 300 points, depending on settings	A point item that can be extremely valuable to players
	Blaster	Gives the avatar a blaster with fast fire rate.	A power-up that makes avatars glow red; its aura flashes and disappears when the blaster runs out; can last 10, 20, 30, or 40 seconds, or permanently, depending on settings
	Crate-o-energy	Restores 1 to 100 energy points, depending on settings.	An equivalent of the energy item*

(continued)

Table 6-6 *(continued)*

Sprite	Name	Effect	Notes
	Double jump boots	Allows the avatar to jump in midair during platformer levels	A power-up that, when collected, gives the avatar an extra (smaller) jump in midair, producing a versatile double jump; can last 10, 20, 30, or 40 seconds, or permanently, depending on settings
	Energy (variants: battery, blue corn, bolt skin, bread skin, candy corn, corn, ham, oil drum skin, pumpkin pie, roast chicken, water drop skins)	Restores 1 to 100 energy points, depending on settings	Keeps avatar alive during energy-based levels and functions well with the backpack
	Freeze blaster	Gives the avatar a freeze blaster with a fast fire rate; overrides the blaster power-up; if the avatar has a blaster by design, the two bullets alternate	Avatars with this power-up glow red; aura flashes and disappears when the blaster runs out; can last 10, 20, 30, or 40 seconds, or permanently, depending on settings; Freeze Duration setting determines how long targets stay frozen, from 2 to 10 seconds
	Health pack (variant: health potion)	Restores 1 to 6 health, depending on settings	Replenishes the avatar's health
	Honey pot health pack	Restores 1 to 6 health, depending on settings	An equivalent to the health pack, resembling a pot of honey
	Key (red/blue/green)	Allows the avatar to remove a lock block of the same color	As long as the avatar has the correct key, can open the corresponding lock on contact; can be consumable or permanent, depending on settings

Sprite	Name	Effect	Notes
	Phasing	Grants the ability to phase	A power-up that, when collected, gives the avatar the ability to disappear while holding the Action button; while phased, the avatar is invincible and invisible, but doesn't move, even defying gravity; can last 10, 20, 30, or 40 seconds, or permanently, depending on settings
	Point (variants: candy cane point, gold nugget point)	Grants 1 to 10 points, depending on settings	The most basic item available
	Starfish point	Grants 1 to 10 points, depending on settings	A flashier version of the Point
	Timer bonus	Adds 1 to 60 seconds to the timer	A power-up, that, when a level has a timer, adds time to it to help you complete the level; can also add time to survival timers, allowing you to complete the level faster
	Treasure chest bonus	Grants 50, 100, 150, 200, 250, or 300 points, depending on settings	A flashier version of the bonus point, with the higher default value of 100

* To get this sprite, go to `http://gamestarmechanic.com/landing/redeem`, *enter the code* **Newgrounds**, *and click the Validate button.*

Applying System Sprites Effectively

System sprites are essential to building complex games, and only a few types of sprites can control the style and feel of a game. To create a game that functions exactly how you want, you need to understand the game mechanics created by way of system sprites. The following sections describe the different system sprites and explain how to use them.

If you're new to designing certain types of games in Gamestar Mechanic, start each level by adding necessary system sprites. Then you can build and test the style of your game before you delve into the more complex work.

Energy Meter

Effect: Sets a countdown gauge that causes a level failure when it reaches 0; it is refilled whenever the avatar collects energy items.

When to Use It: The energy meter resembles a timer, making the game more urgent and engaging, but it's more versatile, with settings for initial energy, maximum energy, and energy consumed per second. In addition, energy-granting items, which cannot restore energy past the maximum value, can be stored in the backpack, which makes for a more multifaceted timer (and should be used in likewise complex levels).

Frag Counter

Effect: Requires the player to frag a certain number of enemies before the level can be beaten. By default, all enemies must be fragged, but the Specify Enemy Count setting lets the counter require between 0 and 9,999 enemies. The specified enemies must be fewer than the number of enemies in the level, unless the level contains enemy-generating sprites.

When to Use It: The frag counter turns obstacles into goals, requiring play-ers to do battle with the challenges ahead. If the counter is set to require All Enemies, the entire level must be cleared out. If the frag counter requires only a certain number of enemies, design your game accordingly, or combine the element with enemy-generating sprites for a powerful survival-shooter effect. Alternatively, you can require zero frags and use the counter as a simple gauge.

Health Meter

Effect: Displays the avatar's health and armor values. The health value turns red when it runs low (for avatars with 1 to 4 health points, 1 health is low; for avatars with 5 to 8 health points, 2 health is low).

When to Use It: The health meter is a commonly used but unusual system sprite. It doesn't change how the other sprites function — it simply informs the player of the avatar's status. However, it's extremely useful because it gauges the players' health and armor points, allowing them to know how close an avatar is to fragging. This sprite is unnecessary when no sprites in the level can damage the avatar, and it sometimes isn't required when the avatar never goes above 1 hit point. If you're unsure about whether to use this sprite, use it.

Population Counter

Effect: The system sprite, which takes the appearance of an enemy, displays how many of that enemy are in the level. The game cannot be won until that number of system sprites enter a certain range.

When to Use It: The population counter prompts the player to manage the population of a specific enemy. By setting the minimum and maximum number of enemies required to win a level, you can build many different challenges. The easiest way to use this counter is to set both the minimum and maximum counts to 0, requiring the player to defeat all of a certain enemy to win. Alternatively, you can use the population counter to tell the player to kill some (but not all) enemies, or use generators to create enough enemies to fill the quota. Lastly, you can set the minimum and maximum counts equal to the number of that enemy, telling players not to frag any of them. Unlike with other system sprites, you can place multiple population counters in the same level.

Score Keeper

Effect: Requires the player to collect a certain number of points before the level can be beaten. By default, all points must be collected, but the Specify Points setting allows the keeper to require between 0 and 999,999 points. The specified number of points must be less than or equal to the sum total of points in the level.

When to Use It: You can use the score keeper several different ways. It must always be used in conjunction with some number of point-giving sprites, spaced throughout the level.

- ✔ If it's set to require All Points, position your point sprites in all the places you want the avatar to explore, requiring the player to see the entirety of the level.

- ✔ If the score keeper requires only a fraction of the total points, try to space out point sprites homogenously throughout the level, either giving each area the same wealth or scaling rewards to difficulty level. This strategy gives the game an open-ended feel that puts power in the player's hands. In addition, you can have a game require 0 points (using the score keeper to have players gauge their own scores) or 1 point (place a point at the end of the level as a goal block substitute).

Players don't know whether you're requiring all points to be collected, so be sure to tell them whenever a certain score is required.

Timer

Effect: Sets a countdown clock; the player loses if the clock reaches 0. The clock can be set from 1 to 599 seconds, depending on settings. The timer can also be turned into a survival timer. (See the following entry.)

When to Use It: The timer adds a rushed feeling to a level. At the sight of this meter, players are urged to complete the level quickly. Use this sprite whenever this type of constraint is necessary to the challenge level of your game.

Timer (Survival)

Effect: Sets a clock to 0:00, which counts up to a set time; the level cannot be won until the clock reaches that time. The clock, which is a variant of the timer (described in the previous entry), can be set from 1 to 599 seconds, depending on settings.

When to Use It: The survival timer has the opposite effect of the classic timer: Players must stay in the level for a certain amount of time before winning. To use this sprite effectively, therefore, players must be in constant danger throughout the level, requiring them to hold out until the timer says that they can win.

Part III
Participating in the Gamestar Community

Find out how to write a meaningful review of someone else's game at www.dummies.com/extras/gamestarmechanic.

In this part . . .

✔ Review other designers' games.

✔ Increase your Mechanic Rank.

✔ Establish yourself in the Gamestar Mechanic community.

✔ Share your games and attract players.

7

Reviewing Games

In This Chapter

▶ Understanding the fun rating and difficulty rating systems

▶ Composing and posting a review

▶ Reading reviews of your games

▶ Giving constructive feedback on other creators' games

*O*ne of the most important social features of Gamestar Mechanic is its review system, allowing you to receive praise and feedback about your games and to play the role of constructive critic for games you play. You may also leave comments, which are the same as reviews but without ratings. This chapter shows you how to write a helpful, balanced review and how to read and interpret reviews of your own games.

I encourage you to add detail to your reviews. You may do this for the first few reviews, but after using the site for a while, it's easy to get in the habit of leaving simpler reviews without any detail. To motivate yourself to leave long, informative reviews, remember that writing reviews is necessary to achieve higher mechanic ranks. As described in Chapter 8, leaving reviews grants you experience points (as long as they contain written feedback), which in turn improves your Mechanic Rank.

Using the Review Interface

Reviews and comments are displayed beneath the game screen while you're playing a game. The following sections explain how to use the review interface as well as leave your own reviews or comments.

To leave a review, you must first have completed Episode 1 of Addison Joins the League.

Viewing reviews and comments

You can view the reviews for a game by going to the page where the game is played and then scrolling down. As many as five reviews at a time can be displayed there, and you can see the others by clicking the Previous and Next buttons in the upper-right corner of the review box, as shown in Figure 7-1.

Click these buttons to scroll through the reviews.

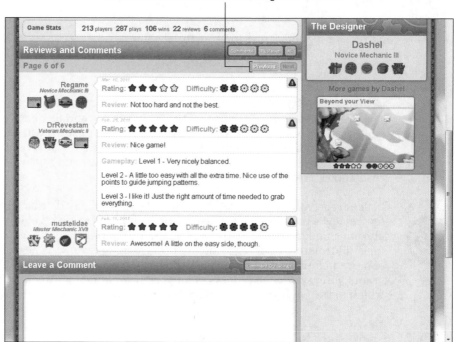

Figure 7-1: Different users write reviews with varying degrees of detail.

If you want to see only reviews and no comments, or vice versa, click either the Comments button or the Reviews button in the upper-right corner of the review box. Clicking the All button undoes these filters, as does refreshing the page.

Submitting a review or comment

Leaving a review is simple: To the right of the game screen is a large box labeled Your Review, as shown in Figure 7-2. It has five stars (Rating), five gears (Difficulty), and a text box labeled Review Notes. Click the highest star and gear that you want to give the game (rightmost is 5 stars, leftmost is 1 star; see the next section for details), and enter your review in the Review Notes text box.

Figure 7-2: The player is in the process of writing a review.

There are also three buttons — labeled Gameplay, Story, and Visuals — which add extra text boxes to the review box. In these text boxes, you can add extra elements to your review, as described later in this chapter. Click the Submit button to post the review.

If you don't want to give a general review, and instead you simply want to say something about the game or to the designer, scroll down the page to the Leave a Comment text box beneath the Reviews & Comments section, as shown in Figure 7-3. Type your comment, and then click Submit to post it.

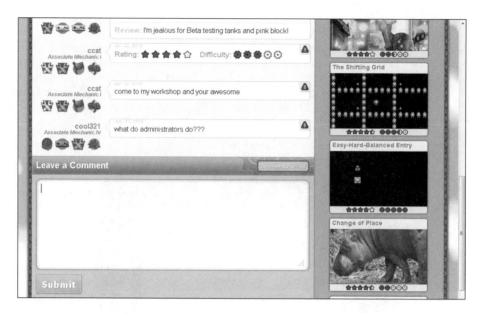

Figure 7-3: The Comment box lets you tell the designer something without attaching a rating.

You can leave only one review per game, but you can post as many comments as you want. Every text box can hold 1,000 characters.

Leave respectful reviews and comments. You cannot delete reviews or comments after you've posted them, though you can edit reviews. After you post a review, the Submit button changes to an Edit button — by clicking it, you can revise your review. The only way your review or comment can be deleted is for another user to click the triangular Flag button in the upper-right corner of the post, reporting it as inappropriate to the administrators.

Rating a Game

When you submit a review for a game in Gamestar Mechanic, you can specify a number of stars (labeled Rating) and a number of gears (labeled Difficulty), as shown in Figure 7-4. The following sections explain how these ratings work in more detail.

Figure 7-4: It takes two clicks to rate a game before you type in your review.

Understanding the star rating system

You can rate a game between 1 and 5 stars, depending on how much fun you had playing it. When rating a game, keep this rating system in mind to determine how you should assess the game:

- **0 stars:** If you don't select a star rating, it appears as 0 stars, indicating that you have no opinion that you want to share. Rather than give a game 0 stars, it's often better to leave a comment instead.

- **1 star:** The game is of poor quality throughout, implementing little or no detail and using no recognizably interesting elements. Use this rating sparingly because Gamestar Mechanic is an all-ages program for designers of varying skill levels. If you feel that you have to rate a game 1 star, be sure to point out how the designer could improve the game. Note that a 1-star review with no text is often flagged as inappropriate.

For contests, games with heavy dialogue, and other non-gameplay-focused genres, don't give a rating of 1 star because the game itself isn't fun. Either rate the game based on the qualities it wants to express, or simply leave a comment.

✔ **2 stars:** The game is in need of improvement in several regards, lacking a good core gameplay or story. However, these games may also have good qualities, which you should point out in your review for constructive feedback.

✔ **3 stars:** The game is a good one, with a solid foundation and entertaining elements, but some levels have notable problems, or some parts just aren't fun. Leave a balanced review for this game, with lots of positive suggestions and ideas on how to improve.

✔ **4 stars:** The game is well designed, with lots of good components and solid ideas. It has a few noticeable errors, which you should point out only after establishing why you thought the game was good. A 4-star game warrants a mostly positive review, but the designer also deserves a clear idea of what could be improved.

✔ **5 stars:** The game is of exceptional quality throughout, with few problems and many virtues. Most or all of the game is particularly impressive. A 5-star rating doesn't require much detail, but it's always helpful to point out why you enjoyed a game — it helps the designer understand which elements were well received, and it makes your rating more meaningful.

Negative reviews can have a rippling effect. A bad review can hurt the average rating of a game, reducing the ranks of its potential players. If you're unsure how to review a game, round up your rating to the nearest star or simply leave a comment.

Getting to know the gear rating system

In addition to the star rating system, Gamestar Mechanic has a gear rating system, which measures difficulty. Displayed to the right of the star rating system, the Difficulty rating is an assessment of how difficult you found the game to play.

Don't worry about your own bias corrupting your difficulty review (rating games at high difficulty because of low skill, or vice versa). The overall difficulty rating of a game represents the average difficulty its players had in completing it — there's nothing wrong with individual bias in the long run.

Use these guidelines for choosing a difficulty level:

✔ **0 gears:** By not leaving a difficulty review, you're indicating that you don't want to share an opinion on the difficulty of the game, such as for a game with more story and visuals than gameplay. You may also refuse a gear review if you didn't complete enough of the game to give an informed evaluation.

✓ **1 gear:** A 1-gear game is quite easy, taking little effort to beat and providing no real challenge. If you can't think of any challenging aspects of the game, 1 gear is appropriate.

✓ **2 gears:** The game is relatively easy to play, with straightforward overall requirements and simple premises. However, you can understand how the game could be challenging to other players, because it has recognizable elements of difficulty in the levels, whether or not you personally see them that way.

✓ **3 gears:** This game is fairly challenging, with gameplay difficult enough to make for an engaging experience. It took some effort for you to win the game, and the level of challenge is moderate.

✓ **4 gears:** This experience was a legitimately challenging one, taking a considerable amount of effort to complete. A game such as this is well balanced for your particular level of play.

✓ **5 gears:** Either this very difficult game required a great amount of effort to complete, or you were unable to complete it because of its challenge. This rating can either be the mark of a satisfying game or a frustrating one, so be sure to point out which one it is in your review.

Adding Gameplay, Story, and Visual Components to a Review

By clicking the orange buttons labeled Gameplay, Story, and Visuals in the Review box, you can add extra sections to your review, as shown in Figure 7-5. These sections are dedicated to certain qualities of the game you're reviewing, and they appear beneath your general review. Use these sections to organize a long review or point out qualities of the game that stood out.

Each component can be as long as 1,000 characters (the same as reviews and comments), allowing reviews to be four times the normal length of a post. You should use the extra sections to rate these particular components of the game:

✓ Gameplay for the experience itself

✓ Story for the storytelling (if any) exhibited in the game

✓ Visuals for the graphical effects

You can evaluate any number of these components where appropriate, as explained in the following sections.

Figure 7-5: A game review with all extra sections used.

Implementing the gameplay component

The gameplay component is often redundant without a story or visual component to go with it, because the review rates the experience of playing and winning the game from the standpoint of how fun it was. When you want to comment on the story or the visuals, work that information into other sections of the review and reserve the gameplay section exclusively for the underlying concepts.

In the gameplay section, you should ask yourself questions like these:

- **Which elements helped make the game fun?** Don't think about the story or visuals, but rather about the mechanics and inner workings of the game. How much did you enjoy the concepts? The five elements of game design (as described in Chapter 5) are useful here.

- **Which areas could be improved?** If you can think of one or two major problems that the designer should fix, be sure to point them out. To stay positive, as with any review, don't put this section at the beginning or the end of the review. Add a positive comment first to set a good tone, and then include something nice at the end to reiterate the virtues of the game. For example:

"I really liked the inventive level design you used in this game. You could make the game more engaging by placing enemies at key areas, such as the hallway in level 3. However, the enemies you did use were very well-designed."

✓ **How did the gameplay affect the story and/or visuals, or how was it affected by them?** Address this question in your review only if you think it's important. Think about how the gameplay linked with the story behind it or the visuals around it.

Adding a story component

The story component is used whenever a game tells a story. These games are quite common, using message blocks or other methods to add a storyline that makes the game more meaningful.

To evaluate a story, ask yourself these questions:

✓ **Was the story engaging?** An effective story should be gripping and worth the time to follow. Think about whether the designer did this well.

✓ **Do you want to point out particular sections of the story?** Think about where in the story you found a particularly interesting, confusing, powerful, or unnecessary segment. Adding specific examples to your review makes it more meaningful.

✓ **Is the story integrated or detached? (How did it connect with the rest of the game?)** If the game combines gameplay and a story, describe how the story improves on, or detracts from, the gameplay and visuals.

Integrating a visual component

This section encourages you to talk about the look of the game in your review — specifically, the background and the visual presentation of sprites.

You can review most games by filling out the Gameplay and Visuals sections, leaving the main section for general notes and overall comments.

To write a visuals section in your review, talk about some of the concepts in the following list:

✓ **Did the game designer choose the appropriate sprites for developing the visuals?** Think about the kind of scene the designer was setting. What colors or textures were used? Could the visuals be improved? Was a certain aspect of the imagery done well?

✓ **Was the background used effectively?** The background should contrast the sprites and, often, set the theme of the visuals. Did the background accomplish this goal? Was there anything special about the background — for example, is it a well-designed custom background? If there was no background (which is rarely appropriate, because the default background is black with no texture or distinguishing features), can you suggest a background that the designer can use?

✔ **Is there space for extra detail? Were the visuals thoroughly detailed and engaging?** If only part of a level is used, it isn't necessarily a problem with the gameplay, though it can lead to visuals that look off. Designers often fill in extra space with collections of blocks or custom backgrounds that form detailed visuals and scenery. Did the designer do this, and was it done particularly well? If this method for filling space wasn't used, is there a place where the designer should have done this? For example, if a level with lots of space involves jumping across thin, concrete platforms in a large, empty space, the designer can help fill in the emptiness by extending the concrete downward and adding buildings or islands. Consider whether the designer's visuals work with the element of space, as described in Chapter 11.

Learning from Reviews of Your Games

Reviews are meant to help designers learn from their experiences and build better-designed games. Thus, you should read reviews on your own games and use the reviews to better understand the best and worst qualities of your work.

Don't let bad reviews lead to hurt feelings. Publishing a game requires an emotional contribution, which can make poor reception difficult to deal with. Just remember that the best reviews are constructive, and use your own judgment to decide which ones help you. People on Gamestar Mechanic are generally friendly, but you should always be prepared for the inevitable bad reviewer.

Reading a low rating

Here are the steps you should take if you receive a low rating on your game:

✔ **Determine whether the rating is legitimate.** Don't waste time on reading reviews that were written only to bully you or other users. If a review is particularly offensive, be sure to report it with the Flag button, as explained in the earlier section "Submitting a review or comment."

✔ **Pick out the useful information that the review is conveying to you.** If someone is alerting you to a problem with your game that you weren't aware of, be sure to read the review carefully. (It doesn't take long because many reviews are quite short.) If someone makes a comment that you've already heard, such as "Too easy!" or "A bit too short," look carefully at the elements of your game to see why users have formed a consensus about this flaw.

Be sure to notice the positive statements that people make about your game, too.

- **Decide which points you agree with.** Think about whether your game would have been better if you had followed your reviewers' advice. To create the best possible version of your game, zero in on the most valuable advice you've received.

- **Keep track of the aspects that you want to fix in future games.** With practice, your design techniques get better and better, and recurring issues get smaller and smaller. Perhaps keep a notebook of known pitfalls to watch out for when working on a game, or practice using individual elements to fill out any skills you might be having difficulty with.

Reading a high rating

A high rating is one to be proud of, but it's also one that you can learn from. Follow these steps to interpret good reviews:

- **Find out what the reviewer liked.** If the reviewer stated a specific quality of the game that's especially good, you should keep it in mind when designing future games. Even if it's a generic comment, such as "Awesome!" or "Fun," you can gain a good understanding of what feeling the reviewer has associated with the game.

- **Think about what you're doing right.** Determine what makes your game fun to play. The important actions here are to pick up on specific techniques that were well received and then consider whether you have made full use of them in your game.

- **Take note of concepts that should be extended or repeated.** Good reviews should be helpful as well as congratulatory. Make sure you identify the strategies you should repeat in future games. Much like the strategy for dealing with flaws, keep your virtues in mind while designing games, or keep a notebook of techniques that you want to implement or reuse.

Writing a Constructive Review

Your reviews of other users' games should serve to help designers with their endeavors on the site, both by praising the skills they're good at and providing insight on how they can improve. Follow these tips to ensure that you give helpful feedback to other designers:

- **Bundle suggestions with compliments.** The courtesy of placing some praise before and after a suggestion for improvement goes a long way toward composing a pleasant and trustworthy review. However, make sure your compliments are *meaningful* — finding particular good qualities of a game is not only helpful for the designer but also good practice for you.

✔ **Imagine the designer's ideal game.** The designer is trying to make a good game. If you find any errors in the game's design, try to help the designer pull her work up toward the level of the ideal game — the game that the designer hoped to create. This form of feedback can be inspiring for designers who are having trouble realizing their gaming dreams.

✔ **Review as you want to be reviewed.** For the most part, all Gamestar Mechanic users want the same thing: to have people play their games and to be able to design better ones. Therefore, you should review games as helpfully and honestly as you would expect others to review *your* games.

Helping students deal with reviews

If you're teaching a Gamestar Mechanic class, as described in Chapter 16, you certainly don't want students to be driven away by bad reviews. Some designers even make games that bribe other users for 5-star reviews in exchange for similar positive remarks, thinking of the rating system as something that's easier to purchase than to earn. In order to help students use the review system, teachers might try going over individual reviews of their games and discussing them. Was the review honest? Did the low rating have good evidence? Teaching these analytical skills is an important step in media literacy, and good preparation for the less-friendly sections of the Internet. Also remember that reviews are meant to help users create better games, so discussing reviews is a useful way to give students ideas for improving on their work.

8
Earning Ranks and Badges

As you progress in Gamestar Mechanic, you can gain several types of permanent rewards and objectively improve your statistics on the site. These achievements permanently benefit your account, either by giving you new sprites or showcasing your accomplishments in your workshop.

You can improve your presence on the site in many ways. Completing the Quest, publishing games, and gaining popularity and followers are important actions that are covered in other chapters of this book. In this chapter, I focus on the following forms of advancement:

- **Gaining experience points and ranks:** Your Mechanic Rank reflects how much experience you have on the site, and you can advance to the next rank by performing actions that earn you *experience points,* or XP.

- **Earning badges and world badges:** Badges indicate special achievements you've obtained on the site. The badge system gives you a number of goals to strive for, which don't have to be completed in order.

- **Winning challenges and contests:** A number of special challenges offer rewards, such as sprites, soundtracks, or backgrounds.

This chapter goes into detail about these different ways you can advance your presence on Gamestar Mechanic.

Gaining Experience Points and Ranks

The abbreviation *XP* is short for *experience points*. In Gamestar Mechanic, you gain XP by performing certain actions on the site, such as publishing your games or leaving helpful reviews on games published by other users. When you gain a certain amount of XP, you progress to the next rank in Gamestar Mechanic.

In your workshop, you can see your current *rank,* which shows how much you've leveled up. (You can see your rank next to your username.) When you first join Gamestar Mechanic, you have the rank of Tourist Mechanic.

Your rank is public — whenever someone sees your workshop, your games, or your reviews, they can also see your rank.

Gamestar Mechanic has a rather unique system for leveling up: Rather than follow a single linear XP progression, you must obtain four different kinds of XP to level up, each of which reflects a different skill you need to learn as a game designer. Obtaining new ranks proves that you have practice designing games to polish your skills, playing games to learn how other designers create fun elements, reviewing games to closely analyze the design of games, and participating in the community of like-minded designers. In addition, many users pay attention to the ranks of their reviewers, and a high rank may intrigue other users to check out your games.

The four types of XP are described in this list:

- **Designer XP (dXP):** You gain this type of experience point by publishing popular games. You are awarded a bit of dXP for every person who plays one of your games. You can also build or repair games in the Quest to earn dXP.

- **Player XP (pXP):** Playing games gives you pXP. Whether you're in the Quest or Game Alley, every game gives you some pXP the first time you play it.

- **Review XP (rXP):** You earn rXP by reviewing other users' games. Providing a simple rating with no text gives you a bit of rXP, but you can get lots of it by leaving detailed reviews (as described in Chapter 7).

    If you enter a bunch of useless text or leave comments such as, "I'm just typing this to get rXP," users can flag your review.

- **Citizen XP (cXP):** To obtain cXP, you must contribute to the Gamestar community and help other designers enjoy the site. An easy way to do this is by playing games that few people have ever played, which helps users who might be struggling for recognition. You can find these types of games in the New Games or Fresh Games sections of Game Alley. By playing and reviewing unnoticed games, you can earn lots of rXP and cXP and help new designers along the way.

    You can also obtain lots of cXP by successfully finding bugs in the website or inappropriate games, reviews, and comments. You can report a bug using the Help button in the upper-right corner, and flag inappropriate content with the triangular ! button next to the game or comment in question. However, you are rewarded only if you report a valid issue.

As you can see, performing different actions earns you different kinds of XP, and you *rank up* (change your Mechanic Rank) by bringing all four to 100 percent. To gauge how much of each XP you currently have, go to your workshop and then click the orange View Progress button next to your rank. The Advancement & Achievements page opens, as shown in Figure 8-1.

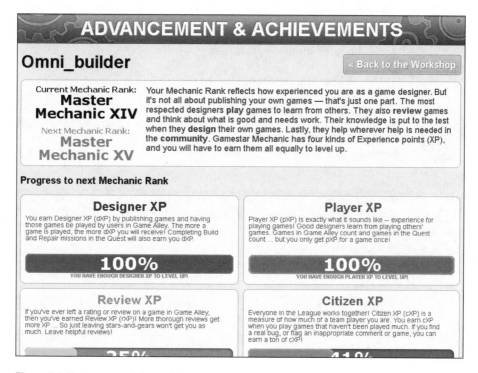

ADVANCEMENT & ACHIEVEMENTS

Omni_builder   « Back to the Workshop

Current Mechanic Rank:
Master Mechanic XIV

Next Mechanic Rank:
Master Mechanic XV

Your Mechanic Rank reflects how experienced you are as a game designer. But it's not all about publishing your own games — that's just one part. The most respected designers **play** games to learn from others. They also **review** games and think about what is good and needs work. Their knowledge is put to the test when they **design** their own games. Lastly, they help wherever help is needed in the **community**. Gamestar Mechanic has four kinds of Experience points (XP), and you will have to earn them all equally to level up.

Progress to next Mechanic Rank

Designer XP

You earn Designer XP (dXP) by publishing games and having those games be played by users in Game Alley. The more a game is played, the more dXP you will receive! Completing Build and Repair missions in the Quest will also earn you dXP.

100%
YOU HAVE ENOUGH DESIGNER XP TO LEVEL UP!

Player XP

Player XP (pXP) is exactly what it sounds like -- experience for playing games! Good designers learn from playing others' games. Games in Game Alley count and games in the Quest count ... but you only get pXP for a game once!

100%
YOU HAVE ENOUGH PLAYER XP TO LEVEL UP!

Review XP

If you've ever left a rating or review on a game in Game Alley, then you've earned Review XP (rXP)! More thorough reviews get more XP ... So just leaving stars-and-gears won't get you as much. Leave helpful reviews!

Citizen XP

Everyone in the League works together! Citizen XP (cXP) is a measure of how much of a team player you are. You earn cXP when you play games that haven't been played much. If you find a real bug, or flag an inappropriate comment or game, you can earn a ton of cXP!

Figure 8-1: You can scroll down this page to see your badges.

This page contains the following information about your rank and XP:

- ✔ **Current Mechanic Rank:** Your current rank is displayed in bold black text at the top of the page.

- ✔ **Next Mechanic Rank:** Displayed in gray, it's the rank immediately after your current one. You can achieve this rank after you earn 100% of each type of XP.

- ✔ **Progress to Next Mechanic Rank:** Four colored bars let you see how close you are to the next Mechanic Rank for each type of experience point. As you obtain certain types of XP, the corresponding progress bar fills up from left to right, and the percentage displayed on the bar increases.

If you achieve goals in a bar that's already at 100 percent, the experience points you earn from that point on will be applied to future ranks.

When all four bars are filled to 100%, you rank up. You can obtain 12 different ranks, from Tourist Mechanic to Gamestar Mechanic, but beyond the first two ranks, you don't gain a full rank by leveling up once. In fact, each rank is broken into several levels marked by Roman numerals, so you might be a Novice Mechanic III or a Veteran Mechanic VII. This means that in order to achieve a new title, you have to rank up the previous title multiple times. The number of ranks required to surpass a title may vary. For example, Tourist Mechanic and Newbie Mechanic have only one level, Intern Mechanic has 5, and the Expert Mechanic and Master Mechanic ranks have as many as 20 levels.

Table 8-1 lists the Mechanic Ranks in order.

These ranks tell other players how experienced you are on the site, and serve as reminders of personal achievement for you. If you're not sure what to do on the site at the moment, try simply filling up your XP bars and gaining the highest rank you can.

Table 8-1	Mechanic Ranks
Rank	*Number of Levels*
Tourist Mechanic	1
Newbie Mechanic	1
Intern Mechanic	5
Novice Mechanic	5
Associate Mechanic	5
Senior Mechanic	10
Lead Mechanic	10
Adept Mechanic	10
Veteran Mechanic	10
Expert Mechanic	20
Master Mechanic	20
Gamestar Mechanic	0
Administrator	0 (reserved for site administrators)

Reading Roman numerals

Rank levels are recorded in Roman numerals, an ancient counting system often used today. In Gamestar Mechanic, these are the three symbols you need to know:

I = 1

V = 5

X = 10

For most Roman numerals, you simply have to add the values of each symbol: VII is 7, and XVIII is 18, for example.

The symbols are usually arranged from largest value to smallest value. However, if you see a number such as IV or IX, it means something different.

The Romans never used four symbols in a row, such as IIII or VVVV. Instead, they rearranged the symbols. *IV,* with the *I* in front of the *V,* means *5–1 = 4.* Similarly, *IX* means *9.* Thus, Roman numerals count to 20 this way:

I, II, III, IV, V, VI, VII, VIII, IX, X, XI, XII, XIII, XIV, XV, XVI, XVII, XVIII, XIX, XX

Use this guide to see your progress in a Mechanic Rank.

Obtaining Badges

In addition to Mechanic Ranks, you can improve your persona on Gamestar Mechanic by obtaining *badges,* which track your achievements on the site.

If you look in your workshop, you see two boxes labeled Gamestar Badges and World Badges. If you click the View All Badges button in either box, the Advancement and Achievements page opens. Scroll toward the bottom of the page to see details about your badges, as shown in Figure 8-2.

The Gamestar Badges section contains all badges you've earned for your account. As you read from left to right and from top to bottom, the badges are listed in order by date earned, starting with the most recently earned badge. You may see grayed-out badges, indicating badges you've not yet obtained.

The World Badges section shows your progress toward each world badge and offers you the option to start or continue your work on them.

I discuss both types of badges in the following sections.

Gamestar badges

Like ranks, Gamestar badges are goals you can pursue by improving your skills as a designer, and they allow you and other users to immediately see your most recent achievements on the site. Most Gamestar badges have a color — the color of the circular background behind it. They can also have a rank, determined by the color of the icon itself. Six such badges are shown in Figure 8-3, displaying four different colors and ranks.

Figure 8-2: The three badges at the end of the Gamestar Badges section have not yet been obtained, so they're grayed out.

The colors of badges are described in this list:

- **Red** corresponds to designing games, matching the color of the dXP progress bar. (Refer to Figure 8-1 to see the progress bars for each XP type.)

- **Blue** corresponds to playing games, matching the color of the pXP progress bar.

- **Yellow** corresponds to reviewing games, matching the color of the rXP progress bar.

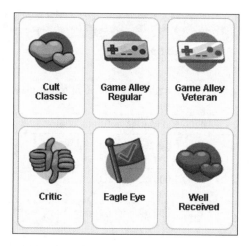

Figure 8-3: Gamestar Mechanic badges allow you to track your achievements.

🖊 **Orange** corresponds to commenting on games or being a good citizen, matching the color of the cXP progress bar.

🖊 **Green** corresponds to online learning, either the official courseware or the world badges, which are described later in this section.

Meanwhile, the ranks of badges are a bit simpler to follow:

🖊 **Bronze** badges have brown icons and are the easiest to earn.

🖊 **Silver** badges have gray icons and are more difficult to obtain than their bronze counterparts.

🖊 **Gold** badges have yellow icons and are more difficult to obtain than either silver or bronze.

🖊 **Platinum** badges have white icons and are the most difficult to obtain; however, few achievement chains go all the way to platinum.

At the time of this writing, 32 badges are available, as described in Table 8-2.

In addition, some badges transcend the 32, and these badges are available for only a limited time. You obtain these badges by winning awards in various contests sponsored by Gamestar Mechanic, using games you've created in Gamestar Mechanic. You can scroll over these special badges, which are markers of your past achievements, to see what they represent.

Table 8-2		Gamestar Badges
Badge	*Rank*	*How to Obtain It*
Blue		
Fresh From the Oven	Bronze	Play a game that had 10 or fewer plays.
Game Alley Cat	Silver	Play 500 games in Game Alley.
Game Alley Newbie	Bronze	Play 5 games in Game Alley.
Game Alley Regular	Gold	Play 1,000 games in Game Alley.
Game Alley Veteran	Platinum	Play 2,000 games in Game Alley.
On the Bleeding Edge	Gold	Play 300 games that had 10 or fewer plays apiece.
On the Cutting Edge	Silver	Play 150 games that had 10 or fewer plays apiece.
Try, Try Again	Bronze	Lose a single level 50 times in a row and keep trying.
Green		
Extra Creditor (Gold)	Gold	Complete every online learning exercise, including both the courseware and the world badges. (See the next section for details on world badges.)
Extra Creditor (Silver)	Silver	Complete all exercises in a world badge, or in a unit of the online learning courseware.
Orange		
Articulate	Silver	Leave 100 comments.
Beta Tester	Bronze	No longer obtainable, this badge was given to all users who played the second beta version of Gamestar mechanic.
Eagle Eye	Bronze	Flag an inappropriate review, comment, or game. You receive this badge only after the flag is reviewed and confirmed.
Eloquent	Gold	Leave 500 comments.
Even Beta Tester	Silver	No longer obtainable, this badge was given to all users who played the first beta version of Gamestar Mechanic, when the site was somewhat unfinished.

Badge	Rank	How to Obtain It
Stop Buggin' Me	Bronze	Report a website bug to administrators. You receive this badge only after the report is reviewed and confirmed.
The Alpha and Omega	Gold	No longer obtainable, this badge was given to all users who played the alpha version of Gamestar mechanic, when the site was still in early development.
Two Cents	Bronze	Leave a comment.
Red		
Cactus	Gold	Publish 50 games.
Classic	Gold	Have a published game that at least 200 people have favorited.
Cult Classic	Silver	Publish a game that at least 50 people have favorited.
Level Designer	Bronze	Publish a game with at least 10 levels.
Off the Charts	Gold	Have a game with more than 1,000 plays.
Prolific	Silver	Publish 20 games.
Published	Bronze	Publish a game.
Sensation	Silver	Publish a game with more than 500 plays.
Smash Hit	Bronze	Publish a game with at least 100 plays.
The Chosen One	Gold	Have one of your games featured by the administrators.
Well Received	Bronze	Have a published game that at least 10 people have favorited.
Yellow		
Critic	Silver	Review 100 games; each review must have some text in it (any amount of text is fine as long as you don't just leave a rating).
Critical Eye	Bronze	Review a game.
Reviewer	Gold	Review 500 games. Each review must have some text in it.
None		
Background Certificate	Gold	Complete the Custom Backgrounds challenge. (Challenges are covered later in this chapter.)
League Intern	Silver	Complete the introductory missions in the Quest.
League Mechanic	Gold	Complete the first five Quest missions.

World badges

World badges take much longer to earn than Gamestar badges because you have to complete a series of tasks. When you click Start Now or Continue in the World Badges section, Gamestar Mechanic shows you the list of requirements to earn that badge. For example, Figure 8-4 shows the list of requirements for the Apprentice badge.

Clicking the orange arrow button on the right side of an unlocked requirement shows you a brief description of that requirement. For example, in Figure 8-4, if you click the orange arrow to the right of Requirement 3, you see the page shown in Figure 8-5. This briefing tells you exactly what you have to do to fulfill the requirement.

The Requirement page sometimes has an extra window at the bottom where you can work on the task. The tasks in this window are much like the Quest, requiring you to build, fix, or design games. Other tasks require you to write about things you've learned, and still others require you to take simple actions elsewhere on the site (such as reviewing a game).

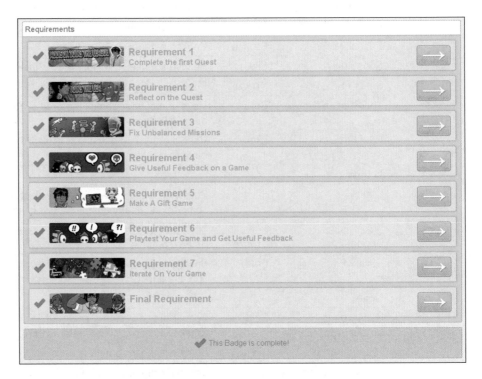

Figure 8-4: World badge requirements.

Figure 8-5: You can view requirement briefings even after you've completed them.

Completing Challenges

A *challenge* is a special task that appears in the Challenges & Contests section of your workshop, as shown in Figure 8-6. Challenges are similar to Quest episodes in that they may require you to play, repair, or build games, but they aren't part of the Gamestar Mechanic storyline. However, they still grant rewards for playing or for designing certain predesigned games and templates.

The Challenges & Contests section contains, as its name implies, both challenges and contests. *Contests* are made available only once and provide the opportunity to submit your games in a competition with other designers, giving valuable real-world rewards to the winners. Usually, only one or two contests are available at a time. An available contest says `Enter Now!` below it, whereas a challenge says `Earn Rewards!`. See Chapter 15 for the lowdown on contests.

To participate in a challenge, click on the image or the title and read the details of the mission, as shown in Figure 8-7. You can access the challenge itself by scrolling to the bottom of the page.

Just like the quests, as detailed in Chapter 4, challenges contain individual missions in which you must play, repair, or design games. By completing all the missions, you finish the challenge and reap the rewards.

Figure 8-6: The Challenges & Contests section in the Workshop.

Figure 8-7: A challenge page explains the mission and allows you to start working on it.

At the time of this writing, 21 challenges are available, as described in Table 8-3.

Table 8-3		Challenges	
Challenge Name	*Free?*	*Reward*	*Times Available*
AMD Impact	Yes	Energy sprites, population counter, and message block; rewards are given at the end of a mission	Always
Autumn	No	Autumn-themed sprites	Always
Background	Yes	New backgrounds, including the Brick Paths template	Always
Bugging Out	No	Bug sprites	Always
Checkpoint	No	Checkpoint sprite	Always
Custom Background	No	Custom background certificate (allows the use of custom backgrounds)	Always
Damage Block	Yes	Damage block	Always
Energy	Yes	Energy items and energy-consuming sprites	Always
Freezer	No	None (grants practice with freezer sprites)	Always
League Hero	Yes	League hero	Always
Level Map	Yes	Ability to generate level maps	Always
Locked On	Yes	Red lock and key sprites	Always
Media and You	Yes	Transmogrifier sprites	Always
Message Block	Yes	Text message block sprites	Always
Mystical	No	Mystical-themed sprites	Always
Spooky	Yes	Halloween-themed sprites	During autumn
Spring	Yes	Spring-themed sprites	During spring
Underwater	No	Underwater-themed sprites	Always
Wild West	Yes	Western-themed sprites	During summer
Winter Animals	Yes	Winter-themed animals (avatars and enemies)	During winter
Winter Holiday	No	Winter-themed sprites, particularly Christmas-oriented	Always

Because you can complete challenges in any order, you can collect the sprites you want ahead of time and complete the other challenges as you need them. However, don't let seasonal opportunities pass you by; if a challenge is closing soon, be sure to complete it if you can.

The Challenges & Contests section of your workshop displays incomplete available challenges first so that you can use them to determine your progress in challenge completion.

9

Meeting the Mechanics

As you progress in Gamestar Mechanic — a task that requires the assistance of a helpful community of users to complete — you may find yourself drawn to certain groups of users. Gamestar Mechanic is designed to make it easy to find your peers and learn from interesting creators: The more time you spend working on the site, the more people you'll meet. In this chapter, I explain how you can make friends on Gamestar Mechanic and become part of the community.

See Chapter 10 for information about how to interest people in playing your games and how to attract players without coming across as intrusive.

Making a First Impression in the Community

Introducing yourself to users on the Gamestar Mechanic site is much different from meeting someone in person. The only thing that other users know about you is the content you've chosen to add to the website. Putting your best face forward, therefore, is important for making people interested in you — if other users haven't gotten to know you, they will start via your online content.

This list describes some of the information that other users can see about you on the Gamestar Mechanic site:

✔ **Your username:** The username that you chose when you signed up for Gamestar Mechanic (as described in Chapter 2) says a lot about you and how you define yourself. Other users can see this nickname stamped on your workshop (as shown in Figure 9-1), your games, your reviews, and your comments.

Figure 9-1: What other users see when they visit your workshop.

✔ **Your published games, especially your Showcase game:** When you design a game, it reflects a bit of your personality. Because games are the most significant and elaborate pieces of content you submit to the site, they're helpful ways to express yourself. Try to build a database of games that describes your ideas, thoughts, or character; let your work help create the personality you want to present. You must also select a Showcase game — which is displayed as a large picture at the top of your workshop (see Figure 9-1) — so consider which of your games best represents you.

If you want to create games for the purpose of relating news, issuing contests, or talking about your ideas, that's fine; however, be sure to update them when necessary, or at least delete them after the content has expired.

Each game is represented by a screenshot, which users click to start playing it. In order to make users interested in your games, try to make this screenshot as descriptive as possible. The screenshot is taken automatically from level 1. If the level is too large to be captured in a single screen, the image is from the top of the level, horizontally aligned with the avatar. This screenshot usually displays a part of the introductory gameplay, but some users design their levels to display interesting pictures or patterns.

✒ **Your reviews and comments:** When you review or comment on a game, the designer is likely to read it. Reviewing and commenting are excellent ways to indirectly introduce yourself to the community and to provide some information about how you communicate. (See Chapter 7 for more information on reviewing games.)

Every element in the preceding list reflects some aspect of your personality, so be thoughtful when you write a comment or review, or create a game. These mediums help you communicate something about yourself and to find people with similar interests along the way.

Gamestar Mechanic sets strict rules against making off-topic reviews and comments. You can add personality to the content you write but, overall, stick to talking about the game.

Embracing the Gamestar Mechanic Community

Gamestar Mechanic hosts a large community of users, drawn together by their games and reviews. The site doesn't support direct chat between users, but that doesn't stop people from connecting — the sharing of ideas and feedback creates a more indirect and creative form of communication between users. This section shows you how to build connections with other users and how to deal with problematic ones.

Building relationships

After you've crafted your online persona (as described at the beginning of this chapter and in Chapter 2), you're ready to start interacting with other users. While there is no official capability to directly communicate with others, here are some ways you can start building relationships on the site:

✒ **Leave respectful reviews.** Kind and well-written reviews encourage people to become interested in you. Because leaving reviews is the closest you can get to direct communication through the site, be sure to make the most of them.

✒ **Find designers that create entertaining and engaging games.** If you enjoy playing a particular game and want to find out more about the designer, consider trying out other games created by that designer. To do so, select a game from the random list of games created by the same user in the lower-right corner of the game screen, as shown in Figure 9-2. Note that other users can do the same with your games.

You can also find out more about a designer by clicking the designer's username in the upper-right corner of the game screen. That takes you to the designer's workshop, where you can find out more about his interests. If you want to follow that user's activity in your news feed, click the Follow button to the right of his username.

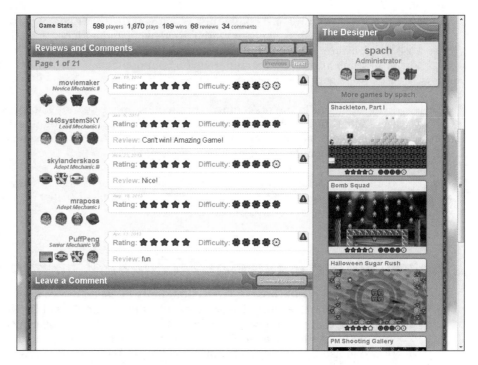

Figure 9-2: Selections from the More Games By section.

You *must* put a good face forward in the Gamestar Mechanic community. In relationships of mutual respect, all participants are rewarded with honest reviews and shared interest in each other's games.

Reporting users for unacceptable behavior

If a user is doing something unacceptable on the site, whether by way of a game, a review, or a comment, you can report that person. This action sends a message to the site administrators and calls attention to the problem.

Types of unacceptable behavior

Here are a few types of unacceptable behavior that you can legitimately report:

- **Personal attacks:** These remarks directly insult or disrespect other people. The comment "This game is boring" isn't a very good review because it doesn't offer any constructive or specific feedback; however, it isn't negative enough to be flagged. A comment such as "You're a bad designer," though, should be flagged. Such personal attacks are belittling and can be particularly damaging to those who are inexperienced with media literacy (being streetwise on the Internet).

✔ **Explicit content:** This content is rare because reviews and comments are filtered, and custom backgrounds must be approved by administrators. However, if you discover that someone has made the effort to hide explicit content in a game, whether it's profane or suggestive, you should flag it. A major draw of Gamestar Mechanic is its safe environment for all ages, which is made possible by users reporting inappropriate content.

✔ **Discriminatory or abusive language:** Even if a remark isn't directed at a specific person, discrimination is a major offense and may make some users uncomfortable expressing themselves. To keep Gamestar bias-free, report anything unpleasant that's being said about a specific group or demographic.

✔ **Plagiarism:** When you plagiarize, you copy someone else's work and use it like it's your own. Plagiarizers usually lift concepts from other users or "borrow" visual elements made by other artists without citation or permission. Parodies do not count as plagiarism.

Don't make too much of a stretch when reporting plagiarism. A game may have been "inspired" by another game or copied inadvertently, so flag only games that exactly replicate large portions of a game. See the later section "Avoiding stealing someone else's work" for in-depth information on plagiarism.

✔ **Personal identification:** If someone posts information about himself, such as his full name or phone number, you should report the incident, for the safety of the poster. Locations such as home addresses or schools are especially troublesome because the user is providing personal information that should *not* be shared with strangers. Read the rules of conduct (`http://gamestarmechanic.com/about/roc/`) to see what information should not be posted.

Reporting another Gamestar Mechanic user for abuse is a serious action, so carefully consider the consequences. If you call too much false attention with your reports, *you* may be the one who is reprimanded instead.

Reporting a user to administrators

If you find reportable content on the site, follow these general steps to report a user as abusive:

1. **Click the Flag button by the review, comment, or game you want to report.**

   In the upper-right corner of every review or comment is a triangular button marked with an exclamation point (!); a similar button is in the upper-right corner of a player page so that you can flag the game itself.

   The Report Abuse page appears, as shown in Figure 9-3.

Thanks for helping us keep Gamestar Mechanic a fun, safe place. Please tell us about what happened.

We take Abuse Reports very seriously and follow up on each and every one. Before you file your report, please take a look at the Rules of Conduct. They will tell you about the types of behavior that are ok (and not ok) in Gamestar Mechanic.

Remember, only use this tool to report things that *really* are against the rules. Making false reports of abuse can result in our moderators taking action against the user who made the false reports.

View our Privacy policy.

☐ I have read the Rules of Conduct **and promise I am submitting a real abuse report.**

Submit Report   Cancel

Figure 9-3: You can report reviews, comments, or games that are offensive.

2. In the large text box, explain why you're reporting the review, comment, or game you flagged.

This step helps the administrators understand where to look when verifying your claim.

3. Click the box labeled I Have Read the Rules of Conduct and Promise I Am Submitting a Real Abuse Report.

By selecting this check box, you acknowledge that you understand what makes an action reportable and that you accept any consequences of ignoring these rules. You can find the full rules of conduct at `http://gamestarmechanic.com/about/roc`.

4. Click Submit Report.

Your report is sent to the site's administrators.

After the administrators read and assess your report, they will e-mail you and send a message to your message box in the Gamestar Mechanic lobby (see Chapter 2). This message lets you know whether the administrators found your report to be valid. It may take a while to receive this message, depending on how busy the administrators are.

If an administrator decides that your report is valid, one of the following actions is taken:

✓ **The user receives a warning.** If the user hasn't made a habit of this behavior, the administrators generally send a warning to the user's message box. This warning details the offense and why the behavior is not acceptable on the site, giving the user a chance to start following the rules without receiving punishment.

✔ **The user is temporarily suspended.** This is a harsher warning that prevents the reported user from accessing the website for a certain number of days.

✔ **The user is banned.** This is only for very severe or repetitive violations of the Gamestar Mechanic rules. Reported users permanently lose access to their account.

✔ **The user is IP-banned.** This punishment prevents banned users from simply creating new accounts. Every computer has an IP address, which can be read over the Internet. If a user gets IP-banned, the user's computer is permanently blocked from the Gamestar Mechanic website.

Filing a successful report rewards you with lots of citizen experience points (known as cXP, as detailed in Chapter 8). It also helps keep Gamestar Mechanic a safe and fun environment for other users.

Learning from Other Designers

If a designer does something you particularly like, you can use this idea as inspiration for your own games.

If you copy someone else's game, you might be accused of *plagiarism,* stealing the idea and passing it off as your own. Avoid plagiarizing others' work, as described in this section.

Getting inspiration

You can gain inspiration from other games in a few different ways. If you're inspired by a unique idea, think of new ways to apply it — just make sure you cite the original game, preferably in the Game Intro or Level Intro page. At other times, you might simply notice specific aspects of rich gameplay or nicely done visuals, inspiring you to focus on these themes in your own games.

If you need further inspiration, play the Quest again. The levels in the Quest contain many original elements and well-designed levels, which are excellent materials for studying the format of Gamestar Mechanic games.

Avoiding stealing someone else's work

When you draw inspiration from other users' games, make sure you don't plagiarize their content. Plagiarism is a serious offense that you should always avoid. Normally, people can commit plagiarism on Gamestar Mechanic only when they actively try to copy someone else's game exactly. However, when you start using custom backgrounds (as described in Chapter 13), plagiarizing someone else's work becomes much easier. That's why you should know what plagiarism is and how to avoid it, in order to avoid breaking the site's rules of conduct.

If you re-create a design mechanic from a game outside of Gamestar Mechanic, it's generally acceptable. Because Gamestar Mechanic is a unique engine, your adaptation of a game such as Super Mario or Final Fantasy would be considered a result of inspiration, rather than stealing. For example, many users like to re-create classic video games, pandering to players' nostalgia. However, plagiarizing another Gamestar Mechanic user's idea is a different story.

Using a well-known mechanic is fine, because some concepts are too commonly used for a single person to claim them. For example, you might place small challenges in all four corners of a room and place a goal in the center. Even if you've seen someone else use this arrangement, you can also apply this mechanic, because it's too simple and well-known for anyone to claim ownership. If you use a more complex or precise mechanic, especially if you copy large numbers of sprites with minimal original changes, this action can be regarded as plagiarism.

Follow this rule of thumb: You can draw inspiration from other users' games, but don't use another game as a template for your own without citing your source. (I define and describe the citation in depth in the next section.)

Adding a citation when using someone else's unique content

If you use unique content created by someone else, whether or not you add your own modifications to it, you should provide a citation to it — don't explicitly try to pass it off as your own design. A citation acknowledges the owner of the content you're using, with a name or URL for the owner. For example, if you use a custom background, you can use the Level Intro message to say *Background courtesy of,* followed by the creator's name or username, and then include a link if applicable. You need to point out that the background you're using was created by, and is claimed by, another person.

You can add citations to your game by using one or more of these features:

- ✓ **Message sprite:** Any sprite that displays a message can be used to display your citation. Just make sure that the sprite can be easily found and reached. You can place a message sprite in each level where you use borrowed content, or cite all of your sources at once in a separate level.

✔ **Level Intro message:** The Level Intro message is a great place to cite content such as custom backgrounds. It is one of the most popular ways to cite individual sources, so you may find it useful if your citation is short enough to fit in the message area, and if you aren't using the Intro Message for a different purpose. (See Chapter 5 for details on adding a Level Intro message.)

✔ **Game Intro message:** You can use the Game Intro message to handle all your citations at one time, especially if all your custom backgrounds are from the same artist. (For more on adding a Game Intro message, see Chapter 5.)

Avoid placing citations at the end of the level with your custom background. If you place them there, players have to complete the level in order to confirm that the background is cited. Especially for difficult games, this action isn't effective.

10

Making Yourself Known within the Community

In This Chapter

▶ Building relationships and renown to attract players

▶ Sharing and embedding games online

▶ Publicizing your games (without being intrusive)

*I*f you want to get more people to play your games, it can help to integrate yourself into the online community. Whereas some games gain popularity by chance, developing a loyal audience is helpful if you want to spread the word about your work. This chapter helps you publicize your games and bring them into the community.

Directing Gamestar Mechanic Players to Your Games

If you don't want to wait for people to play your games, you have the tools to take matters into your own hands. The following sections help you understand how to gain potential players and popularity while forming relationships and community in the process.

Keeping your games on the Game Alley main page

As soon as you publish a game, other players can see it in the New Games section of Game Alley, granting you the opportunity to gain many potential players immediately. However, your game can also appear in several other sections of Game Alley, which you can see by scrolling down the page. Each of these sections can increase your game's popularity by showing it on the front page.

To keep players coming to your game, get your game listed in at least one of the sections on the front page of Game Alley (see Chapter 2 for more on these sections). To do this, follow these suggestions:

- **Publish multiple games.** The most direct way to keep your games in Game Alley is to publish more games. This strategy sometimes leads players to your workshop (as described in the next section).

- **Aim for the Up and Coming Games section.** Having your game in the Top Rated section is an outstanding feat, but that position is difficult to achieve and easy to lose. The Up and Coming Games section, geared toward relatively new games with good reviews, is a nice boost for popularity. New games with high star ratings are continually added to the Up and Coming Games section, so if you can garner a few good reviews from the start, you have a good chance to reach this section.

- **Strive for getting your games into the Featured Games and Challenge Winners sections.** Though these sections are the most difficult to enter, they're the most valuable tools for promoting your game. Here's a description:

  - *Featured Games* generally update every week, but they sometimes take a few months to change. If you manage to get a game featured, a great achievement that usually entails getting an administrator to notice your game, you get a head start in popularity.

  - *Challenge Winners* is even better, and even more difficult to achieve, because it requires winning official game design contests. See Chapter 15 for more information on these contests.

It is extremely difficult to get your games featured. If your game is particularly unique or well-balanced, the administrators could decide that it's a good example and feature it. However, don't be discouraged if your games don't get featured (it's often a matter of luck), and never waste the administrators' time asking them to feature your games.

Leading players to your workshop

Game Alley is often an inconsistent way to gain *plays,* or having your game played by other users. Gamestar Mechanic has so many designers that Game Alley can do little more than accommodate a few of their games at a time. To gain more plays beyond Game Alley, you need to direct players to all of your games at one time. Players tend to find you and your games when they

- **Play one of your games:** A player who tries out one of your games and enjoys it is likely to click on your username to view your workshop or to check out the random selection of your games that's displayed on the page.

✒ **Hear about you from other players:** If you're active in the Gamestar Mechanic community, other players notice you. Interest in your games can spread whenever you're mentioned, *favorited,* or recommended. Players who favorite one of your games endorse it in their workshops, granting you a piece of their popularity and recommending you to other players.

✒ **Follow you:** Players who are following you can see your new games in their news feeds as soon you publish them. (I discuss this topic later in this chapter, in the section "Gaining Followers.")

No matter what you do to get yourself recognized in the community, you're adding an outlet by which players can link to your games. Follow these tips to help drive them toward your work:

✒ **Publish new games.** When your game is on the front page of Game Alley for even a little while, players can see your games as gateways to your other works.

✒ **Review games.** Your reviews contain a clickable username that links others to your workshop. When you write helpful reviews, users may sometimes link to your workshop to find out more about you as a person and designer.

✒ **Build connections.** Simply interacting with others is a good way to find potential players. Building relationships based on mutual interests is beneficial to everyone, by providing interesting games and helpful reviews, as described in Chapter 9.

Directing Non–Gamestar Mechanic Users to Your Games

If you want to widen the audience of your game, you can attempt to attract an audience from outside the Gamestar Mechanic community. You do so by sharing your games with friends or over other public websites. In the following sections, I explain the benefits of sharing your games with outside groups and detail the ways in which you can share games.

Publicizing your games outside Gamestar Mechanic

Sharing your games with non–Gamestar Mechanic players has several advantages. Depending on the sort of communications system you use, the benefits of publicizing in this way can range from sharing with friends to attracting a large audience.

Public websites are great for discussing your game with potential players. Though Gamestar Mechanic has limited possibilities for communicating with the public, the Internet is often a good source of publicity. Here are some ways to publicize your games online:

- **Share via forums or blogs or other websites to which you can upload freely.** In particular, it usually costs nothing to start a forum thread showcasing your games. (In case you want to discuss other topics, many forums contain an Off Topic section that you can use.)

- **Start a blog to support your games.** A blog attracts all sorts of readers, depending on how you market it. However, this strategy requires a healthy level of *media literacy,* the skill of finding your way around media such as the Internet.

- **Look for supplementary online groups that might be interested in your work.** You can design games for your friend's web content or join a group that shares or discusses games. (Gamestar Mechanic can be useful for sharing and promoting creative projects by way of fun, easy-to-make games.) If you reach out, possibly sharing some of your best games to inspire interest, you may find yourself integrated into a rewarding resource and community.

- **Contact friends on social communities outside Gamestar Mechanic.** When you contact them regarding your games, they can become well-trusted game testers who provide useful, fresh perspectives on your work.

Some Gamestar Mechanic games can be difficult for newcomers to play and require lots of practice to master. When showing your games to people who are inexperienced with Gamestar Mechanic, especially if they aren't familiar with sprites, make sure that they can easily understand how to play the game. You must explicitly define the avatar's abilities and challenges, usually by way of sprites such as text message blocks. If you also want to tell players about the game controls, keep in mind that these controls are automatically displayed on the Pause menu and at the beginning of every level.

One of the easiest ways to share a game is offline, giving players a seat at your computer and possibly guiding them through levels when needed. However, giving people the privilege of using your account is a gamble for all but your closest friends. A safer option is to allow people (especially large groups of people) to play your games without requiring Gamestar Mechanic accounts, as described in the next section.

Sharing games online

Gamestar Mechanic offers you a number of methods for sharing stand-alone versions of your games. You can see your options in the sidebar on the right side of the game's page, as shown in Figure 10-1. By using the buttons there, you can easily set up links outside of Gamestar Mechanic that point to your game and allow viewers to click and play it.

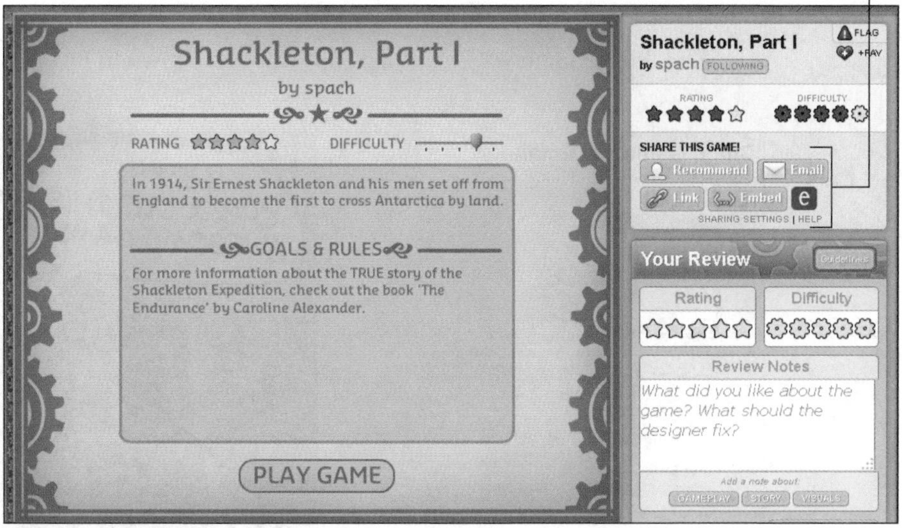

Buttons for sharing your game

Figure 10-1: Use the Share buttons to tell others about your games.

Here's a rundown of what happens when you click each of these Share buttons:

- **Recommend:** Suggest this game to another player.
- **Email:** Share your game with someone by sending a link via e-mail.
- **Link:** Generate a link to your game and then share the URL with other users.
- **Embed:** Create code that inserts the game window directly into another website — this requires the uploader to have access to HTML code.
- **Social media:** You may see one or more small buttons after the ones just described, marked with symbols representing various forms of social media (such as Facebook and Twitter). The one shown in Figure 10-1 is for Edmodo, but your selection can change based on the social media accounts that are linked to your Gamestar Mechanic account.

The following sections explain these buttons in more detail.

Email

If you want to send your game only to certain friends, Gamestar Mechanic lets you do it. If you share a game via e-mail in Gamestar Mechanic, the message contains the title and author of the game as well as a link for the reader to play it.

To share your game via e-mail, follow these steps:

1. **Click the Email button (refer to Figure 10-1).**

   The Share Game via Email page appears, as shown in Figure 10-2.

Figure 10-2: The Email feature lets you share a game in less than a minute.

2. **Enter the required information.**

   You can enter as many as five e-mail addresses, separated by commas. You can also enter your own e-mail address, if you want, so that you can confirm that the game reached your recipients.

3. **Click the Send button.**

   Or click the Cancel button to return to the player page of your game without sending any e-mail messages.

Link

If you click the Link button, you can generate a static link to your game. Anyone with an Internet connection (even non–Gamestar Mechanic users) can use this link to play the game.

To generate a link to your game, follow these steps:

1. **Click the Link button (refer to Figure 10-1).**

   Gamestar Mechanic generates a custom URL for your game in a text box below the Share buttons, as shown in Figure 10-3.

Figure 10-3: Note that the Link button doesn't open a separate page.

2. **Copy the link from the text box.**

3. **Share the link with others.**

Embed

If you want to take an approach to sharing your game that makes your link more immediately interesting, you can create windows outside of Gamestar Mechanic to allow players to try your game from anywhere. Following this strategy means that your game isn't represented only by text, but rather by an interactive screen that brings the Gamestar Mechanic experience directly to players.

To use the embedding system, you must have editor access to a website that allows HTML tags. It's usually a blog or website of your own or an HTML-enabled forum. If you aren't sure whether HTML is allowed, you can always try it out; embedding a game requires just a little copying and pasting — no experience with HTML code is needed.

When you *embed* a game, it appears on the website or forum as a large game screen with a blue arrow button in the center, as shown in Figure 10-4. Anyone who clicks the blue arrow, whether or not that person is a Gamestar Mechanic user, can start playing the game on that screen. This sharing method allows people to play your games without linking to a new website, which many people are hesitant to do.

Figure 10-4: The Gamestar Mechanic teachers' page uses embedded games as samples.

To embed a game on a website, follow these steps:

1. **Click the Embed button (shown at the top of Figure 10-1).**

   Gamestar Mechanic generates the HTML code necessary to embed the game into your website or forum, as shown at the bottom of Figure 10-5.

2. **Copy the HTML from the text box.**

3. **Paste the text into your website, blog post, or forum.**

   Your game appears wherever you embed the HTML.

Sharing on other sites

Some popular websites are directly supported by Gamestar Mechanic, which means that you can link to them directly from the corresponding share buttons. As mentioned earlier, the websites that are supported depend on the accounts you have linked to your Gamestar Mechanic account. By clicking the corresponding button, you are taken to Facebook, Twitter, Edmodo, or another social media site, where a link to the game is set up for you to post.

Figure 10-5: The Embed button functions similarly to the Link button.

Gaining Followers

If a number of people regularly play any new games that you publish, your games will become much more reliably popular. To develop this player base, you must convince players that checking out your newest games is generally worth their time. You can do this either on the Gamestar Mechanic site itself or outside of it — and this section tells you how to do both.

One of the most direct ways to gain a viewer base is by attracting followers. If Gamestar Mechanic users are so inclined, they may decide to *follow* you (receive notifications about your activity on the site), which updates them, in their news feeds, on your recent work. This action indicates that they're interested in being a part of your regular audience.

To gain followers, follow these tips:

- **Build a positive persona.** Followers tend to follow those who have consistently good reputations. If you leave poor reviews or publish games that aren't worthwhile (such as games made only to draw attention to yourself), other players may not want to be updated about you. As long as you act pleasantly and monitor the quality of your public content, you should have no problem operating at your full potential.

- **Think about your effect on a user's news feed.** Consider your potential followers' perspectives. You want these people to follow you so that their news feeds are updated on your activities, including any new games you've published. Then after you've gained a group of followers, you need to think about how to keep them. Avoid cluttering your followers' news feeds by leaving lots of unnecessary comments and recommendations or republishing the same game too many times. The best way to maintain your followers is simply to avoid potentially irritating behavior.

- **Publish games that stand out.** You don't have to be an outstanding game designer to earn followers, but you do need to be a unique one. You can try making games that use your own, unique concepts, style, and flair and attracting those who recognize the added fun in nuance. If you're not yet experienced enough to make an exceptionally original game, you can always set your work apart in other ways. For example, a little detail and balance can create a great experience — a well-designed game is unique in its own regard.

If you use a custom background in your game (as described in Chapter 13), your followers may see the game in their news feeds before it's released (because the backgrounds have to be manually approved before the game can be made public, and the administrators check your backgrounds only after you publish). Thus, after your game is published, look for ways to edit and republish the game so that it returns to your followers' news feeds as a finished product. Just don't spam your followers with too much news; otherwise, they may unfollow you.

Part IV
Designing Masterpieces

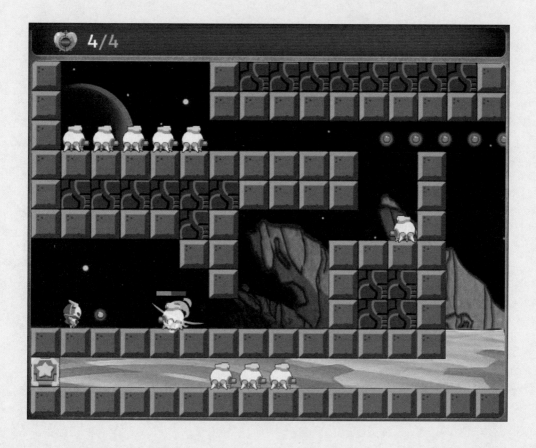

Learn some ways to develop interesting game structures at www.dummies.com/extras/gamestarmechanic.

In this part . . .

- ✔ Understand the components of a well-balanced game.
- ✔ Iterate and improve on a game.
- ✔ Develop stories and visual components.
- ✔ Generate new ideas for games.
- ✔ Master the essentials of designing a truly fun game.

11

Understanding What Makes a Good Game

In This Chapter

▶ Exploring the five elements of game design

▶ Designing the aspects of a game

▶ Iterating and improving on a game

*G*amestar Mechanic is easy to use because, to create a game, all you have to do is place sprites on a grid and change a few settings for each one. Making a game that's fun to play, however, requires some strategy. To get the best experience from Gamestar Mechanic, you need to understand the basics of game-building — especially how to use the Edit and Clone tools — before reading this chapter. (You can find this information in Chapter 5.) In this chapter, you find out about the components of a good game and about the artistic processes behind building one.

Building with the Five Elements of Game Design

In Chapter 5, I introduce you to the five elements of game design that are essential in the Gamestar Mechanic template. If you have a general understanding of game design, you may find the five elements intuitive. If not, be sure to apply them to produce the best possible games, refining your ideas and showing the community their full extent.

The five elements of game design are described in this list:

✔ **Space:** The enclosure where the action happens. The space usually consists of the set of empty squares between the walls of the level — where the dynamic sprites in your game can move and function. Spaces can be tight hallways or open fields, and they can take on extra traits with the Edge Bounding and Wrap Around level settings (which are explained in Chapter 5). The shape, size, and feel of a game space determine how the contained sprites can function and how the game tends to "feel" objectively.

✔ **Rules:** The restrictions that the player must abide by. You can create rules by using system sprites (such as the timer) or through your arrangement of sprites (walls, enemies, or avatar settings). Because rules determine the course that the player must take to beat the game, they form the general outline of the game's challenge.

✔ **Goals:** The requirements that the avatar must complete in order to pass. You can create goals with goal blocks or system sprites, such as the score keeper. (See Chapter 5 for more on goal blocks and system sprites.) You can also construct goals through your placement of sprites. For example, if a goal block is trapped behind a blue lock, finding the corresponding blue key becomes a secondary goal.

✔ **Components:** The objects in the game, from avatars to walls to items. Components can be single sprites, such as keys or enemies, or combinations that serve more complex purposes (such as an enemy that fires into a portal in order to engage the avatar from afar). Components can define the gameplay, portray the story (for example, enemies used as characters), or enhance the visual elements (such as motion blocks, phoenix blocks, and energy generators that produce interesting dynamic scenery).

✔ **Mechanics:** The core actions of your game that the player must take in order to win. If the player unlocks certain walls with corresponding keys, that's a mechanic. If the player avoids enemies or other hazards, that's a mechanic. Jumping over gaps and racing to complete goals in time are mechanics as well. Some games require the player to apply multiple mechanics in order to win, while others give the player practice with one or two.

The five elements are all pieces of a system that is your game; if you change one of them, you change the others as well. For example, the space of a level can set some of its most fundamental rules, telling the player where the avatar is able to move. A good game develops a strong synergy between the five elements: The game space allows enough room for the other elements, the rules and goals keep the player on track, and the components and mechanics neatly set the overall structure of your game. If you find something interesting to do with a certain element of your game, be sure to design the other elements to complement your idea.

For more information about the individual elements of game design, check out Chapter 5 — the elements are also introduced and explained in the first Quest.

The elements of game design are tools for better understanding the components of a well-balanced game. The following sections examine the five elements in the context of creating good games.

Defining a good game space

Game spaces can vary in size and shape, whether they're loose or tight or square or rounded, for example. A good game space is one that neatly frames the gameplay of the level, allowing both the avatar and enemies just enough space to function the way you want them to. Space affects the other elements of your game by defining where they are in the level, and how much room they have to function.

Figures 11-1, 11-2, and 11-3 show three variations of a single-screen game, each with a different game space. Notice that the game space tightens as you progress through the three games. The spaces contribute differently to the gameplay, as explained in this list:

✔ **Game in Figure 11-1:** The avatar has a lot to do here, though little of the space is necessary. This loose game space is especially useful for open-world games where the player can explore and find new venues, challenges, and rewards throughout the level. A game of this type may look odd without supporting visual elements, but the gameplay is still fun and functional.

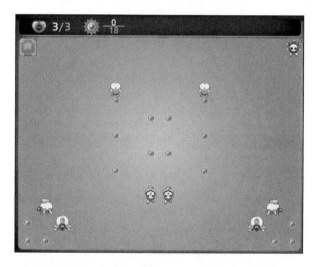

Figure 11-1: A loose game space allows for easy exploration.

In games with large open spaces, give the avatar a high speed value. (See Chapter 5 for details on changing sprite settings.) Otherwise, players may become bored when they wander without challenge. On levels with multiple screens, make sure that the player knows generally where to go — never let an avatar get stranded in empty space.

✔ **Game in Figure 11-2:** This type of game has a balanced space — somewhat restrictive and somewhat free. Walking enemies are placed under tighter motion patterns, and turrets close the gaps between safe areas. The visual elements are well suited for moderately sized rooms, and the walls direct the avatar's course while allowing some freedom of movement.

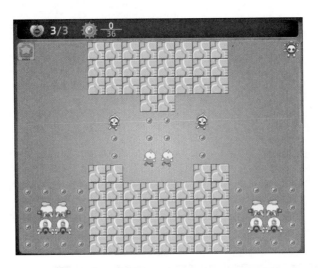

Figure 11-2: A moderately strict game space sets solid guidelines for the level while giving the player some room to move freely.

✓ **Game in Figure 11-3:** In this cramped room, the game space is outlined by enemies as much as by blocks. Two enemies with circular motion patterns close off most of the squares where the avatar would normally be safe. Many of the challenges are severely restricted, requiring the avatar to take specific routes in order to survive. The phasing power-up, an item that lets the player evade enemies by blinking in and out of the level, makes the player's job easier and justifies the use of more restrictive gauntlets. Nevertheless, the player retains freedom of choice — the player can choose from several different routes, some of which may be easier for players with certain skills.

Game spaces like this are helpful for portraying dense enclosures, and they can produce experiences that sharply contrast those created by loose spaces.

Developing the goals of your game

The goals of your game lead the player through a level. They plot the avatar's course and string together all the game's components. The most important aspect of designing goals is that the player knows what they are. A player should have a general idea of where to look for the goal block, as well as what points to collect, enemies to frag, keys to find, and so on. For example, placing a goal block at the end of a series of challenges is much better than placing one in a huge, empty room, because the player knows generally where the avatar should head.

Phasing power-up

Figure 11-3: A tight game space creates a tense and strict environment.

The way people play your game is determined by the goals you set for them. Players always know the goals of a game: They're automatically told if a goal block is in the level; they can see the system sprites of the game; and they notice when their paths are blocked by locks, enemies, phoenix blocks, and so on. (See Chapter 6 for more on these different sprites.) Goals are therefore important for guiding players where you want them to go. This means that goals are vital in making the player experience the spaces and challenges you've designed.

You can implement the following three types of goals in your game, which produce varied results:

✓ **Sequential:** The player completes this type of goal *in sequence,* or in a certain order, and cannot work on a goal until the previous one has been completed. Figure 11-4 shows a game with several goals in sequence: Get the red key, get the blue key, and get to the goal block. Sequential games can be fun to play as long as each goal is fun. Though this method is helpful for beginners, experienced designers can find it useful as well.

✓ **Parallel:** Not all goals can be completed by taking a single action. For example, the player may have to collect five red keys to pass through a hallway or frag 20 enemies to win. With parallel goals, the player can make progress toward more than one goal at a time. In Figure 11-5, the player must frag all enemies and collect all points to win — these two goals are parallel because the player must complete both, though one is not a requirement for the other. The player can frag all enemies first, collect all coins first, or even work toward both goals at the same time, collecting and fragging sprites as they come.

Figure 11-4: A game with sequential goals.

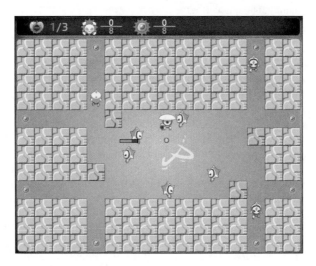

Figure 11-5: A game with parallel goals.

A game can have both parallel and sequential goals. For example, in the game in Figure 11-5, you can add a goal block (making the game a two-step sequence, with the first step a parallel set) or split up the enemies and points with keys and locks (dividing the parallel goals into a sequence of parallel goals).

✏ **Disjoint:** This type of goal achieves sort of a balance between sequential and parallel goals — players complete the goals one at a time but in any order they like. Figure 11-6 shows a game in which players must collect points in small rooms, each of which they can access at any time — players can follow any sequence they like in order to win. The four goals in the example are especially disjoint because only three are required to win. (Note the 3 points required by the score keeper.) Though each goal helps the player make progress toward victory, no single goal is fundamentally necessary. Disjoint goals are useful for making games that implement several ideas — only one goal can be completed at a time, but the goals aren't presented linearly.

Figure 11-6: A game with disjoint goals.

Some games use innovative combinations of goals, connecting various sequential, parallel, and disjoint structures. In complex arrangements, *flowcharts* (graphs that can map various routes of a system through cause and effect) and *Gantt charts* (scheduling charts that can map both linked and overlapping objectives over a function of time) can be useful for mapping out goals — just make sure that players can still follow them.

Setting appropriate game rules

The rules of your game have the same purpose as the goals: They guide the player. The difference is that goals are positive reinforcements that serve as paths for the player, whereas rules are negative reinforcements that serve as walls. A good game needs both elements in order to be fun: a positive aspect to chase after and a negative aspect to overcome.

Rules must be restrictive enough to challenge the player, but not so unforgiving that the player becomes frustrated, nor so arbitrary that the player invokes a cycle of trial, error, and punishment. The purpose of rules is to restrict the player in ways that are both challenging and fun to overcome (for example, don't touch enemies, don't let certain sprites get fragged, or don't leave the game borders). Rules are also used to govern the other elements of a game: They keep the avatar within a space, guide the player toward the goals, bring order to the components, and make the mechanics more challenging to perform.

Gamestar Mechanic already has several rules that exist in any game, such as the game is lost if the avatar is fragged, sprites cannot move through solid objects, and the avatar must stay in the game space. However, you can add your own rules to make the game more interesting.

You can create rules in the following ways:

- **Add system sprites.** System sprites can create both goals and rules. For example, the timer sprite causes the player to lose if a certain amount of time runs out. The population counter can be a goal, a rule, or both — it's a rule while the condition is satisfied, and a goal when it isn't. (You can find out more about system sprites in Chapters 2 and 5.)

- **Change the level boundaries.** The Edge Bounding and Wrap Around settings (described in Chapter 5) are useful for designing the rules of your game. These settings determine where the player can go inside or outside the screen. In addition, if you unbind the bottom of a platformer game, the player loses if the avatar falls down, off the screen.

- **Change the limitations of the avatar.** By modifying the avatar's health, speed, and capabilities (as described in Chapter 5), you establish restrictions on what the player can do. Make sure the avatar is suited to complete the level, but weak enough to challenge the player. You can also change the level's gravity to tweak the avatar's capabilities.

- **Use special sprites.** The Naviron VIP sprite (and the corresponding Minion Naviron VIP) has the special ability to add a new rule to the game: If a VIP is fragged, you lose. These sprites (which are described in Chapter 6 and obtained in the premium quests) are quite suitable for specific sorts of games.

Selecting good components for your game

The components of a game are important not only to the gameplay but also to the story and visual elements. Some components are relatively easy to select; for example, if you want moving platforms in your game, you can simply add motion blocks. Some decisions are more difficult to make because Gamestar Mechanic contains so many different sprites with similar abilities that can create vastly different gameplay, stories, and visuals.

To choose which components to add to a game, keep these tips in mind:

✔ **Use and reuse a set of components.** A good game doesn't have to have lots of components. As long as you find a few ideas you like, you can apply them throughout your game to extract their full value. Reusing components is a useful technique as long as you change them up every once in a while. For example, if you supply a nemesis for the avatar to fight, you can repeat the battle with more health or damage blocks on the ground or add another innovation. If you add a lock-and-key component, you can use that idea several times in succession, placing the key behind a different challenge each time.

Components don't have to be complicated — single sprites are fine, for example. Just make sure you get the most out of the ones you choose.

✔ **Balance individual components.** After you've created some components, you have to balance them, by being able to change the qualities and quantities of various components to make them neatly interact with the avatar and with each other. (For more information about balancing components, see the section "Balancing the Different Aspects of a Game," later in this chapter.)

✔ **Construct your story in Gamestar Mechanic the way you visualize it.** Ask yourself what you want to portray in your game. Components can be integral to the connection between the story and game; events and characters can be defined by your choice and arrangement of sprites and can even integrate with the gameplay. Consider the components of a story (such as characters, conflicts, themes, and progressions) as they relate to components of game design (such as sprites, challenges, styles, and game progression).

✔ **Build a visual style.** Components can contribute to visuals as well. Different objects — animate or inanimate — create an overarching theme that defines your game's aesthetics. The colors and textures of the sprites you add aren't the only items that define the visual elements. You can also arrange them, or make them move, in interesting ways. Determine what patterns you can add in the unused space of your game and what visual value you find in the sprites themselves. For example, the game shown in Figure 11-7 uses sprites of different colors to make the level look like a cluster of interlocked squares, and the equally colorful margins of the level expand the theme beyond the game space.

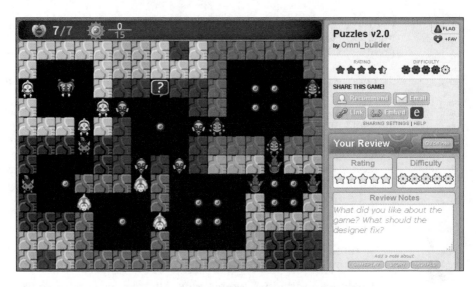

Figure 11-7: This game has a visual style featuring colorful blocks over a black background.

Building your game's mechanics

The mechanics of your game — which define the way your player acts — are generally the most important aspects to implement. If you have trouble setting up the mechanics of your game, try these suggestions:

- **Apply basic mechanics in your own way.** Even a simple platformer game can be an inspiring, original work if you add your own flair. Use visual elements, balance, and other mechanics, such as point-collecting or enemy-dodging, to turn simple mechanics into original ones.

- **Give the player several ways to use a mechanic.** You learn a number of mechanics in the Quest, the template games, and other games. Try building on one you're familiar with, even if it's a simple one such as jumping or dodging.

  For example, the game in Figure 11-8 applies the dodging mechanic (specifically, running in a circle to dodge rotating enemies) with four different enemy pinwheels. The pinwheels at the bottom of the level are more nuanced in that they also include the point-collecting mechanic, keeping the idea interesting. By showing players the same concept in different styles (small pinwheel, large pinwheel, small pinwheel with points, large pinwheel with points), you can expand a single mechanic into a versatile technique that the player can experience in several different ways.

- **Build around a sprite.** After you become more experienced with Gamestar Mechanic, you can apply what you know to invent your own mechanics. To do this, select a sprite (or multiple sprites) — a score keeper, an enemy, or an avatar, for example — and break the sprite down into the essentials you want to form into a working game. You might find a creative way to arrange the points, apply the enemy, or provide a challenge for the avatar.

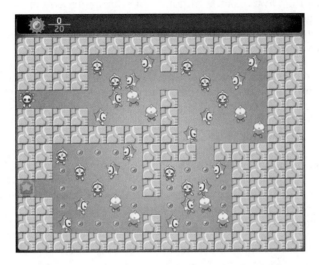

Figure 11-8: Expanding on a mechanic helps make games more interesting.

✓ **Try to construct an experience.** If you know generally what you want your game to feel like, it's a matter of technical experience to be able to approximate it by using sprites, as explained in Chapter 13. If you focus on creating certain feelings or impressions in your game, you can design a more immersive experience.

Balancing the Different Aspects of a Game

Balance is one of the most important qualities of a fun game in Gamestar Mechanic. The balance of a game refers to how well it's moderated and how well it avoids being too much of any one thing; a balanced game is not too easy, hard, overcomplicated, or eventful.

Adding balance to a game means scaling the different metrics of the game so that they stay level between two extremes. If a game is too easy, rushed, linear, or confusing, for example, a player might see it as unbalanced. This is what makes balancing a game important: You don't want it to have too much of any single quality, making the game unfair or uninteresting to players. If you design a well-balanced game, players are more likely to enjoy it.

Many elements of a game — difficulty, pacing, choice, and attributes — often require balance, as explored in the following sections.

Balance of difficulty

The most common example of balancing a game is balancing its difficulty: Don't make the game so easy that it's boring, and don't make it so hard that it's frustrating. To tweak the difficulty of your game, you must be able to make small changes to it without becoming too attached to certain details. Remove enemies, adjust the player's health, and redesign unbalanced areas, for example, until your game is more moderate in challenge.

You are the creator of the game, and the creator often finds the game easier to play than others do. Don't make the game so difficult to complete that even you can just barely beat it. If lots of people leave reviews saying that your game is too difficult, think about whether you should make it easier, and consider how difficult you want it to be.

Also keep in mind that Gamestar Mechanic users have varying skill levels. There isn't a specific level of difficulty that all games should strive for because the difficulty of a game is relative: A beginner may find a game very challenging, while an expert may find the same game easy. Balancing a game for inexperienced players is therefore a different sort of goal than balancing one for experienced players.

If you feel that you need to change the difficulty level of your game, use one or more of these methods:

- **Add or remove challenges.** Delete or add a few enemies, or open or close gaps in the floor for the avatar to jump over, for example. Move a key health pack a little farther out of reach, or make it a bit easier to obtain. If any challenge seems to be too little or too much, balance it with more or fewer complications.

- **Adjust the settings of a challenge.** You can use many methods to change how sprites or arrangements function without adding new ones or removing them completely. For example:

  - Change the health, speed, fire rate, and other qualities of enemies.

  - Make motion blocks move slower or faster.

  - Change the widths of platforms to make them easier or harder to jump across.

  - Calibrate each challenge you give the avatar so that it's not too easy or hard.

- **Modify the avatar's abilities.** Change the avatar's speed or health. Adjust the level's gravity to change its jump height. Grant abilities such as phasing or shielding to make some areas easier. This strategy is a useful way to change the difficulty of a setting if you're hesitant to change the rest of your level.

Figure 11-9 shows a game with several levels of difficulty. It consists of three horizontal passages, from easy (top) to hard (bottom). Note how the middle passage achieves a balance between the two: The game space is tighter than above but looser than below, and the enemies combine elements from both of the other floors. The game as a whole is balanced because the difficulty ramps up steadily, with each floor tuned for a certain player skill level.

Figure 11-9: A balanced game, with three levels of difficulty.

If you want to earn the apprentice badge for your account, you must be able to design a game with three levels, each tuned to a different difficulty. You can use Episode 5 of the Addison Joins the League quest for more practice with balancing games.

Balance of pacing

The *pacing* (or rate of progression) of a level is also a metric with two extremes. If the game drags on slowly, players lose interest; if it's rushed, players get confused. A game with good pacing has mechanics that progress at a prompt but consistent rate.

You should consider a few different types of pacing while balancing your game:

- ✔ **Consistent action:** Give the player a sufficient amount of action throughout the game. Avoid making long progressions with no challenge — every part of the game should be interesting to the player. If one area of your game is reserved for telling a story or showing off visual elements, that's okay, but be sure to divide up these intermissions with actual components of gameplay.

✔ **Well-paced information:** *Pacing of information* refers to understanding the player's knowledge and experience and providing challenges and follow-up to match. Most games transmit information to the player. Whether it's an elaborate story or the strategy behind an evolving gameplay concept, games are useful in this way. This information has to have an element of pacing, however: Giving the player too much information at once makes the corresponding levels difficult and confusing.

✔ **Progressive difficulty:** A good game becomes increasingly difficult as you play. Pacing this slant in difficulty is necessary not only to keep the game interesting but also to make it accessible for players of all skill levels. Good games are easy to learn but hard to master, so players can appreciate the expansiveness of the gameplay right from the start and be engaged all the way through, even if they can't complete a level and have to stop playing partway through.

Players who can't complete your game should at least be able to complete all levels of their ability. Because Gamestar Mechanic supports users of all ages, you must organize levels by difficulty (from low to high). Also make sure that the difficulty of your game rises steadily, instead of flattening out or jumping up quickly.

The View Stats feature, explained in Chapter 5, helps you analyze the empirical difficulty of each level of your game.

How many levels are sufficient?

Deciding how many levels to include in your game can sometimes be difficult. If your game has too few levels, you may not be able to do all you want in your game; however, if the game has too many levels, players may not make it all the way through. This is a balance problem in itself: What is the correct number of levels for your game?

To solve this problem, consider what your levels represent. If you're making a game that has increasing difficulty, simply add levels after the easiest one until you make a level hard enough to stop at. If you're showcasing several different ideas, such as in a game with a different concept on each level or a series of puzzles, make a level for every concept you can think of, possibly adding a few comprehensive levels throughout that connect your concepts into a fuller experience. If your game portrays a story, add a level or two for each major event, matching the pacing of the game with the pacing of the story.

Remember that some players are looking to play long games and others want short games. To gain a diverse audience, don't exclusively publish long games.

Balance of choice

Many games allow the player to make choices that affect the game's dynamics. Some games purely test accuracy or reflexes with no room for choice, and these games can be extremely fun. However, choice gives players more control over the game, even if it's a simple choice, such as a difficulty meter. *Balance of choice* gives the player a sufficient number of choices and balances the outcomes of each choice.

Choices don't have to be strictly defined. For example, Figure 11-10 shows two simple games with different levels of choice. The first game has very little choice and relies on the player's reflexes — the only choice is how fast players choose to go, which means that the player controls the difficulty. This game is by no means a bad one, but the second game might be more fun for players because they can use many different strategies of running and jumping to advance past the enemy.

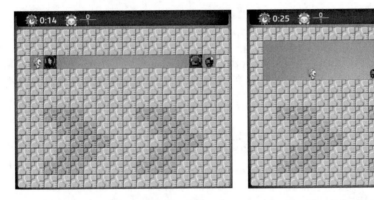

Figure 11-10: The number of choices players have can affect the level of fun in the game.

If the player has too few choices in your game, it might become less fun as it progresses. However, having too many choices can become confusing and frustrating. Consider the strategies in this list when you're balancing the choices in your game:

- ✔ **Establish well-defined goals.** To create a fun game that the player chooses how to complete, make sure the player understands the goals of the game and the effect of each choice in achieving these goals.

- ✔ **Give meaning to every choice.** If you're explicitly defining choices for the player, each choice must be equally valid. If you're quizzing the player, make the incorrect choices sound realistic. If you're giving the player several ways to win, make each of them valid. As detailed in Chapter 18, don't give your players *sham options,* choices that don't meaningfully affect the player's experience.

✔ **Give the player control over the important parts of the game.** Players expect to be a part of the game, so give them choices that affect how the game plays out. Give players enough space to decide how to reach the goals, frag the enemies, or find the points. Maze games work because players are constantly given choices of different routes to take, and while there may be only one correct way, players must think hard in order to take the right action, making the choices their own. Your game doesn't have to be an expansive web of split paths and complex strategies, but there should always be some leeway for the player to win the game in various ways.

✔ **Provide freedom to the player.** Players can find it liberating when you give their avatar freedom of motion. In open spaces, give players the incentive to jump about and try various techniques. To do this, test your game in a few different ways. In closed spaces, try using split paths and small rooms to let the player exercise freedom of choice.

Balance of attributes

The concept of *balance of attributes* is important for both gameplay and aesthetics. It refers to avoiding the use of extremes that might corrupt the cleanliness of your design. By setting the attributes of your sprites and levels to appropriate values, you can make a game feel realistic to its context.

Balance of attributes often comes in handy for the following types of settings:

✔ **Avatar:** If your avatar is too fast, too slow, or has too much health, the game might seem a bit off. Usually a moderate avatar speed is best, and you can always change the health of your avatar to fine-tune the difficulty of your game.

✔ **Enemy:** You don't have to make the strongest enemy in the game, or the weakest possible enemy in the game, to convey different levels of difficulty. Balance enemy statistics so that enemies move the way you want them to move.

✔ **Parallax:** Try out different parallax values to change the feel of your game's visual elements.

✔ **Gravity:** The default value for gravity is 1, which allows the avatar to jump extremely high — however, this ability is rarely appropriate. An avatar that hangs in the air too long makes the dynamic of the game unbalanced. Usually, you should make the avatar jump a few blocks at a time and design the level around that ability.

See Chapter 5 to find out how to change the settings mentioned in the preceding list.

Iterating and Improving on a Game

To produce particularly high-quality games, you need to *revise* your creations, creating a better version of your original work. In game design, this is referred to as *iteration,* which literally means the process of repeatedly applying a function. By going over the design process multiple times by drafting and revising, you can produce better iterations of your game.

Iteration is vitally important when designing games. The process of iteration involves building better versions of your game based on where you think it can be improved. You can practice a few different kinds of iteration, as described in the following list, to design more refined games:

- ✔ **Debug.** Test your game thoroughly before publishing it. Repair any errors you made in designing it. This process is the simplest form of iteration — smoothing out bugs in your design.

  Ask a trusted friend to play the game so that you gain a fresh perspective on your game.

- ✔ **Accept feedback.** Even after publishing your game, you should think about its iteration. A player who leaves a good review may also suggest how your game could be improved. Considering this advice is a useful exercise.

- ✔ **Return to your older games after some time has passed.** If you've grown more experienced in game design, you may start noticing problems in the games you created early on. Iterating your old games is an excellent way to cement the progress you've made in game design.

In terms of experience, revising an existing game is just as useful as drafting a new one. By applying your critical thinking skills to a work of your own, you'll be better equipped to design well-rounded games in the future.

The page at `http://gamestarmechanic.com/teachers` has free PDF resources for teaching — and learning — the concepts of game design. You can download lesson plans to work on, which contain some interesting resources.

12

Designing and Redesigning Games

In This Chapter

▶ Diving into the game design process

▶ Creating your best game

▶ Designing gameplay that's fun

▶ Coming up with engaging stories

▶ Assembling detailed visuals

*T*he process of designing a Gamestar Mechanic game may be simple, but the potential design strategies are limitless. To build better games, you must understand the basic process of designing games and then the techniques for improving them.

This chapter describes how to build your best game by designing entertaining gameplay, developing an engaging story, and incorporating attractive visual elements, as well as how to implement the process by which you can achieve the best of your ability and beyond.

Understanding the Game Design Process

After you gain a lot of experience in designing games, the process of designing a game should be firmly implanted in your mind, and you should have a sense of the characteristics that make up a good game. To take your design to the next level, you must find ways to improve on the design methods you already know.

Suppose that you start building a game by adding a long line of blocks. You add an avatar on the far left end and begin thinking about the combinations of enemies to put along the path. Whether by following this method or another one, you always try to follow this general formula when building a game. This approach may be well and good, but only by truly analyzing the concepts and adding innovative detail, can you move beyond this design pattern and improve your skills in doing so.

Designing an innovative game from the beginning is difficult: Faced with a blank grid and a bunch of sprites, it's difficult to figure out what to do first, so this section provides tips on getting started and following through with the rest of the design process. You can also visit Chapter 5 for a description of the five elements of game design, and read Chapter 9 for advice on learning from other users and their games.

Developing individual challenges

Many games are simply collections of *challenges* — groups of sprites that the avatar must pass and/or resolve. These challenges can be in any order or shape, and they represent the individual trials you present to your players. To build your best game, you should develop individual challenges as design practice.

A challenge doesn't have to consist of much content — it can be small and simple, or broad and complex. It might be a gauntlet of enemies that move in a way that hinders the avatar. The template games in your workshop — Dragons and Pinwheel — are advanced examples of such enemy patterns. A challenge might also be a maze or a simple collection of enemies that the avatar has to defeat.

Individual challenges are so versatile that I can't give you a list of steps for creating one, just as I can't give you a list of formulas for designing the perfect game. I can, however, give you the following tips that can help you create well-designed challenges:

- ✔ **Learn from examples.** Look at the Template Games section of your workshop, at Game Alley, and even at games outside of Gamestar Mechanic, to either emulate the challenges or add your own ideas.

- ✔ **Remember the five elements of game design.** As detailed in Chapter 11, the five elements are useful not just for analyzing challenges but for creating them as well. Use your space well, choose components carefully to create interesting mechanics, and work in a way that plays off your level's goals and rules.

Have a challenge function in multiple ways. For example, you might use destructible blocks to change the gameplay of a room before and after the avatar acquires a blaster. You could also make a challenge in which the player navigates the level, picks up a sprite such as an item or a VIP, and then brings that sprite back to the start of the level. By either revisiting the challenge at different angles or difficulties or making the player circle around and navigate its more intricate concepts, a robust challenge is difficult to make but rewarding for players.

✔ **Play with ideas.** Whether it's in your game, in a separate draft, on paper, or in your head, think of ways to use sprites efficiently and effectively. Find ways to make your challenges fresh and interesting — with practice, and the content of this book, you can turn your ideas into realities.

Designing from the bottom up

When you need to turn a series of challenges into a full level, the most direct way is from the bottom up. The *bottom-up* process involves building a game as a series of small pieces and linking them together to produce the final creation. This simple and efficient approach to designing a game is important for beginners and helpful for veterans.

To build a game from the bottom up, follow these general steps:

1. **Come up with some small challenges.**

   Compose a gauntlet of enemies, a little puzzle, a door that requires two keys to enter, or whatever else you want to add to your game. Follow the advice in the preceding section, "Developing individual challenges," to design these challenges.

2. **Incorporate one or more challenges into a level.**

   You might place the challenges in a line, a branching system, or another type of path that leads the player through your challenges and toward the goal.

3. **Tie it all together.**

   Try to make challenges intersect, if you want. Build passageways to connect challenges, and add more challenges to unused space.

You can use this intuitive approach to make any game: Design each level obstacle by obstacle and goal by goal. Using the bottom-up method, you can try new approaches and build basic games in a series of challenges; however, this method is commonly and effectively used for building large, complex games.

Consider the game shown in Figure 12-1, which was designed with this approach in mind. The level is divided into multiple segments of separate challenges: The avatar passes through two small cells, navigates across a hallway, and makes its way up to a group of two rooms that can be completed in any order. Games of this sort can be designed easily from the bottom up: The designer creates the cells at the bottom of the level first and then allocates the remaining space to the remaining hallways and rooms. This technique doesn't require you to think about the whole level at one time (just the part you're working on), though it can lead to interesting results.

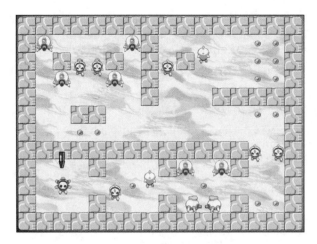

Figure 12-1: A game designed from the bottom up.

Designing from big to small

The method of designing from big to small is a technique for experienced designers, and it's a helpful way to create elaborate games. The *big-to-small* method requires you to build the form of the level and then work down to the function. This design method can be challenging if you misjudge the spatial requirements of your game, but the payoff can be deep, well-shaped game-play and immersive visual elements.

To design a game from big to small, follow these steps:

1. **Build the outline for the level.**

   Set up the format for the type of level you want to design: Set the dimensions of the level, draw out the rooms with block sprites, and define the position of any large structures or gameplay elements that you want to include. Think about what you would want your level to look like if you handed someone a tour map of it. If you're confident enough, you can detail many of the overarching visual elements.

   Completing the Level Map Challenge can be useful for this step.

2. **Divide the level into sections.**

   Figure out where you want to place your goals and obstacles. Sometimes, you need only one section; at other times, you may want to create a section, complete the next step, create another section, and so on.

3. **Build the challenges in each section.**

   After you complete your template, start working more narrowly until you have a challenging game that fills the whole level with interesting ideas.

The big-to-small approach is particularly helpful when you know how you want an entire level to flow but aren't yet sure of the components. When designing components, don't be afraid to edit your game plan to fit your ideas — if you find a creative way to make a component work, it can improve the outline.

This approach works well when developing games with large, elaborate levels, but it can also be applied to make a game less linear. Whether the outer layer is a map, a mechanism, or another structure, the big-to-small approach can help you visualize your game without getting distracted by details. Figure 12-2 shows an example of a game that seems to be designed from big to small: The structure consists of a number of rooms connected by passages, and the pieces of these structures are filled out by elevators and small challenges.

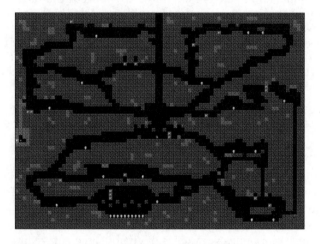

Figure 12-2: A game designed from big to small.

 Many designers work both from the bottom up and from big to small when designing games. For example, you might create the general structure of a game and then work from the bottom up to construct each section. You might also come up with an interesting short-term concept and then use the big-to-small approach to build a game around it. Don't feel that you're limited to just one of these approaches, and apply whichever one you feel is appropriate.

Making Your Best Game

Note that this section is not titled "Making *the* Best Game," or even "Making a Great Game." You can make an exceptionally fun game only by practice, so in this section, I show you how to use your current design skills to their full potential.

To make your best game, you must ensure that it follows good game design techniques (visit Chapter 18 to see ten things you should avoid) and truly lives up to your vision of it. To do this, follow the advice in this list:

- **Optimize your gameplay.** If certain parts of your game are meant to be challenging (such as mazes or enemies), but offer no difficulty or too much difficulty or simply consume too much time, be sure to rewrite them. Alter the difficulty level, change the sprites' positions and settings, or replace the challenge with one that you find more effective. You don't have to make your game constantly challenging — many games tend to rise and fall, spacing out the key challenges with breaks or segments dedicated to the story and visuals; however, be sure that your game is enjoyable wherever it needs to be.

  Test your game, and make mental notes about areas that are boring or frustrating so that you can fix those problems. Additionally, look for helpful reviews from friends or peers to avoid bias. You might also look for minor annoyances to fix, such as a message block that the player is forced to trigger multiple times. The more effort you put into details and revisions, the closer your game will approach your ideals. Whether your game is ready to publish is up to you to decide.

- **Fill out your game's visual elements.** Powerful, striking visuals are essential to a game. Fill in unused spaces with engaging images that flesh out the visual theme of your game. (You can find out more about how visuals fit together later in this chapter.)

  A background is almost always a positive influence on the game — the generic black background can bias players against your game.

- **Find play-testers.** To design a game that reflects the best of your abilities, you must sort out which of your ideas work and which ones need improvement. Testing your games yourself is often not sufficient — find people who can supply constructive feedback. The reviewing and commenting system on Gamestar Mechanic is also useful, prompting players to point out the virtues and flaws in your game; you can keep these points in mind for future games.

Designing Fun Gameplay

The word *fun* is difficult to define, because everyone experiences it differently. This section gives you ideas on ways that might help you capture this elusive element in your game.

To provide a good experience for your players, try these methods when designing your game:

✓ **Analyze and expand on a game you know.** Think of a game you've played and enjoyed. Why did you enjoy it? What made it truly fun? Consider the fundamental elements of the gameplay and structure of the levels — how many features could you take away and still find the game enjoyable to play?

The next step is to apply this structure to your own game. You face two challenges here: Re-create the structure of the game you like in Gamestar Mechanic (but be careful not to commit plagiarism, a topic I cover in Chapter 9), and expand on it by incorporating your own, original ideas. The former takes some practice in using the Gamestar Mechanic format, and the latter is more complicated. Is there anything you wanted to see in your template game? Is there a feature, such as a story or a system, that you could replace with your own concept? Game design is a dialogue, with lots of people building on each others' ideas — try to find something of your own to contribute.

REMEMBER

Don't copy levels or stories exactly, unless you're doing an homage to a classic game. If you are, be sure to mention that to your players, and check Chapter 9 to make sure you're not plagiarizing.

✓ **Determine what you want to see in a game.** You want the player to be in control of something. Through the avatar, the player should be able to accomplish certain goals but still be impeded by challenges along the way. What do you want to see in this game? Usually, a puzzle or a platform-jumping challenge can stand on its own because it gives the player a challenge that results in the satisfaction of completing it. What happens, though, if you want more immersive or diverse experiences in your game? When you imagine an avatar moving through your game, what do you see it doing, and what might stand in its way? If you can deconstruct and define your interests, you can accommodate them with truly unique design concepts, if you really work at it.

✓ **Build prototypes.** Gamestar Mechanic requires you to have a complete game in order to publish it. But until you publish it, you can play around with it however you want. Try building *prototypes* — arrangements that don't form finished games but contain components and mechanics that interest you. Add an avatar and try out your playground — run around without a defined goal. If you find an element you like, you have the foundations of a game. Build around a prototype, using goals to guide the player and filling out the essential components, to make a complete game that lives up to your imagination.

Writing Engaging Stories

Sometimes, you might want to incorporate a story in your game. This section gives you some basic tips for writing good stories and effectively weaving them into your games.

Understanding the components of a story

When you design a game that tells a story, either via text or closely linked gameplay and visuals, both the game and the story should be complete works — interwoven ideas that could function just as well on their own. You can tell your story with pictures or actions that occur in the game, but it must be a finished story in order to make the game complete. To build a good story, include the elements described in this list:

✔ **A conflict:** Your story's conflict might be between two groups of people, three individuals, a person against himself, or any other combination. But if you can think of only one side of the conflict, the story may not be able to surprise the player, and the resulting game may not be challenging. Think about what causes the conflict in your game, what challenges the player must resolve, and what force the player stands for (such as good, evil, a character, a faction, or another alignment).

You can create enriching stories by combining multiple types of conflict. For example, try tying a physical conflict (such as a protagonist fighting an evil nation) with an associated mental conflict (such as the protagonist discovering new abilities and dealing with their implications).

✔ **A few surprises:** To get players interested in your story, show them something new and exciting. These surprises don't have to be major — you can surprise someone by simply creating an interesting world, an engaging dialogue, or a unique theme. Add twists and unexpected ideas — as long as you keep the story fresh and interesting, you can hold your audience's attention as long as you want.

✔ **A sense of constant progression:** If you emphasize a certain component of your story — a character, a place, a time, or an object — you should make sure it changes and develops over the extent of the game so that the players continue to find it interesting. For example:

• A central character who is important to the story should change or become more complex as the game progresses.

• If you invest a lot of time in writing about the events of a certain place or time, make sure the story flows with game-changing events.

• If you focus on a particular object for a long time, explain it and analyze its implications, to keep it from becoming boring and negligible.

To make a story that keeps the audience interested, let the individual components of the story change and progress.

Connecting stories and games

When people play your games, the first thing they expect is gameplay. If you want to tell a story through your game, make sure that the game is still interactive: There should always be some gameplay to keep the player engaged.

In order to balance gameplay and story, try integrating one with the other. By telling the story through the gameplay or making the gameplay more meaningful through the story, you can make a game that is both interesting and involved.

As discussed throughout this book, Gamestar Mechanic supports both simple and complex games that are built from collections of sprites that players learn to navigate quickly. This system can sometimes make it difficult to create an integrated story. However, with a little work on your part, an engaging story can be used to make an even more engaging game, with the gameplay and storyline enhancing one other.

To integrate your story into your game, follow the advice in this list:

- **Reflect the story by way of your gameplay.** Some designers try to alternate between building story and building gameplay, keeping the elements separate so they don't interfere with each other. In fact, the story and gameplay can help each other: A story gives meaning to action, which in turn lets the player truly live the story. You can also use gameplay to tell the story, applying active play in place of reading or listening.

- **Communicate your story in intervals.** It can be challenging to tell a story through a game — after all, many players are focused more on the gameplay. To discourage players from rushing through the story, try spacing out the text throughout the game. Don't give players a wall of information that they need to pass in order to play the game; instead, add messages throughout the game to break up the story, making it more compelling and better integrated within your game.

- **Realize your story with visual elements.** Why describe something when you can create it? Use visuals to the best of your ability to truly build the story. If any component of the story can be made into a picture, try to describe it by way of the aesthetics of your game. For example, construct the buildings and landscapes in which your story takes place, and adapt them to have goals and recognizable gameplay. In more character-oriented scenes, you could represent each character with a sprite and edit them to roughly act out what you want them to do. This strategy immerses the player in your game and cuts down on the amount of text you have to use.

Assembling Visual Elements

Visual elements add ambience to a game. They allow the player to experience sounds and images that enhance the gaming experience.

Understanding what visuals add to a game

Visual elements can improve a game in a few ways. They can

- ✔ **Provide visual meaning to gameplay:** Visuals are helpful for establishing ambience and beauty around your gameplay. By elaborating on the elements of the game, visuals greatly improve pure mechanics with elegant presentation. Every game should have at least some visual appeal, but you can decide how much emphasis you want to put into it.

- ✔ **Draw out a story:** A picture can be more effective at telling a story than words. If you have an absorbing idea for a story, visuals are an excellent way to communicate your idea to players. In addition, ambient design is useful for building your world outside the main storyline — make players feel like they're exploring your creative universe.

- ✔ **Be aesthetically immersive:** Elegant visual elements can catch the eye of players, building interest in your game beyond just the gameplay and storyline. This is what makes visuals an important component of a game: They immediately grab the players' attention and make them love to simply look at your work.

Developing visuals for your game

Developing artwork is a fun experience, and you can easily implement visuals in Gamestar. Try these methods to get started:

- ✔ **Add building blocks.** Many games have chunks of space that are reserved for buildings, pillars, thick walls, or other elaborate objects. This is common in games featuring large detailed areas, where challenges are spread out over expansive levels. When you have space to build your visuals, and no gameplay is required there, the design process becomes more like building blocks: You assemble large objects by using a collection of meticulously chosen smaller ones. By setting aside spaces where you have the freedom to build whatever you want, the building block method is a simple and useful strategy.

- ✔ **Experiment with sprite combinations.** Blocks in Gamestar Mechanic don't just have single colors, but rather gradients and unique textures. So you can produce interesting results when you use only a few sprites together. For example, maybe you find that concrete and white blocks go well together. Or using bricks and glass over a light blue background is an attractive design. If you can find unique combinations of colors and textures, you can create an interesting design.

- ✔ **Build a scene.** It sometimes helps to have some sort of theme behind your game, from either the story or the gameplay, such as "medieval" or "outdoorsy." If you have a plan for what the area should look like, you can construct it more easily. You can build your gameplay and develop the scenery around it, or build the scene and develop the gameplay to explore it.

You can use several of these methods to develop whatever kind of game you like.

Using visuals effectively

In addition, visuals have a few general rules that you should always remember:

✔ **Avoid colors that clash.** Sometimes two colors clash, such as the red objects against a bright green background on the left side of Figure 12-3. Try not to use combinations like this one. Instead, use a background that goes well with as many sprite colors as possible.

Keep in mind, especially when using a custom background, that light or dark colors can be quite useful because they blend well with almost everything. Bright colors can be tricky to use neatly, so it helps to water them down a little.

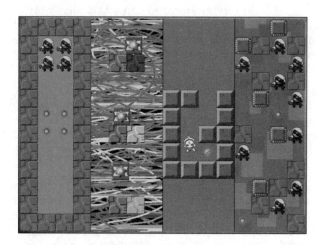

Figure 12-3: Color and space can have an impact on how players feel about your game.

✔ **Don't clutter the level.** If you have lots of colors, objects, and moving sprites in your game, players may become distracted and frustrated. The second area from the left in Figure 12-3 shows a cluttered level: The background and sprite colors are distracting, and the motion blocks are shaky, making it hard to pinpoint the level's structure. In general, don't use visuals that make it difficult for players to focus. Concentrate your efforts on the overall structure of the level instead and change anything that you find particularly distracting.

✔ **Define the game space.** Space isn't just an element of gameplay. Space and perspective make vital contributions to visual style, defining the area in which your game takes place. Fortunately, Gamestar Mechanic makes perspective fairly straightforward: Space out your sprites to create an expansive feel, and clump them together for a tight feel. A primary use of visuals is to define the game space — provide an aesthetic frame for your gameplay, giving the game a refined and complete look.

Note the second area from the right in Figure 12-3. The game space is defined as a small room surrounded by empty space, which looks a bit mismatched. To fix this problem, you can either expand the room and give the avatar more space to move about or fill out the area around the room with extra detail. This technique better defines the game space and gives the player a sense of perspective.

✔ **Use backgrounds that contrast rather than blend.** Another potential problem with backgrounds is blending: If a color in your background is similar to a monochrome sprite, the sprite may become hard to see. For example, a bright red background can make enemy bullets almost invisible (refer to the right side of Figure 12-3). Also, a background with tiles similar to certain sprites can confuse players trying to see which sprites are real. The background should make sprites stand out rather than absorb them.

✔ **Use blocks as architecture.** Use blocks and other sprites to design buildings, landscapes, and other structures. If you add a minimal number of platforms or walls and use the background only to define your visuals, the level may feel incomplete. Place lots of blocks in your level to establish the setting — sprites don't have to affect the gameplay if they serve the purpose of making the game look better.

✔ **Define the palette.** Many games require only a small selection of decorative blocks. These blocks form the *palette* of the level — the basic colors and shapes that define the look and feel of the environment. If you use a lot of different types of sprites for detail, the level might look inconsistent. Clearly define the palette for each level — consider the sprites that you need in order to construct each major structure, and use the others primarily for detail work.

Nonsolid blocks (such as the item generator) are helpful for designing visual elements that the avatar can move through instead of circling around. Use animated sprites such as enemies, Phoenix blocks, and moving blocks to add a dynamic feeling to visuals.

13

Seeking True Mastery in Game Design

....

In This Chapter

▶ Filling out an idea

▶ Creating a game that provides a complete experience

▶ Finding ways to improve your games

▶ Applying custom backgrounds

▶ Exploring more game design resources

....

*I*t's impossible to know absolutely everything about game design. Game designers use various methods to create a fun experience (as explained throughout this book), but it's implausible to rigorously define the exact formula for making fun. This is what makes game design an interesting science: It's a language of formulae and processes so vast that this book has only scratched the surface of its concepts.

This chapter describes how to gain mastery in game design. You see how to expand on existing concepts, study the techniques of game design, use custom backgrounds for a deeper experience, and practice the known components of a full gaming experience. The concepts in this chapter are applicable to all skill levels.

Developing an Idea for a Game

Finding an idea for a game design can be difficult. You need an idea that is creative but loose enough that it can be applied in a number of ways. Here are some ways that you can generate new ideas for games:

▷ **Look at a single element of game design.** The Quest strongly emphasizes the overarching elements of space, goals, rules, components, and mechanics (terms that appear often in this book). When you try to define one of these elements in your own words, your interpretation will likely be different from that of other Gamestar Mechanic users. If you have an interesting way of thinking about space or of putting together components, your thought process itself can be a helpful element of originality. For example, you could think of a level as a series of inter-connected cells, and create a delightfully organized yet nonlinear game.

✔ **Build around a sprite.** The Gamestar Mechanic Class Project system (as described in Chapter 16) includes two projects that are applicable to this method: Build around an avatar and build around an enemy. An easy way to develop an idea for your game is to design one around a sprite. Think about all of the sprite's assets — its functions, set-tings, and tricky abilities — and then put those capacities to every test you can think of. For example, if you have a sprite that can jump and shoot, give it some platforms to run and jump across while plac-ing various enemies in its way. This process can take some experi-ence and practice, but it's a helpful way to gain mastery with certain sprites.

✔ **Build around a core mechanic.** The core mechanic of your game is the action the player most readily associates with the game — for example, jumping, shooting, racing, or solving. Consider the experience you want the player to have, what you want the player to be able to do, and then design a game that offers this mechanic.

✔ **Develop patterns.** You can use sprites and levels in interesting ways if they're in the right arrangement. The first step in using this method is critical analysis: Think about the root concepts of levels and sprites, such as damage, gravity, and collision and the proper-ties of each one. For example, choose an avatar with a high health value (Acheron sprites such as the Acheron scout can have very high health values), and then build a puzzle where the avatar has to find the best route to escape the level with minimal damage. As another possibility, build a maze that uses pitfalls as one-way passages, or make a battle with a giant sprite over a platform broken up by narrow gaps so that smaller enemies can jump up at the avatar through cracks in the floor.

Any action in Gamestar Mechanic — whether it can be used by, for, or against the avatar — can be expanded into a challenge by using the ele-ments of game design. Though this process can take some practice and skill, it's a useful way to move from technical understanding to creative mastery.

If you're still having trouble finding the inspiration you need, you can always try expanding on an existing idea. Find an interesting concept or structure, and build around it until you construct a full game.

Looking to other designers for inspiration

If you want to implement an idea from another designer, you don't have to completely reimagine the concepts of that person's game design in your own game. Though many people have spent their lives building templates, structures, and examples of games, still more have made contributions by building on those concepts. Many game designers do this subconsciously: For example, every game that falls into a genre is an extension of that genre's defining entry.

Taking inspiration from other games can be fruitful, but make sure you expand on these ideas in some way — don't just copy parts of their designs. If you find a neat idea, you should apply it only if you feel that you have something to contribute. You should understand how and why the idea works: What do you find appealing about it? What experience does it create? What can you add to that experience?

Other designers can teach you all sorts of concepts, from the small scale to the large scale. For example, you may notice that some designers use the Phoenix block, a block that can repair other sprites, to turn destructible blocks into impassable walls and require the player to destroy the corresponding Phoenix block in order to pass — then you can apply this strategy in your own games. Alternatively, if you see a game with an interesting overall structure, you might try to apply similar elaborations to make your games less linear.

Warning: Give credit where credit is due! See Chapter 9 for information about plagiarism and how to avoid it.

This method is especially popular with puzzle games and the like. For example, if you were to discover that a reversible, one-way door adds interesting consequences to a classic labyrinth game, you might try to find other ways to apply this door, putting all these variations together in a game with many levels.

You can build on other ideas as well, adding creativity to almost any game. Suppose that you notice this particular idea: A stationary sniper placed along a thin path produces a clever challenge for the avatar to navigate the corridor. Figure 13-1 shows a game based entirely around this idea. The series of horizontal paths are filled with league snipers and connected by walls and holes, producing a labyrinth of connected challenges. The player must make his way to the bottom of the level, collecting all the points along the way, so the designer can place every imaginable arrangement of the idea.

Other games, especially large ones, rely on several original ideas. A long, level-by-level game may introduce a new concept every few levels, or a battle game may combine unique aspects of combat, enemies, and character development. Gamestar Mechanic is no exception: After you discover a good idea, it can often help to find more ideas that intersect neatly.

Figure 13-1: Expanding on an idea can make for an interesting game.

Turning Your Idea into a Game

After you have an interesting idea for a game, the next step is to expand on it. After you invent your concept, creating the corresponding game is more technical and straightforward. This section shows you how to turn a simple idea into a complete game.

Suppose that you want to build a game with a *league hero,* a platformer sprite with a moderately powerful blaster (see Chapter 6). You come up with this interesting idea: If you place several identical snipers in a column so that they fall on top of each other, the resulting super enemy fires dense bullets that require several hits to destroy. The reason is that the snipers fire in unison and occupy the same space, so they pack clusters of bullets into a single strike.

You can turn this concept into a number of games that are fun to play. Think about where to position these enemies for the greatest effect. Also, consider how you can arrange them to make various contributions to the level. Play around with the possibilities. For example, a sufficient number of snipers can force the avatar to jump over the bullets and get close to the enemies or sneak behind them to frag them. You can apply this idea in lots of ways — the arrangements in Figure 13-2 show a few interesting examples, each of which provides a different way to challenge the player to frag the snipers.

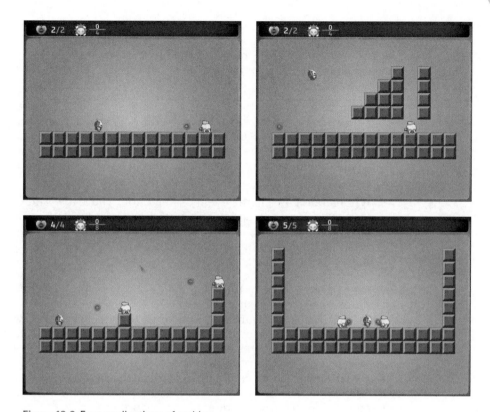

Figure 13-2: Four applications of an idea.

Each example in Figure 13-2 consists of four identical enemies stacked on top of each other. These enemies fire four identical bullets at the same time, which are much more difficult for the avatar to deflect. Figure 13-2 shows how this concept can be expanded in at least four different arrangements:

✔ **Arrangement 1:** Shows the player standing opposite the enemies over a fairly straightforward platform. The enemy shoots without moving, and the player's speed is very slow. This makes the player's best course of action to run toward the enemies while jumping over the bullets, because the avatar has an opening to attack only when it's close to the enemies. This structure makes a fighting game more like a dodging game, and you can improve on it by adding more enemies or placing gaps along the platform for the avatar to jump over.

✔ **Arrangement 2:** Similar to the first arrangement except that the extra blocks make it impossible for the avatar to attack the enemy from the front without receiving lots of damage. To win, players must jump over the bullets until they reach the staircase made of blocks and then navigate to the right side of the screen and frag the enemies from behind. Because the enemies are easily defeated on only one side, this concept opens up a lot of possibilities for navigation or maze games, either top-down or platformer.

- ✔ **Arrangement 3:** Features enemies that are raised above the main platform — the avatar can hit or be hit only when it's on the same level as the enemies. Each jump must be timed carefully, therefore, by weaving each shot between the enemies' attacks. This concept is valuable for testing the avatar's timing and shooting skills at the same time.

- ✔ **Arrangement 4:** Sets the enemies in motion. The avatar and enemies are positioned in a cage, and the enemies run back and forth while shooting powerful bullets. This arrangement puts players in a challenging fight, requiring them to jump nimbly around the level while still finding time to damage the enemies.

Now you have templates for the components of your game. Your only remaining task is to arrange them, as shown in Figure 13-3. You can recognize some segments of this level from Figure 13-2, such as the rightmost enemies (which apply the concept from the third arrangement). However, other parts are adapted to fit the style and shape of the level, such as enemies at the bottom of the room: The level doesn't have enough space for them to be stacked vertically, so they're placed in a horizontal line to produce the same effect. See how the avatar has to navigate toward the goal block; each individual challenge in its way is derived from the same tricks used in Figure 13-2.

Figure 13-3: An expanded idea.

You can reproduce the game shown in Figure 13-3 by using only the free content of Gamestar Mechanic, so you don't have to pay anything to make a game like this one. Try to reproduce this game in your toolbox so that the result is a fully functioning game. Placing the sprites in the right spots is fairly straightforward, but you may have to make your own decisions when adjusting the sprites' settings. You can even try to improve on this game by rebalancing or expanding it. This exercise is a good one for beginners: To reach the height of your creative ability, look at games by other users and try to re-create them (just don't publish the ideas as your own).

Turning an idea into a game is a process that's similar to following the core concepts of Gamestar Mechanic design, because you're given all the base components and then you must arrange them in a challenging and fun way. Follow these tips to make the most of your idea:

- **Manage your space and levels.** You can showcase the applications of your idea in several ways. You might add a new application with each level, using many levels to break up the material you want to use. Or you might create large levels that use the idea in several ways (refer to Figure 13-3, where the snipers are applied in multiple different arrangements in the same level). Think about the best way to deliver your idea to your players, and ask yourself these questions:

    - Should the levels follow a linear or nonlinear progression?

    - Should the concepts be separated by space or by level?

    - How fast can players receive my information?

    These questions address your game in a general sense, but they become much more important when you build on a unique idea — innovative concepts take time to develop and teach to your players, so you must pace your game properly.

- **Map out the gameplay with the elements of game design, as described in Chapter 5.** The components and mechanics of your game are mostly centered on your idea. Here are some questions to ask yourself to make your idea into a complete and well-balanced game:

    - Can I apply any other concepts to bring my idea to life?

    - What sort of game space would work best for guiding players through my idea?

    - What goals can be achieved by implementing my idea?

    - What rules are necessary for my idea to function?

- **Design a complementary story and visual elements, if applicable.** An idea can often be connected to a story or a particular visual style, which makes it blend into the game better and produce a fuller experience (as explained in the next section). Outline the structure of your game with a series of events, or build visual elements that fit with the style of the idea. The concepts portrayed earlier, in Figure 13-2, have a fairly generic look about them, but their application in Figure 13-3 adds an interesting style that's dark and futuristic.

Creating a Full Experience for Players

After you've fleshed out the essentials of your game, the next step is putting them all together. A truly fun game is one that feels complete — the gameplay, visuals, and other elements must mix to create a full experience. This step in the game design process finalizes your work and ensures that the player is engaged throughout the game.

Follow these tips to create a full experience and ensure that your game is complete:

- **Don't let the gameplay drag along anywhere.** A full experience doesn't let the player's mind drift away from the game because of boredom. Look at each segment of your gameplay, and decide whether a player would be interested in it if it stood alone. Then, if you find a part to be too long and boring, add a challenge to it by placing better enemies or rebalancing the goals and rules of the game. Your game doesn't have to be constantly engaging through gameplay alone — you may want to dedicate segments to the story, visuals, or simply short breaks between the challenges. Just make sure that you keep the player interested when you *do* want to focus on gameplay.

- **Don't leave large, empty spaces where you can add visual elements.** Sometimes, you just want to use a fraction of a level — you may want the player to navigate a thin hallway or a tiny room. However, this doesn't mean that you should leave large parts of the level blank, because the player can always see a full screen's worth of your work. Fill out blank spaces with blocks or enemies that justify the amount of space you're reserving for gameplay. For example, if you're composing an indoor level, fill empty spaces with blocks such as concrete, interesting patterns, or even separate rooms that make the area look bigger.

  The only time you want to leave large sections of space blank is when you're deliberately making the game feel spacious — for example, if you're depicting an expansive sky or a wide cave.

- **Use a background on every level.** The background is vital to a full visual experience because it details the setting behind the sprites. Backgrounds add much-needed depth to a game by showing that sprites are functioning in a particular location rather than floating in undefined space.

- **If you add a story, always tell the player what's happening.** Withholding information about your story is sometimes a technique for preserving mystery, but you should make sure that the story is understandable enough to be engaging. A full storytelling experience provides players with all necessary information — either by way of level messages or message-displaying sprites — to understand what the gameplay and visuals represent, and why they should care about the characters and events.

- **If you've deliberately designed part of a level to have no gameplay, use a good substitute.** In certain levels, you may want to slow down the action a little and develop the story and visuals with no gameplay. For example, you might dedicate a level to fleshing out the story or send the player down an elaborate, empty hallway to build up to a boss battle. Having a lack of gameplay works fine when used sparingly, but you must always substitute the lost gameplay with an equally engaging element. The straightforward parts of your game should therefore include an interesting story or neat visuals to tide over the player until the gameplay appears again.

Evaluating and Revising Your Game

You should revise your game before publishing it, to ensure that you're providing the best possible experience. Some users even revise their games after publishing, releasing newer and better versions. One of the most useful things you can do when revising your game is to ask yourself a few questions. By formally scrutinizing individual portions of your game, you can identify problems much more easily and improve your game effectively.

Identifying areas where you can improve your game

Revising a large game can be challenging. If you evaluate your game from a big-picture perspective and then skim the levels for errors, you can easily overlook certain problems.

To ensure that you catch errors and develop a well-rounded game, ask yourself a series of questions to test different aspects of your game. Here are several examples of questions you can ask about your game — or, even better, you can acquire a game-tester to answer the questions without bias:

- Did you enjoy playing the game?
- What makes each challenge of the game difficult?
- What core concept or concepts does the game focus on?
- How tight or loose is the game space? Is this a good choice?
- Does the game space fit with the visual elements?
- What does the game look like? Can the visuals be more detailed?
- If the game tells a story, is it told consistently throughout each level of the game? Does it enhance the game experience?

- Is this game mentally stimulating? Did your mind wander while playing?

- How many different types of sprites (just a rough estimate) are in the game? Do all sprites fit the theme? If you have little variance, do you like it that way?

- What abilities does your avatar have? How often do you use each ability?

- How big is the level? How much of it is used?

- Which system sprites did you choose for your level?

- How do the backgrounds affect the appearance of the levels? How do the visuals change from level to level? While moving around in a large level, what does the background parallax say about the game space?

- Does the game live up to your design expectations? If not, what do you think could be better?

Fixing problems revealed in your games

As you answer the questions in the previous section, you may find some problems or issues to fix. Sometimes, fixing problems in your games is straightforward: For example, change the avatar's settings, repair misplaced sprites, or add new challenges to unused areas. If you simply can't figure out how to improve on a section that you find problematic, try these tips:

- **Redesign the section.** Rebuild your idea with components you're more comfortable with. For example, if you design a roomful of enemies and the gameplay turns out to be a bit too slow and trivial, create a few enemies in key positions, and relocate the other enemies to match the new setup.

- **Remove components that don't work.** If part of a level is problematic, remove some factors and rebuild it differently. For example, if you design a complex game with lots of system sprites (a timer, an energy meter, a score counter, and a frag counter, for example), you may want to factor out one of these goals or rules to simplify the game so that it's easier to fix as a designer and to understand as a player.

- **Add new mechanics.** If part of a level feels empty, fill it out a little. For example, you can add a racing mechanic by using a timer, or lead players where you want them to go by implementing a point-collecting mechanic.

- **Collect opinions from other players.** Even a simple suggestion such as "Needs to be easier" or "Needs more enemies" can show you what players are expecting from your game. Look particularly at reviews along the lines of, "Level 3 was much harder than Level 4 and seems out of place." Reviews such as these aren't biased by the player's absolute skill level.

Using Custom Backgrounds (Premium)

If you complete the Custom Backgrounds Challenge, which is available for Premium accounts, you earn the ability to use any picture you want as the background on your levels, as long as you can save it as a file in either the JPEG or PNG format. This feature has many different applications and can be used in complex ways. This section helps you understand some of the ways you can apply custom backgrounds to improve your game's design.

Obtaining custom backgrounds

Adding a custom background is liberating — you can use absolutely anything you want (as long as it's appropriate for all ages). However, you have a nearly infinite selection of backgrounds, which can be intimidating. The next couple of sections describe methods of obtaining custom backgrounds.

The Gamestar Mechanic image database

The Pics4Learning website (www.pics4learning.com) provides Gamestar Mechanic with a custom background search engine that's easy, free, and safe to use: No inappropriate images are available, and you can use images freely as long as you don't try to directly gain money from them. Open your toolbox, and then follow these steps to search for an image and import it into your game:

1. **Click the Settings button for the level.**

   The Level Settings dialog box opens.

2. **Under Background, click the Choose a Custom Background button.**

3. **Choose Add New Background⇨Search for an Image.**

4. **In the Search box, enter a search term and press Enter to find a set of custom backgrounds.**

   The Pics4Learning database contains fewer images than other options. Be sure to use simple search terms, such as *floor* or *cave* or *sky,* to find lots of results.

5. **Select the background you want to use and then click Choose to add it to your background library.**

6. **Click Choose again to add the selected background to your game.**

Google and other universal search engines

Internet search engines give you access to every online image available. However, to use an image as a custom background in Gamestar Mechanic, you need to ensure that it is either labeled with a Creative Commons license or is in the public domain. You can do that by searching specifically for images with those usage rights.

If you're searching with Google, follow these steps:

1. **Go to** www.google.com/advanced_image_search.

   The Advanced Image Search page appears, as shown in Figure 13-4.

2. **Enter your search terms in the boxes at the top of the page.**

3. **From the SafeSearch drop-down list, select the Filter Explicit Results option to filter out any terms that are too explicit.**

4. **In the Usage Rights drop-down list at the bottom of the page, select the Free to Use Share or Modify option.**

5. **Click the Advanced Search button.**

   The search returns a huge selection of images.

6. **If you find an image you want to use, save it to your computer.**

   You find out how to upload this image in the later section "Uploading a background to your toolbox."

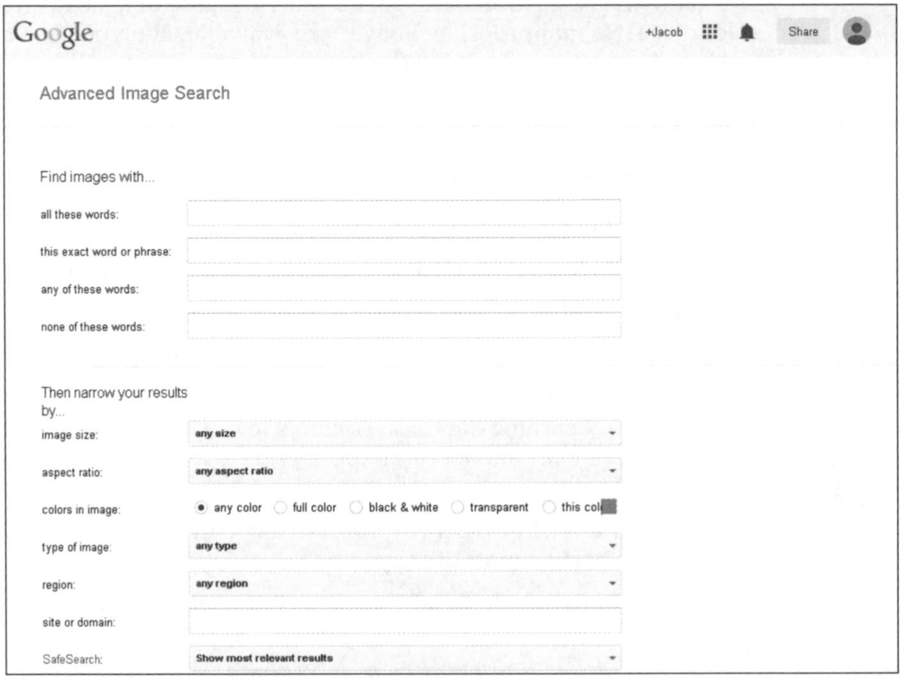

Figure 13-4: Google's Advanced Image Search fields.

Creative Commons lets image owners grant options for use without your having to contact them directly. But you need to look at the Creative Commons license for each image: Some let you use them only if you're not creating images that make money; some let you use them as long as you give credit; others let you use them but not modify them in any way. Check out `http://creativecommons.org` for more information.

Designing your own custom background

To design your own custom background, you need to use programs outside Gamestar Mechanic. You must use a program that lets you create image files and save them to your computer. Programs such as Microsoft Paint are free and come supplied with your operating system; others, such as GIMP and PicMonkey, can be downloaded. Some programs, such as Dungeon Painter Online (`www.pyromancers.com`), are specifically designed for game backgrounds.

When drawing a background, don't overdo it. The sprite — the most important part of your game — is meant to stand out visually, so use shapes and colors that work well as a background and don't distract the player.

Drawing a background from scratch can be difficult, especially when you want it to fit in with a Gamestar Mechanic game. You can always modify existing images by scaling and recoloring them into new works; however, the rules of plagiarism still apply. Some free programs give you sets of tiles that you can arrange into high-definition backgrounds and save to your computer.

A single screen in a Gamestar Mechanic game is 640 pixels wide and 480 pixels tall.

Uploading a background to your toolbox

When you upload a custom background, it's stored in the Gamestar Mechanic database, where you can access and use it at any time. To upload a custom background, you must first save the image as a file on your computer. Your Gamestar Mechanic account is permanently linked to all the image files you've uploaded as custom backgrounds. After you submit an image file to Gamestar Mechanic, you can access it again at any time to use in other games.

To add a new background to the list, follow these steps:

1. **Go to your game's page and click the Settings button for the level.**

2. **In the Level Settings dialog box, scroll down to the Background section.**

3. **Click the Choose a Custom Background button.**

    This button appears only if you've completed the Custom Background Challenge in your workshop.

Figure 13-5 shows the Choose a Custom Background dialog box that appears.

After your game is published, you have to wait for every custom background (that isn't designated with a green check mark) to be approved by the administrators. *Marked* backgrounds have been used in, and approved for, another of your games, and you can reuse them as you like.

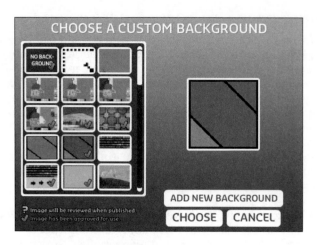

Figure 13-5: Your custom backgrounds.

4. **Click the Add New Background button.**

5. **Click the Choose a File to Upload button.**

   A second dialog box appears that lets you access the files on your computer.

6. **Find the image file you want to use, select it, and click Open.**

   The actions you take in this step depend on your computer's operating system.

7. **Wait for the image to appear on your screen.**

   This step may take some time for large files. Try changing the file type, if you need to. Your image editing software may also have an option to compress the image you're editing into a smaller file size. When the file appears, don't worry if it looks skewed or cramped — all you're seeing is a screenshot that ensures that you have the right file, so it won't look that way in your game.

8. **Click Upload.**

After you upload the background, you can use it in any level of any game. All you have to do is follow Steps 1–3 in the preceding step list, click on the background in the Choose a Custom Background dialog box (refer to Figure 13-5), and click Choose.

The list of custom backgrounds is sorted from oldest to newest. You can find the first backgrounds you uploaded at the top of the list, and find the most recent ones at the bottom.

Gamestar Mechanic identifies image files only in JPEG or PNG format. If you try to upload a background but Gamestar can't find it, follow these steps:

1. **Check the file type.**

   Examine the properties of the image file, and see whether it's referred to as a PNG file, JPG file, or JPEG file, as shown at the bottom of Figure 13-6. If the file format is incorrect, continue to Step 2 in order to fix it. If the format is correct but you still can't find the file, you may be looking in the wrong folder on your computer.

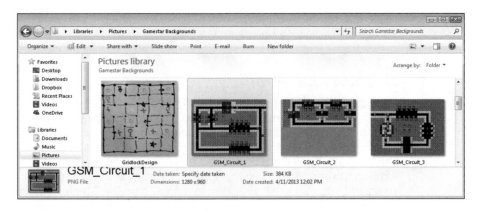

Figure 13-6: Select a file to view its properties.

2. **Open your file.**

   You can open it in Paint or any other image-viewing program.

3. **Save the file again in the correct format.**

   On Windows, this is File⇨Save As⇨Save As Type⇨PNG File (or JPG File)⇨Save. You now have two files of the same image, though only one should be noticed by Gamestar Mechanic.

Adjusting Settings for Backgrounds

After you've added a background to your game, you can further customize the background by using two additional options in the Level Settings dialog box: Background Scrolling and Background Style, as shown in Figure 13-7.

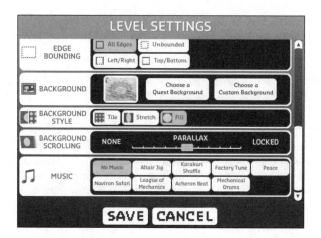

Figure 13-7: The Background Style and Background Scrolling settings change how the background functions.

Background Scrolling

The *parallax* is an important property of the background in games in which the Multiple Screen option is selected. Editable by the slider under the Background Scrolling section of the level settings, parallax determines how far the background is from the sprites. In large levels, the sprites scroll so that the main screen is centered on the player, but the background can scroll at a different rate. Many classic platformer games such as Super Mario use this trick, and you can see it in action in many Gamestar Mechanic games, such as the Naviron Elevator mission from Episode 2 of the Addison Joins the League quest. The parallax thus determines how quickly the background moves relative to the avatar. You can set it to None (the background doesn't move) or Locked (the background scrolls with the sprites) or any spot between them.

The three types of parallax are described in this list:

✔ **None:** The background remains where it is, even as the level scrolls — this means that the game's sprites are displayed over a single stationary image. This type can look mismatched if all the sprites start sliding but the background doesn't. Thus, if your background has this attribute, make sure that the background feels disconnected from the sprites of the level.

✔ **Locked:** The background scrolls along with the sprites as though it's connected. Thus, if a sprite is placed over a certain part of the background, it remains there no matter how the player moves around. This is often effectively used in top-down games, since the background then becomes the floor which the sprites walk over. Locked backgrounds are used in the "Puzzle Garden of DOOM!" mission from the Dungeon of the Rogue quest finale.

This type of background can depict items that are aligned with the sprites of the level, such as walls or floors. You can make this type quite detailed, by drawing paths and features that connect neatly with the sprites. However, don't depict anything as though it's off in the distance, because it makes the perspective of the game look odd. For example, if you draw a mountain in the background, it might look like the player can cross from one end to the other in a couple of seconds, because the mountain scrolls by too fast.

✓ **Somewhere in between:** As the player scrolls through the level, the background scrolls at a fraction of the speed of the sprites. The Parallax background gives the illusion of being at a distance from the sprites — the slower it moves, the farther away it seems. Try different parallax values to calibrate how far away you want the background to be.

Background Style

Custom backgrounds can be compromised by improper scaling, making them pixelated or mostly hidden. As explained in Chapter 5, you can scale backgrounds in the Background Style level option in three ways: Tile, Stretch, and Fill. This section tells you how to select and apply a style to your custom background and incorporate parallax setting and level size.

Tile

The *tiling* background technique is reserved almost entirely for custom backgrounds (because most quest backgrounds aren't properly enabled for tiling). Making a background repeat without scaling is quite a useful skill — the image you select acts more like a single tile than a full background.

Suppose that you make a tiny background consisting of a light gray square with a dark gray outline. The resulting background would consist of many of these tiles set in a grid pattern. This background can be used in interesting ways — by drawing smaller backgrounds than normal, you can create large tiled patterns easily.

You can also use larger tiles — the size of a screen, for instance — to create large levels with a background for each room. The Tile feature isn't necessary to get the background you want, but it can be quite a convenient tool for doing so.

Most backgrounds look mismatched when tiled, because of the seams between the tiles. Either place outlines around tiles to separate them from each other, or design the background so that each side connects neatly with the opposite side. In Figure 13-8, the happy-face background (in the left image) has outlines around each tile; the sky background (in the right image) is designed so that each side connects seamlessly.

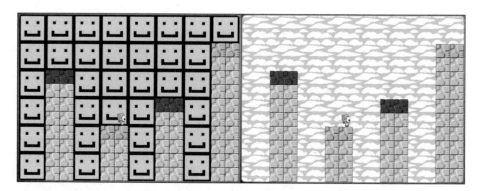

Figure 13-8: Tiled backgrounds can give depth and consistency to your games.

Stretch

Though the Stretch background style is not as commonly used as others, it has some interesting applications. If you apply a background that's too small for the level, the Stretch feature "pulls out" the background both horizontally and vertically to fit the stage, as shown in Figure 13-9. This effect is different from Fill (described next) because the process doesn't try to maintain the background's *aspect ratio* — it can be stretched in one way more than the other.

Figure 13-9: This game's background is stretched out sideways to fit the level.

The Stretch feature is most commonly applicable in high-resolution quest backgrounds, especially abstract ones that can look interesting when stretched out. However, you rarely want to use this feature with custom backgrounds.

Calculating the dimensions of Fill-type backgrounds

Though the Fill background style is the default style (and arguably the most useful), it introduces complications when you try to fit the background to a level. For example, if you create a room that's two screens wide and two screens tall (four times the size of a default room) but the parallax is set to the default, a single screen background gets scaled up by 50 percent (rather than double in size, as you might expect). Try it out to see what happens.

A single screen or room is 640 pixels wide by 480 pixels high.

A simple formula can help you determine the factor by which a background is expanded to fit a level. First, however, let me define a few terms:

Let p be a number from 0 to 10 representing the parallax of the level; 0 is None and 10 is Locked, which means that the notches on the Background

Scrolling slider represent all integers from 0 through 10.

Let d be whichever number is larger: the Level Width value or the Level Height value.

Using these terms, you can calculate the scale factor of a background that is the size of a single screen (640 pixels wide, 480 pixels high) to equal $1+(d-1)p/10$.

For example, in a 1-by-5 room with parallax 8, a 640-by-480 background would be expanded to $1+(5-1)8/10=4.2$ times its normal size.

The quality of a background can drop when it's stretched. If you want to choose the dimensions of a background in a large level, consider the dimensions you would use for a single screen, and then multiply by the scale factor from the preceding equation.

Fill

The default (and arguably the most useful) background style is Fill — a useful go-to style for both quest and custom backgrounds. Fill resizes the background until it's just large enough to fill the room (accounting for parallax). One problem to watch out for is that Fill-type backgrounds are centered on the level; if you put a square background in a wide level, the top and bottom parts of the background are cut off.

Background cutoff can be helpful for quest backgrounds. If you want to make a level in the sky, you can combine a high level width with a plain background to produce a more "airborne" picture.

Finding Additional Resources for Studying Game Design

The following sections can help you find additional ways to improve your game design techniques.

Learning other design languages

The Gamestar Mechanic platform has a lot of predesigned code that lets you design more easily, but it's limited to certain types of games. Other design platforms can be more difficult to use, but more robust. These platforms run on programming languages — some are object-oriented, some work better with lists, and some have features specifically attuned to certain purposes, for example. Some game designers build their games from scratch using robust languages such as C++ or Java, which you can learn in a school program or search for on the Internet. These languages can produce anything you can imagine, though they can take a while to pick up. Other designers work from specific engines, and learn languages specifically suited to their games — for example, the Game Maker program lets you create any sort of game you like much more easily than with generic programming languages (see www.gamemaker.nl).

Learning multiple design languages is a way to further your experience in game design, because every language supports a certain set of games. Some professional designers even write multilingual games, creating elegant works with several features by patching together multiple kinds of code. The game design experience you gain from other languages can also help you improve your skills on Gamestar Mechanic.

Analyzing and emulating games

You can draw inspiration from a huge number of games outside Gamestar Mechanic. As with the practice of learning another programming language, emulating another game is a useful way to practice game design. However, remember not to plagiarize other people's ideas, as detailed in Chapter 9.

Using Gamestar Mechanic to emulate a game is similar to re-creating a known structure with building blocks; however, you have to be able to emulate the interactions and motives behind the game's components rather than just the components themselves. Practice manipulating the components used in other games to become more comfortable with design, and, eventually, to build better games of your own.

Other users have accomplished this task in interesting ways. Sprites such as portals and transmogrifiers have been applied to create various mechanisms and menus, whereas classic platformer games have been remade in Gamestar Mechanic many times in many ways. But even then, you don't have to emulate a game entirely to draw inspiration from it — a single mechanic can inspire hundreds of possibilities for new creations in Gamestar Mechanic.

Moving on

You can find many resources to help you design games at Gamestar Mechanic and in general. The practice of game design has inspired many books, courses, and practices that you can find online, in libraries, or from other sources.

The quests in Gamestar Mechanic give beginners a good starting point, but if you want to further expand your horizons, you can communicate with other game designers to find out a bit about their thought processes. Some independent game developers even maintain blogs where they talk about their works and their works in progress, so if you're following a block in anticipation of a new game, you can use it as inspiration.

You can find out all about designing in Game Maker specifically and programming interesting games in general by reading *The Game Maker's Apprentice*, by Mark Overmars and Jacob Habgood. In addition, Jesse Schell's *The Art of Game Design* is an extremely useful book about the deep concepts of designing, with lots of interesting information and an included deck of 100 lenses (ways to view and analyze a game) that you can learn and study to improve your work.

You can also go to `http://gamestarmechanic.com/teachers` to look at teachers' resources, which reiterate a lot of fundamental information that you may find useful. Teachers of all subjects have a lot of interesting things to say about game design, especially because it links to many other fields, from economics to computer science to critical reading. Just as you can use game design to learn creativity, critical thinking, systems thinking, and media literacy (as I explain in Chapter 1), you can study these fields to develop an overall intuition for game design. Jane McGonigal's *Reality is Broken: Why Games Make Us Better and How They Can Change the World* is an inspirational book that derives insight on game design from similar insights on reality, and it shows you how to shed light on all sorts of real-life problems through mastery of games.

Part V
Going Deeper in the Gamestar World

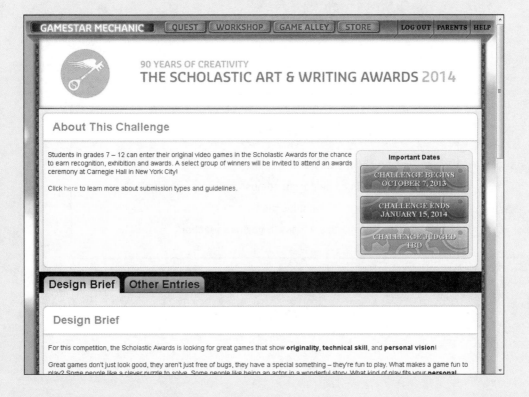

Find out how teachers can design a Gamestar Mechanic lesson plan at www.dummies.com/extras/gamestarmechanic.

In this part . . .

- Find out about premium accounts.
- Participate in game design competitions.
- Join a Gamestar Mechanic class.
- Create and manage a class (if you're a teacher).

14

Examining Premium Content

....

....

The Gamestar Mechanic store offers a number of premium packs that you can purchase. The Addison's Complete Quest premium pack adds a huge amount of content to your experience, as detailed in this chapter. You can also purchase less-expensive sprite packs, which give you access to specific groups of premium sprites, some of which are not available in the Addison's Complete Quest pack. In this chapter, I explain what premium content is available for you to purchase, show you how to upgrade your account, and give you an overview of premium sprites.

Exploring Premium Content

With a free Gamestar Mechanic account, you have a wealth of features at your disposal; you have access to the Addison Joins the League quest, and you can make and publish as many games as you want while interacting with the Gamestar Mechanic community. But after you become more experienced with the site, you may discover that you need new challenges. For experienced players, purchasing premium content is often a good choice because it provides plenty of useful new sprites, as well as features such as custom backgrounds.

Looking at your premium options

The Gamestar Mechanic store offers the following premium content:

✔ **Addison's Complete Quest:** Upgrading your account to this premium pack — for a flat fee of $20 — gives you unlimited access to these features:

- *Two new quests:* These quests begin a new story arc to help you master advanced concepts in game design.

- *More than 100 missions:* The new quests contain a wealth of games designed by the Gamestar Mechanic administrators.

- *More than 20 backgrounds:* You also unlock as many as 21 new backgrounds from Quest missions to use in your games.

- *Custom backgrounds:* A new challenge is unlocked in your workshop, letting you design your own backgrounds for your games. (See Chapter 13 for more on custom backgrounds.)

- *More than 100 sprites:* You can unlock as many as 104 new sprites as you progress through the quest. You can also access the Locked On Challenge, which grants you two bonus sprites from the gateway pack. Even if you already have some of these sprites, you can always find useful new ones, such as the Naviron knight and the Karakuri phoenix (discussed later in this chapter).

- *Two soundtracks:* You can unlock two new, instrumental soundtracks: the airy Altair jig and the darker Acheron beat.

✔ **Sprite packs:** If you're looking for a less-expensive option, you can purchase individual sprite packs, which give you access to groups of premium sprites beyond the ones found in Addison's Complete Quest. Figure 14-1 shows the sprite packs that are available at the time of this writing, ranging in cost from $1.99 to $2.99. The Mystical sprite pack, for example, contains 11 sprites representing the medieval and mythical, as well as the Naviron informer and health pack from Addison's Complete Quest.

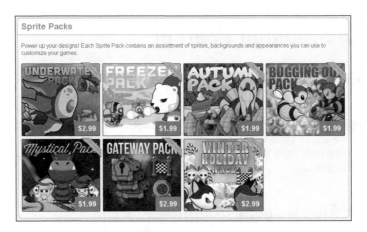

Figure 14-1: The seven sprite packs, each marked with either a banner labeled Owned or a button labeled Add to Cart.

Deciding whether to purchase premium content

Here are a few points to keep in mind as you consider whether it would be worth your while to purchase premium packs:

✔ **To get a feel for how a Premium account might translate to game design, play some games that were designed by Premium account holders.** Then you can evaluate what other users are doing with their Premium accounts. In Game Alley, you can find a lot of games created by users with Premium accounts. You'll recognize the games because of their unique sprites and backgrounds. By playing interesting premium games from experienced users, you can see what sprites and opportunities the premium content offers you.

✔ **Fully explore what you can do with the sprites in the free version of Gamestar Mechanic.** If you find a major obstacle in your design process (for example, there are no health packs or checkpoints available in the free version, so you can't make levels too long and challenging), see whether some games in Game Alley feature sprites that clear this obstacle (sprites such as health packs and teleporters are very useful for surpassing the limits of the free toolbox). If you aren't sure whether you want to purchase premium content, use the free version as much as you can — when you reach the limits of your creativity, you can become inspired to try out the premium sprites.

✔ **Plan out how you might use premium features to design a game.** The best way to decide whether you would benefit from a Premium account is to find lots of ways in which you want to use it. You can practice applying premium content by designing games for contests, as described in Chapter 15. Some contests give you access to premium-level sprites even if you haven't purchased premium packs, so you can see what the interface is like.

Purchasing Premium Packs

If you decide that you want to upgrade your account by purchasing Addison's Complete Quest or other premium packs, follow these steps:

1. **Click the Store button at the top of any Gamestar Mechanic page, or go to**

   ```
   http://gamestarmechanic.com/store
   ```

2. **If you want to see specific information about the pack, click the image corresponding to the pack you want to buy.**

   The description page appears, as shown in Figure 14-2.

Figure 14-2: This page gives a description of the pack and a list of the challenges and sprites it contains, which you can expand by clicking the plus-sign (+) buttons at the bottom.

3. **Click the Add to Cart button.**

This button is below or on the image for the sprite pack (depending on whether you followed Step 2).

If you don't see the Add to Cart button, you may already have this feature.

4. **Follow the instructions to pay for your purchase.**

If you aren't yet 18 years old, a parent or guardian must complete the credit card purchase.

After you purchase a product from the store, the new quests and challenges become available in their respective places: Quests are available on the Quest page, and challenges are available in the Workshop. You have no hardware to install or files to download, so you can access these features right away.

Using Complicated Premium Sprites

A major feature of premium packs is access to advanced sprites. If you select an item in the store, you can see a list of all available sprites in that purchase. These sprites can be difficult to understand and apply, but used well, they can unlock a wealth of possibilities, such as epic boss battles and intricate puzzles. This section gives you an overview of some of the premium-level sprites. All sprites described in the following sections are available when you complete the Addison's Complete Adventure content. For a description of all the sprites, see Chapter 6.

Megasprites

The enemy class known as the *megasprite* is four times the size of other not-so-mega sprites and occupies a 2-by-2 square on the grid, as shown in Figure 14-3. You can place a megasprite on your grid only if all four of the squares it's being placed on are empty. A total of eight different megasprites are in Addison's Complete Quest: They are either pacing *megachasers* or sharpshooting *megasnipers* (one per school). (See Chapter 6 for more on megachasers and megasnipers.)

Megasprite

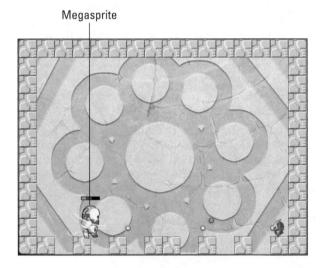

Figure 14-3: Megasprite game.

Megasprites have a number of unique characteristics:

✔ **They cannot be spawned.** Enemy generators and enemy spawn points (described in Chapter 6) are too small to create megasprites. This means that megasprites work best as boss battles, since they can only be destroyed, never created.

✔ **They have increased health boundaries.** Whereas most enemies can have a maximum of only 10 hit points (outside of the Quest missions), megasprites can have as many as 15, depending on the sprites. They also have an increased minimum health, which varies between mega-sprites: Only Acheron megasprites can have 1 hit point (as well as the megadragon from the Mystical sprite pack).

✔ **Some megasnipers have better shooting damage.** Usually, all bullets deal 1 point of damage, and this value cannot be changed. However, cer-tain megasprites shoot more powerful bullets: The Acheron megasniper deals 2 points of damage, and the Altair megasniper deals 3. In addition, the Acheron megasniper shoots three bullets at a time: one straight ahead and two angled to each side.

✔ **They pass over gaps.** If you add a megasprite to a platformer game and
have it walk toward a pit that's one block wide, the megasprite passes
right over the pit. You can use this to your advantage, making platforms
that certain sprites fall through and others do not.

If you make a platformer game in which the avatar is on the same platform as
a megasniper, the megasniper's bullets fire slightly higher than normal ones,
making them difficult to block.

The megadragon from the Mystical sprite pack (a pack containing many sprites
beyond Addison's Complete Quest, available in the Gamestar Mechanic store) is
a useful addition to the megasprite family. It has triple bullets that deal 1 point
of damage apiece, and its health and damage sliders have the widest variety
(1 to 15 health; 0 to 10 damage). It can also fire bullets at superfast speed,
similar to the Acheron megasniper.

Naviron defender and Naviron guardian

The special avatars known as Naviron defender and Naviron guardian (see
Figure 14-4) are sprites with green clothes and yellow shields that can block
attacks when you hold down the Action key. The *defender* is a top-down
sprite that blocks in whichever direction it's facing; the *guardian* is a platformer sprite that can block left or right.

Naviron defender

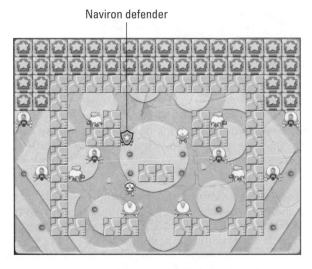

Figure 14-4: An avatar hidden behind its raised shield.

The *shield,* which is treated as a solid object, gives these avatars some interesting properties: The shield deflects enemies and absorbs bullets. The guardian can squash enemies by jumping on them while shielding.

Naviron knight and Naviron hero

Similar to the Naviron defender and guardian, the Naviron knight and Naviron hero sprites have a shield (activated by pressing the Action key) and a sword (activated by pressing the Attack key). (See Figure 14-5.) The sword can extend a short distance and, unlike bullets, can damage every enemy in its range. Hitting an enemy knocks it two squares backward.

Naviron hero

Figure 14-5: An avatar with a sword and shield.

These sprites do lots of damage to groups of enemies, and they can hit twice with each strike if the enemy is against a wall and cannot be pushed. If you use one of these sprites, be sure to design the game around its powerful abilities.

If one of these avatars picks up a blaster (described later in this chapter), it becomes quite powerful. However, you cannot hold down the Attack button to fire as you normally can, because the bullets are in sync with your sword strikes.

Naviron lancers and Naviron sentries

The Naviron lancer and Naviron sentry enemies make Naviron unique, by replacing the traditional chasers and snipers with two melee fighters: the spear-wielding lancer and the shield-bearing sentry, as shown in Figure 14-6. These sprites have many interesting properties:

Naviron lancer   Naviron sentry

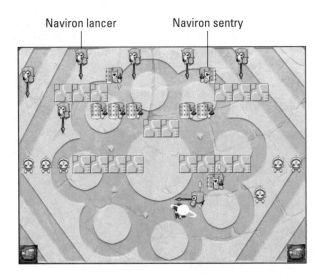

Figure 14-6: Lancers and sentries.

✔ **Each sprite consists of two components:**

• The lancer's spear, which is almost a sprite of its own, sticks out in whichever way the sprite is facing, effectively doubling its size. However, the lance is unimpeded by walls and doesn't prevent the lancer from navigating tight places.

• The sentry's shield is held close to its wielder. Only the sentry's body does damage, whereas the lancer can hurt the avatar with both of its components.

✔ **They both push the avatar around:**

• The lancer's weapon pushes back the avatar with every hit. However, it can do only as much damage as it's programmed to do, regardless of whether the avatar is pushed against the wall. Its range is as long as its lance, which is slightly shorter than the sword wielded by Naviron knights and Naviron heroes.

• The sentry pushes the avatar as it walks, dealing no damage but possibly destroying the avatar by pushing it into a wall or another shield.

✔ **They can guard.** These two enemies have a unique Movement Style option, labeled Guard, that lets them stay in place while watching a triangular area in front of them, depending on which way they're facing. If one of these enemies sees the avatar, an exclamation point (!) appears over its head, and it starts chasing you. Fortunately, you can dodge it or escape it, causing it to become confused and then return to its position.

✔ **They're stronger against shooters than sword users.** Both the lance and the shield can absorb bullets, making them difficult to defeat with a blaster. You have to sneak up on them and attack from the side or back. Alternatively, shooting the lancer just above or below its weapon damages it. The Naviron knight, using a sword instead of a blaster, is quite effective against these enemies: Its sword is longer than the Lancer's lance, so if you use it at the right time, you can damage and knock back a Lancer before it can do the same to you. The sword can also push the Naviron sentry back with its attack, even if the sentry blocks. The knight's shield is also effective: The lancer can push a shielding knight without dealing damage, giving the knight time to escape, and the shield causes sentries to change course.

Karakuri phoenix

The *Karakuri phoenix* destructible block can repair other sprites. After placing this block on the level you're designing, you must click on another sprite that you want to attach the block to. When the attached sprite is destroyed, it becomes transparent, and two red orbs spin around it (indicating that it's being resurrected), as the phoenix block turns red as well (indicating that it's resurrecting the sprite). After a set amount of time, depending on the phoenix's Resurrection Duration setting (which you can set with the Edit tool), the sprite returns to the game with full health. This can be done with enemies or destructible blocks — you can even have a phoenix block resurrect another phoenix block. Phoenix blocks work at any range, so the sprite they resurrect keeps coming back until the phoenix block is destroyed.

Figure 14-7 shows an example of how the phoenix block can turn a shooting game into a dodging game. The gray-and-red blocks spaced throughout the level are all phoenix blocks, and each one is linked to one of the enemies. The phoenix block in the figure is bright red because it is in the process of resurrecting a destroyed sprite. The player must defeat seven enemies on each side, but the enemies on one side are regenerated by the phoenix blocks on the other side — you cannot destroy any of the enemies (they'll just revive themselves) until you destroy the phoenix blocks opposite them. In the figure, the player tries to destroy the phoenix blocks at the top, shooting the invincible guards to stun them as they regenerate.

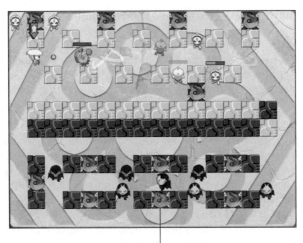

Karakuri phoenix

Figure 14-7: Phoenix block game.

If you set the resurrection duration to 0, the phoenix block effectively makes its linked sprite invincible unless the phoenix is destroyed. This is useful when making a glass door that requires the phoenix block to be found before it can be opened, or for making an indestructible enemy with a consistent motion pattern. However, this setting allows the linked sprite to gain back only 1 hit point after resurrecting.

Transmogrifier

This advanced block, the transmogrifier, has the ability to shoot! Its maximum firing rate is extremely fast, and it can fire in any direction, including all four at once. However, its bullets have special properties: They hit and damage enemies rather than avatars, and when they frag an enemy, that enemy changes into another sprite of your choice with full health! The transmogrifier is quite versatile because it can turn its victims into dangerous enemies, helpful informers, stronger or weaker opponents, or even items that the avatar can collect.

Figure 14-8 shows an example of enemy-making transmogrifiers that turn a shooter game into an interesting exercise in population management: All enemies in the figure are running around in a circle, but the transmogrifier at each juncture changes them as they pass by. The player can change the cycle and edit the population of each enemy by touching or destroying the transmogrifiers.

Transmogrifier

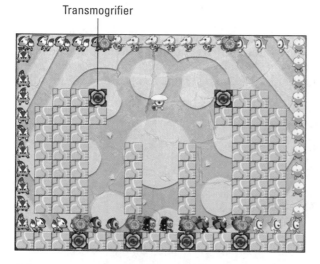

Figure 14-8: Transmogrifier game.

To modify the effects of the transmogrifier's bullets, select the transmogrifier with the Edit tool, and click the Edit Settings button in the Transmogrify Bullet option. This action opens a new editing page containing the most of the transmogrifier's unique settings. You can

- Set the bullet's damage (which cannot be done with any other bullet).
- Pick the sprite in which to transmogrify targets.
- Edit the settings of the sprite.

You can set the transmogrifier to create either an enemy or an item from its targets.

If you want to edit the settings of the Transmogrify Into sprite, do *not* click Pick Sprite by mistake! You will have to readjust all of your sprite's settings, which return to the default.

The transmogrifier can also be affected by the avatar. It can be destroyed, and can even be toggled when the avatar bumps into it. By touching the transmogrifier, you make it turn transparent and inactive; move away and touch it again to reactivate it.

If you want your transmogrifier to cleanly destroy an enemy without changing it, have the transmogrifier bullet turn the target into a Naviron grazer or Naviron gnasher (both of which have an energy meter) with Start Energy 1, Energy Usage 50 or more, and Damage 0.

Power-ups

A number of square power-up items are available in Addison's Complete Quest, granting the avatar improved abilities when it touches and automatically picks up the item. All active power-ups, including keys, are displayed in the upper left corner of the game screen, as shown in Figure 14-9.

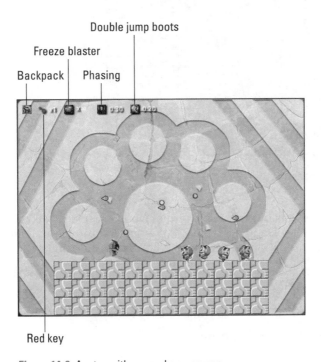

Double jump boots

Freeze blaster

Backpack   Phasing

Red key

Figure 14-9: Avatar with several power-ups.

Armor pack

The *armor pack* gives the player armor, allowing it to take more damage. The red beam in the health meter turns white and is covered by a large, white number denoting armor points. Your avatar cannot lose health until its armor is depleted.

Armor isn't accumulative: If you have X points of armor and you pick up an armor pack worth Y points of armor, your armor becomes whichever of X and Y is greater. This makes armor helpful, but no substitute for health.

Backpack

A more indirect item, the *backpack sprite* lets you see a tooltip the first time you collect this sprite on a level. When you have a backpack, you don't use any items you collect (except keys). Instead, they're stored in an inventory that's accessible with the inventory key (I), which lets you click on items to use them. Using the backpack, your players can use health packs only when needed and save power-ups for the right moments.

Blaster

The *blaster* is an obtainable weapon that causes the avatar to glow with a red aura, allowing even defenseless avatars to fire bullets at an extremely fast rate. This item can last indefinitely, or it can burn out after 10 to 40 seconds, depending on how you structure your game. You can also apply a blaster to an avatar that can already shoot, which can be advantageous to avatars with low fire rates. If you give a blaster to an avatar that doesn't normally use one, the power-up can be overridden by the similar freeze blaster (described later).

Double jump boots

Effective only in platformer games, the *double jump boots* allow the avatar to jump twice before hitting the ground. While in midair, the avatar gets an extra jump. This jump isn't as strong as the first one, but it allows for better maneuverability.

For maximized jump height, don't jump twice in quick succession — wait until the peak of your first jump before launching the second.

Freeze blaster

The freeze blaster power-up grants the avatar a *freeze blaster* (a weapon similar to the blaster), which fires bullets that encase their targets in ice. You can use frozen targets as walls or platforms, but they unfreeze from 2 to 10 seconds later, depending on the blaster's Freeze Duration setting. If you freeze a frozen sprite, the ice around it thickens, and the timer counting down to the enemy's release resets. If you freeze a sprite that's overlapping with other sprites, the unfrozen sprites are fragged instantly. In a platformer game, you can freeze an enemy in midair so that it falls and squashes other enemies.

The freeze blaster is a built-in feature of the Altair iceman, Altair freezer, frost wizard, and frost mage, as well as some enemies. However, like the blaster, the freeze blaster increases the fire rate of the default freeze blaster, and an avatar with both blasters can fire with alternating attacks.

Frozen sprites are unaffected by collisions, but they can still be damaged by weapons. However, a frozen avatar is unaffected by freeze blasts, whereas frozen enemies are affected.

Phasing

A property of all Karakuri avatars except Naja, *phasing* lets you share the phasing ability with other avatars. While this item is active, the Action button causes your avatar to freeze in place and become invisible. Nothing can harm you while you're phasing.

Shield-bearing sprites can still deflect enemies while phasing.

15

Entering Game Design Contests

In This Chapter

▶ Searching for contests

▶ Creating your own, unofficial contest

▶ Designing a game to enter in a contest

▶ Taking a look at the benefits of entering contests

▶ Composing a design document

*G*ame design contests are competitions in which users submit games to a panel of judges, who evaluate the games and select winners to receive awards for their work. Contests often require participants to create games focused on certain topics or styles. Gamestar Mechanic hosts many contests, from carefully judged, company-sponsored competitions to unofficial ones planned by users on the site.

Contests take place over a specified period. If you miss the due date for one contest, you have to wait for another one. Official, sponsored contests offer the best rewards, but each one generally only comes around once a year, so take these opportunities *seriously*. This chapter explains how to perform at your best for contests and helps you understand why you should do so.

Finding Contests

Contests are relatively easy to find. The official contests are strongly advertised, and many Gamestar Mechanic users make contests of their own.

Looking for contests sponsored by Gamestar Mechanic

You can find contests sponsored by Gamestar Mechanic in the Challenges & Contests section, which you can find by scrolling down in your workshop until you reach a group of eight large challenge icons and titles. Click on an element in this group to identify the type of challenge or contest it is. If it's a contest, the contest page should resemble the one shown in Figure 15-1.

Note that the front page of the Challenges & Contests section sometimes contains only challenges, if no active contests are available. Challenges aren't usually judged; they often simply require you to play games rather than design them — though they can be useful for unlocking new sprites and features and for trying out new techniques.

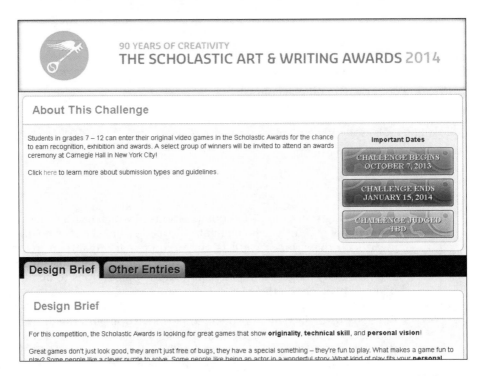

Figure 15-1: The contest page. Though the header is labeled About This Challenge, this is true for both challenges and contests.

On the contest page, you can find information about how the contest runs. The page is divided into sections, though some sections are hidden until you click on the appropriate tab. You can find various sorts of information from these sections:

- **About This Challenge:** This section of the page presents an overview of how the competition works.

- **Important Dates:** In the upper right corner of the contest page, you can see a list of dates that represent, from top to bottom:

  - The day the contest started

  - The day all entries are due (also appears in seasonal challenges)

  - The day the results are published, which is shown only for contests (doesn't apply to challenges)

If you see the initials *TBD* (indicating *to be d*etermined) rather than a date, the date isn't available yet.

✔ **Design Brief:** This tab displays detailed information about the contest, such as a description, guidelines, recommendations, and information about how the contest is organized.

Check the design brief again before submitting your entry to see whether you should do anything else to enter the contest. Contests are often run by way of Gamestar Mechanic from other websites, which have different requirements for entry.

✔ **Create an Entry:** This tab lets you view one or two options for submitting a game to the contest. (This tab is available only before the due date of the contest.)

- *Build a New Game Template:* Usually, you see this button on the page, which opens a special version of the toolbox, where you can design your game. If you click the Save button on a template, your draft appears on the Create an Entry tab for you to work on later.

- *Choose a Game from My Workshop:* Depending on the restrictions of the contest, you may see this button as well; click it to see a list of your published games, and select a game to submit to the contest.

✔ **Challenge Missions:** This tab is available only in certain contests. It lets you see specifically made missions that teach the values expected by the contest. Try to complete these missions whenever they're available.

✔ **Other Entries:** After the judging is complete, this tab provides links to winning entries, which you can click on to play those games. If you've entered the contest, a link to your entry is also provided.

Looking for user-created contests

Some game design contests are created by Gamestar Mechanic users and published on the site in the form of games. These are *not* official contests; they're organized for fun by Gamestar Mechanic users who set the rules and decide the winners. Users do this by publishing the rules and results through games, which contain message blocks outlining the details of the contest, as shown in Figure 15-2. These contests often require entrants to submit their games by recommending them or by posting the name of their submitted game in the Comments section. The contest host decides how to judge and select winners, and usually publishes the results by creating or editing a game to display them.

User-created contests are beneficial for both the host and the participants. When you submit your game, the contest's judges are sure to play it, and they often leave reviews. Whether you win or lose, this process is a good way to advertise your games.

Figure 15-2: This message block outlines the rules of the contest.

The best way to find these contests is to search for games using the keyword *contest* or *competition* in Game Alley. By looking through the search results, you can find a number of contests to enter at once and reap both short-term and long-term rewards: Simply entering can get people to play and possibly review your game, and users often check out your workshop if you have a winning entry. And some contests even allow you to reuse a game you've already published. All it takes is a review or a comment to get started: Comment on the contest game to let the contest manager know that your entry is ready (and follow any special instructions set by the designer).

When you search for contests in Game Alley, the results are sorted from newest to oldest. Focus on the newest ones because their due dates probably haven't passed yet.

Starting Your Own Contest

Users create contests because they consider the process fun and interesting. If you want, you can make a contest yourself. Follow these tips:

- ✔ **Decide how to restrict entries.** How do you want entries sent in? Are you looking for a particular sort of entry, such as platformer games or games with a limited selection of sprites? Consider your own skill level because you want to be able to complete all the submitted games — if you're a beginner player, for example, request some easy games. Also consider whether you want users to design new games for your contest, or allow them to enter games they've already published. Requesting new games ensures more topical — but fewer — entries.

✏ **Build a game that provides all necessary** information about the contest. Use message block sprites, as well as the Level Intro and Level Win messages, to tell players how to participate in the contest. Ask yourself what your entrants need to know:

- When are the games due?

- What restrictions did you decide on?

- How should the games be submitted?

- How are the results published?

Think about these questions ahead of time so that you can organize this information to make it as clear and concise as possible.

✏ **Evaluate your own ability to manage the contest.** Always carry out what you promise: Play the games submitted to your contest, publish the results in a timely fashion, and issue any rewards you might have offered. Don't run a contest that gets you in over your head — for example, you might limit the number of entries to your contests or enlist help in the judging process.

Running a contest can be a great way to meet interesting people, and to get people interested in you. In particular, contests are good at attracting users who like to share interesting games. However, remember that users often play your games for a fun challenge, so if you run too many contests (which usually means publishing games with no gameplay), people may not want to follow you or visit your workshop as often. Delete games that pertain to contests you're no longer hosting, and use these no-challenge games sparingly to keep people coming back to your workshop. Adding one or more fun little levels to your contest game doesn't hurt, either.

Building an Effective Game for a Particular Contest

After you enter a contest, the next step is to put together a good game as your entry. You'll notice a few differences about designing a game for a contest than designing a game normally:

✏ **You may have a different set of sprites.** If you work from a template for an official competition (which opens a special version of the toolbox), check to see what sprites you have to work with. (See Chapter 6 for a rundown of different sprites and their abilities.) Some official contests grant access to new sprites, and some have extra limits on what sprites you can use. User-created contests cannot do this strictly (because they're no more than games asking other people to submit entries). However, some users only accept entries that use certain sprites or combinations of sprites.

✔ **Your entry is being judged, possibly by those who haven't played many games at the Gamestar Mechanic site.** Give your game a moderate difficulty level, and explain any difficult concepts. You don't have to provide the keyboard controls for the game (they appear automatically at the beginning of every level), but keep your audience in mind.

✔ **Most contests are centered on a certain topic.** Make sure that you understand what the judges want to see in a game. This section gives you some tips for how to design such a game. See Chapter 5 for the basic principles of designing a game, and check out Part IV for a look into the deeper concepts of elegant design.

A common strategy for building a game is to expand as much as possible on an idea you like. However, building a game for a contest sometimes requires a different approach. Professional game designers often have to design according to a *prompt,* a provided structure in which the designer must build his game, whether it's the request of the client or the restrictions of the design engine. Similarly, when designing a game to submit to a contest, you often have to meet certain guidelines — your prompt is generally included in the contest's Design Brief. To create a game that satisfies the contest requirements *and* is fun to play, try the following method:

1. **Find an interesting aspect of the contest prompt and use it as inspiration for your game.**

   Rather than think of the contest prompt as a restriction (and try to mold your outstanding idea into one that fits the contest), use the prompt as inspiration. Do the contest judges want educational, original, or themed games? Think about these guidelines first and foremost, and find an interesting way to translate them into a game. Your game structure will be much more interesting to you *and* the judges if you work with the prompt, not in spite of it.

2. **Develop a strong outline for your game.**

   When you develop a contest game, a balanced and elegant structure is a vital quality. Strive to create a game that's well organized and easy to follow so that players understand the main points you're trying to make.

3. **Build the individual levels.**

   Be sure you can work out the smaller portions of the game as well as you've planned it in the big picture. Keep detailed notes of how you've organized the game, fix mistakes carefully, and track the flow of your game. To make a game that stands out in a contest, maintain a steady flow of information from the game to the player.

Preparing for Particular Official Contests

Several contests supported annually by Gamestar Mechanic form a majority of the contest opportunities. Many of these contests allow games from platforms other than Gamestar Mechanic. You can improve your chances of winning a contest if you understand the goal of the contest and develop your game entry accordingly.

Even if you aren't eligible to enter a contest (usually because of your age or grade level), you can still submit an entry and publish it on the Gamestar Mechanic website. (You just can't sign up on the contest site and have the chance to win.) Then you can create a practice entry for the contest, and possibly gain experience using new sprites that are available from the template.

The Scholastic Art and Writing Awards

The Scholastic Art and Writing Awards contest (www.artandwriting.org) is a large, annual, national competition that features all forms of art, writing, and general creativity. To enter — as long as you're a student between Grades 7 and 12 — follow these steps:

✔ **Go to** www.artandwriting.org/the-awards/how-to-enter.

The instructions page appears, detailing the sign-up process, eligibility requirements, and judging criteria. You can reach this page by clicking the Skip Intro button at the bottom of the main page and then clicking the How to Enter button in the upper right corner.

✔ **Check out the "What else do I need to know?" section.**

In particular, you may find the following paragraphs helpful for creating a good entry:

What Is Originality

What Is Technical Skill

What Is Personal Vision or Voice

The contest design brief on Gamestar Mechanic also gives you a helpful overview of the contest and its guidelines.

✔ **Follow the steps in the section labeled "How do I enter a work in the \<year\> Scholastic Art & Writing Awards?"**

To follow this advice, you have to memorize your school's zip code, register an account at www.artandwriting.org/ors/registration, and mail in printed submission forms after you complete your entry. You might want to save the link to this webpage so that you can review the rules when needed.

To enter, you must be

- ✔ **Part of a public, private, or parochial school or a home-school program or an out-of-school program**

  If you belong to more than one, you can select one to represent.

- ✔ **Enrolled in school in the United States or Canada or in an American school abroad**

The regional-level awards for this competition generally give you some recognition, as well as a special badge for your Gamestar Mechanic account — however, national-level work can also provide cash and scholarship rewards. If you're competing for national-level recognition (rewards are listed at `www.artandwriting.org/the-awards/scholarships-and-prizes`), consider attending the winners' award ceremony in New York.

You can use the Gamestar Mechanic Custom Backgrounds feature for this contest, but do not use it to "borrow" someone else's content in your entry without permission and citation.

If you use another person's work in your game without citing it, your entry may be disqualified. See Chapter 9 for information about how to avoid this problem. Strict rules, and tips for avoiding plagiarism, are available at

`www.artandwriting.org/the-awards/copyright-and-plagiarism`

As stated in the design brief (refer to the earlier section "Looking for contests sponsored by Gamestar Mechanic"), the Scholastic Art and Writing Awards contest is looking for games that show the characteristics described in this list:

- ✔ **Originality:** Creativity is greatly valued in the Scholastic awards. If you exhibit novel ideas in gameplay, story, or visual elements, you can make your game stand out among other entries. It helps to have some experience on the Gamestar Mechanic site so that you're familiar with the sort of games published on Gamestar Mechanic and you can come up with something new.

- ✔ **Technical skill:** Another way to make your game stand out is to refine your work, putting lots of details into the design and carefully balancing the game. When your game is ready to be submitted, it may not yet be completely balanced and detailed. Before you publish, be sure to detail and calibrate the gameplay in each level, to make your game look as professional as possible. This process can take some practice as well: Practice reviewing games and analyzing where components can be expanded. Getting people to play your games can be a great help, especially if they give you specific feedback about what you did well and what you could improve.

✔ **Personal vision:** The last metric of a good Scholastic Awards game is the vision behind it. Establish a long-term goal, and use it to create your ideal work. This criterion judges the experience you're building for players: Does it fit your vision of your game? Is your game as fun as you imagined? Be sure to have other people test your game, to ensure that your vision makes sense to others as well as to you.

The Scholastic Art and Writing Awards ensure that all entries are judged fairly, with no bias toward individual designers or topics. You should therefore feel free to express yourself in any way you want — make the judges interested in your game by being interested yourself.

The National STEM Video Game Challenge

The National STEM Video Game Challenge (visit www.stemchallenge.org) focuses on education; the organization looks for game designers who use their work to learn or to teach others, gaining important life skills in the process. STEM is an acronym for *science, technology, engineering,* and *math* — subjects that the competition attempts to teach via students' interest in game design. Every winner receives a laptop with game design and educational software, as well as $2,000 to a school or nonprofit organization — only one person can win with a Gamestar Mechanic game. More information is provided at www.stemchallenge.org/about/the-challenge, or in the contest's design brief at the Gamestar Mechanic site.

To participate in the STEM Challenge, you must be a student between grades 5–12 or be between ages 9–18. You also need permission from a parent or guardian (if you aren't yet 18 years old). When you finish making your game, follow the steps at the STEM Challenge site to enter. For a Gamestar Mechanic game, you need to provide a link to your entry — see Chapter 10 for information on generating the URL.

The STEM Challenge is all about finding skilled game designers who can apply their expertise toward practical goals. The design brief, as described in the earlier section "Looking for contests sponsored by Gamestar Mechanic," lists a few characteristics that the judges look for in games:

✔ **Engagement:** Your game should offer a feeling of *immersion* (complete involvement), drawing the player into the world you create by way of your game. When testing your game, do you ever feel detached or indifferent? If so, your game can be more immersive. Continue working to find ways to gain your audience's attention so that you can show off your imagination to attentive players. Immersion is generally achieved by keeping the player's mind active: Make sure that the player is always either challenged by gameplay or entertained by way of a story and its visuals. For example, break your game down into a challenging section, followed by a short update on the story and setting, followed by more challenges, and so on.

✔ **Innovation:** STEM Challenge judges like to see games that have a creative vision. Focus on creating interesting gameplay puzzles, original stories, and intricate landscapes to create a masterpiece for the contest. (See Part IV of this book for specific information on how to do this.)

✔ **Balance and uniqueness:** Find a balance between innovation and fine-tuning. Be bold, but support your ideas. To make your game unique, get creative and come up with something that hasn't been played out. To make your game well balanced, carefully execute your chosen concepts and make sure that they contribute to a well-scaled game. For example, you might find a new way to design a strategy game — to balance it, you can introduce each element of your idea in a separate level by starting with some basic tutorials and working up to your greatest vision.

✔ **Communication:** Your game should progress smoothly, giving players an experience that communicates the goals and rules in a way that they can understand and follow easily. For example, you should always tell players where they need to go — a goal block in plain sight needs no introduction, but elements such as hard-to-find goals and system sprites generally need to be pointed out, either in the level intro or via message blocks. Heed the advice of *play-testers* — people who try out your game and let you know when they see something that needs to be clarified or fleshed out.

To build a suitable game for the STEM contest, showcase your expertise by creating the sorts of games you know and love: Apply your best effort in your game, detail and balance it as best you can, and implement interesting concepts that speak for themselves. Similarly, if you try to incorporate science, technology, engineering, or mathematics into your game, try to apply a topic that you would particularly want to learn about.

If you want to incorporate a unique new mechanic, practice and tweak it until you master it. Add some progressive structure to your game, making sure that the entire game is well formed (not just its individual levels). The STEM Challenge seeks kids who can make a difference, and you can prove this by expressing your interest and passion in the concepts and strategies that you apply in your game: Be professional and be creative, and revise your game wherever you can improve on one of these qualities.

AMD Challenges

The AMD Foundation (AMD stands for Advanced Micro Devices, in case you're curious) is a technology design company supporting a number of contests that are unique in their specific focus on a single concept and its value in everyday life. At the time of this writing, competitions have been held to design games that model resource management, energy systems, nonviolent solutions, and media — and that raise public awareness and support peace.

Though these challenges don't appear at regular intervals, the Gamestar Mechanic administrators will let you know when new ones show up, via news posts that you can see in your news feed or in the Gamestar News section of Game Alley. You can find the AMD website at www.amd.com; information about the supported game design contests is at the Gamestar Mechanic website, in the contest's design brief.

To join the AMD Challenges, you must be younger than 18 and live in the United States. Create a design document to include with your submission (see the section "Writing Design Documents," later in this chapter). However, the most important part of AMD Challenges is the topic choice: The site lists a general subject that your game must reflect, and you can respond with whatever sort of game you want — though you must address the problem completely.

The AMD Challenges pose the interesting dilemma of how to model a real-world scenario — or discuss a real-world problem — through a game. The first step is to analyze the problem that's presented. Ask yourself these questions:

✔ **What problem and solution am I focusing on?**

It can be difficult to completely address a broad subject, so think about a basic concept within the topic (whether it's a specific example, a simplified model, or a story based on the topic) to turn into a game. Suppose that you want to make a game about pollution. Do you want to deal with air pollution? Water pollution? City waste management? Do you want to use a combination, where each level represents a different subtopic? Which problems do you think would make the best game?

✔ **What elements of that challenge can be converted into a game?**

Start thinking about what your gameplay would look like. Try modeling your solution — figure out its components, its process, anything that makes it interesting — and imagine what it would look like as a game. What could the avatar represent, and what could enemies signify? Which elements should be told by way of story and visuals, and which could be integrated into the gameplay? Likewise, think about which factors you could leave out.

✔ **How should I structure the game?**

What are you trying to accomplish, and how would you progress in doing so? To make a point or explain a topic, you should have some sort of structure and organization: Do you want to make a level for each component of the system? Do you want to organize your points chronologically? Once you understand how you want your game to work, you can progress with a greater sense of understanding and direction.

When you're ready to build your contest game, you may find that the process is a bit different from designing a game without guidance from challenge rules. To teach a concept by using a game, you need to address a problem and solution with the same playfulness and optimism with which you would approach a video game. But analysis and problem-solving *are* games — if you're in the right mood. Your job is to put players in that mood.

Contests in general

The three preceding sections cover the large, recurring competitions supported by Gamestar Mechanic at the time of this writing. However, other contests can become available, and you should understand how to effectively turn any prompt into a game. Follow these steps whenever you encounter a new contest:

1. **Read the rules, requirements, and recommendations carefully.**

   Don't rush off to get started after reading the first step of the prompt. Review the criteria that the judges are looking for in your game so that they stay in the forefront of your mind. Write them down, if you have to.

2. **Find a quality that you like about the topic.**

   If the contest is simply looking for good games in general, try to find an original idea that you think would impress the judges. If the contest is based around a certain topic, find a quality that you love about that topic — one that inspires you. This process marks the first step in developing your game and lets you use the restrictions as ideas to your own advantage.

3. **Build a little bit each day.**

   As long as you work on your game consistently, you can gain lots of ideas and thoughts by sleeping, taking breaks, and extending the design process over a long period. Ideas that are fresh in your mind can become even better if you let them "marinate" a while. Leave a little bit of time before the due date to review your game and change any elements that you realize could be improved.

4. **Proofread.**

   Find a few game-testers, and ask them for opinions on your game's strengths and weaknesses. Try to figure out whether a judge with no experience on the site would find the difficulty level manageable. Be sure to scrutinize every element of your game, in case you're overlooking a flaw or still have room to improve your work. Also, recheck the guidelines for the contest, and make sure that you have gathered everything you need in order to submit the game. Compose a design document, if necessary. (See the section "Writing Design Documents, later in this chapter.)

5. **Turn in your entry.**

   Publish your game and follow any other steps listed in the design brief, as described earlier in this chapter, in the section "Looking for contests sponsored by Gamestar Mechanic."

Designing a game for a class project

If you're a student in a Gamestar Mechanic class, your teacher may assign class projects, which are similar to contests. The parameters of a project are a lot like the parameters of a competition. The only difference is that class projects are constructive, not competitive.

If you're looking to design a good entry for a class project — or if you're a teacher and you want to design effective but nonrestrictive rules for a project — this chapter can help you understand what constitutes such a prompt. See Chapter 16 for more information about classes and projects.

Examine winning entries in previous AMD contests to gain inspiration — or to form a better idea of the criteria and the sorts of games the judges like. Just remember not to copy large chunks of other people's entries, which may result in your disqualification.

Exploring the Benefits of Participating in Contests

Submitting your games to contests can benefit you in many ways, whether or not you're playing to win the contest. Here are some possible rewards:

- ✓ **The chance to publish a game with extra sprites:** Many contests provide premium sprites, seasonal sprites, sprites from packs at the store, and others for designing your entry. Whether you win or not, you can publish a game on Game Alley with these resources, and it stays public even if you don't own some of the sprites you used.

- ✓ **More players for your games, including professional judges:** Your entry is listed in a special channel on the contest page until the judgment date. From there, other Gamestar Mechanic users can play your game. In addition, you get to have your game played by the official contest judges, guaranteeing plays by people who truly know games.

- ✓ **Contest rewards:** If you're one of the winners (most contests have many different winning positions), you can bag a lot of neat prizes, from T-shirts to laptops to participation in award ceremonies. This huge accomplishment can also lead to many opportunities later in life, from recognition to resources. (The Scholastic Art and Writing Awards even provide scholarship money.) Being a contest winner can also help you out when writing an application or a résumé. In addition, winning games are featured in Game Alley for a long time, where they can gain tons of players. See the Judging & Prizes section of the design briefs for specific information — you usually need to scroll down to the bottom of the Design Brief page to see it.

Writing Design Documents

A competition may ask you to write a *design document,* which gives an overview of the concept, vision, and meaning of your game. The document has no required format or length (so you don't have to write an essay). Just be sure to get all your points across in an organized way.

You can use any text editor to make this document. The most versatile text editors are Notepad (for PCs) and TextEdit (for Mac computers), which can be opened on almost any operating system. Some competitions may not accept Microsoft Word documents, for example, so be sure to verify which types of files are accepted. (Notepad and TextEdit are always safe options.)

A common method of creating a design document is to list a number of sections, each containing a short paragraph or two. The document looks something like this:

Game Title

Section 1 Title

Explanation

Section 2 Title

Explanation

. . .

Final Section Title

Explanation or conclusion

Here are some ideas for sections you may want to include in your design document:

- ✔ **Abstract/Overview:** Add a summary of your game at the beginning of the document. Determine the critical information that the judges need to know about the concept of your game, and limit it to one or two descriptive sentences that clearly communicate your vision to the judges. You can expand on this vision in a different section (as suggested in the following bullet).

- ✔ **Vision (The Big Idea):** Explain the core concepts of your game. Spell out everything you want your game to be, by describing the kind of experience — and lasting effect — that you want to give to players.

✔ **Essential Mechanics:** After describing the values of your game as a whole, start detailing the individual elements of your game. Describe some of the mechanics you've implemented that are essential to the game. If you're making a simple run-and-jump game, think about the templates that you used to build challenges for the player. If you're modeling a system, for example, you can name important components of that system and how you've implemented them in your game. Or write a bulleted or numbered list of actions in this section.

✔ **Model and Connections:** This section is useful if your game is based on a system or topic or another, similar game, or if you want to connect your game to deeper ideas. Take some time to describe the process of putting your game together, and the subjects your game is connected to.

Sometimes, you have to include a link to your game in the design document. Use the Link button to do this, as described in Chapter 10.

Never copy the URL of the player page, which requires the viewer to be logged in for access. If you provide the wrong link, the judges can't consider your game, and you may not even be informed about it. Make your hard work count — do not use any link of this form for a contest:

```
gamestarmechanic.com/game/player/. . .
```

Make design documents for all your games, even if the contest doesn't require them. Writing out your ideas as though you were teaching them can open new avenues of thought and give you new ideas for your game.

16

Teaching and Learning through Gamestar Mechanic

In This Chapter

▶ Understanding the Gamestar Mechanic class system

▶ Joining and participating in a class

▶ Creating and managing a class

A good class is like a good game: Students should be motivated *and* have fun. Gamestar Mechanic offers the opportunity for teachers to create classes to teach game design or use the principles of game design to teach other subjects (such as science or writing). Teachers can track students' progress on the Gamestar Mechanic site, assign creative projects, and guide discussions among students.

Though you don't have to be in a class to fully enjoy the Gamestar Mechanic website, a class is a helpful way to build design skill under close guidance. Your games are evaluated by your instructor or your peers, or both. Large Gamestar Mechanic classes are offered in many schools around the world, though users can pay to set up smaller classes instead. If you're looking to join or create a class, contact a local or online community to find teachers or students, respectively. You can also check out the Gamestar Mechanic teachers' community at

```
http://gamestarmechanic.com/teachers/community
```

If you're a student, the first few sections of this chapter are aimed at you. If you're a teacher, you may be more interested in the remainder of the chapter, beginning with the section "Creating and Managing a Class As a Teacher."

Joining a Class As a Student

If you're offered membership in a Gamestar Mechanic class, a class teacher will provide you with a link to join the class. Joining a Gamestar Mechanic class is always free to the student, unless the teacher requests payment for his service. The following sections give you an overview of the different types of invitations and show you how to join and participate in a class.

Receiving an invitation

You can be invited to join a class by receiving one of these three types of invitations:

- **Free:** When you receive an invitation, you also get a link like this one:

  `gamestarmechanic.com/join/<class shortname>/free`

  The italicized content is replaced by the shorthand name of the class. By following the link, you send a request to simply add your account to the class.

- **Premium:** This type is similar to the free invitation, except that the link is

  `gamestarmechanic.com/join/<class shortname>/premium`

  A teacher can offer a limited number of Premium packs. If you receive an invitation to a premium class and join it, you receive the entire Addison's Complete Quest package, containing two quests and more than 130 missions, for free — essentially, your teacher is paying for you to have the full Gamestar Mechanic experience.

- **Teacher:** You receive this type of invitation if you're asked to teach the class. The link for this activation is

  `gamestarmechanic.com?activation=...`

  (I give you the lowdown on teaching a class later in this chapter.)

Rather than let you request permission to join the class, the teacher activation link relies on a code that appears at the end of the address. Do *not* share this code with anyone until you activate your Teacher account.

Accepting an invitation

Class teachers can give you the option to join a class by providing you with the necessary link. Some teachers publicly advertise their classes and allow you to request the link, whereas others send exclusive invitations. To join a class, you must satisfy these requirements:

- **Have a Gamestar Mechanic account:** If you try to join a class without being logged in to your account, the site prompts you to either log in or register a new account.

- **Have permission from a class enroller:** After you follow the link provided by the teacher and complete the necessary steps to join the class, the teacher has to approve your request — not just anyone can join a class. Be sure that the class leaders know who you are when you attempt to join.

✔ **The restrictions of the class:** Sometimes, you must meet certain qualifications for joining a class. For example, you may have to enroll in an associated class outside Gamestar Mechanic (for example, a school course for which Gamestar Mechanic is a resource), pay a fee, or have a basic understanding of the principles of game design. Be sure to check the class requirements so that you know whether the class is the right one for you.

When you're invited to a class, you receive a link that takes you to a page like the one shown in Figure 16-1. On that page, verify the class you're joining and the username you're using to join. If all the information is correct, click the Join button to request permission to add your account to the class.

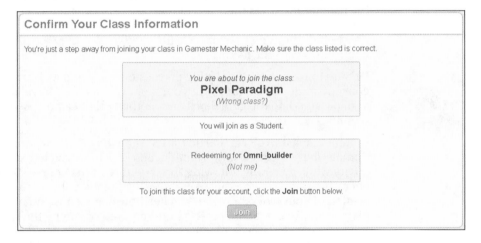

Confirm Your Class Information

You're just a step away from joining your class in Gamestar Mechanic. Make sure the class listed is correct.

You are about to join the class:
Pixel Paradigm
(Wrong class?)

You will join as a Student.

Redeeming for **Omni_builder**
(Not me)

To join this class for your account, click the **Join** button below.

Join

Figure 16-1: Make sure that the class name and username are correct.

Participating in a class

After you've been accepted into a class, you find a few new items that you can access:

✔ **Class Projects section:** Displayed in your workshop similarly to Challenges & Contests, class projects are assignments specific to your class. The teacher may talk about these projects beforehand or simply put them in your workshop for you to try out. Projects usually don't tell you to take a specific course of action; instead, they require you to design a game that creatively fulfills a certain goal. By clicking on the name of a project, you can view the briefing and instructions from your teacher and find a template for designing your game. You can also see games that fellow students have submitted for the project.

✔ **A new section in Game Alley:** At the bottom of Game Alley, you can see a new section labeled with the name of your class. This section updates you on all the new games published by you and your classmates. As with other games in Game Alley, you can click on the games there to play and review them.

✔ **New content:** The Premium pack can unlock a lot of new content for you. Also, some classes give you access to all sprites automatically.

The goal of a class is to reinforce directed study while providing a group of peers with whom you can share games. To participate in a class, you should

✔ **Participate in live discussions.** Classes often have discussions in which the teacher instructs the class in real-time, either in person (via a physical classroom) or long-distance (via an online communications system). The best of these discussions are interactive, and they rely on students' contributions to the lecture.

Be sure to talk *and* listen during discussions — you may learn some new concepts that you can apply in your games. Discussions are also helpful in understanding the guidelines and methods that can be useful in completing class projects.

✔ **Complete class projects.** Participation is a vital component of classes. Completing projects is important because it allows you to express creativity while generally following the structure of the course. Be sure to check the due dates on these projects. If you look at the Class Projects section of your workshop, you can see how many days you have to complete each project. Some projects are required of you by the teacher, but teachers sometimes create optional projects to complete only if you want to. You should generally consider projects to be required unless the instructor says otherwise. You can still publish non-project games if you're in a class.

✔ **Leave constructive reviews for classmates.** Reviewing is not only an important skill to learn but also a powerful tool in classes. To think critically about a particular subject or project, look at other students' work and analyze it without bias. (See Chapter 7 for information on effectively reviewing games.)

✔ **Find ways to improve your games over time.** Classes don't focus only on designing games and getting people to play them — you have to be able to learn and improve your methods. Read reviews of your games and take notes on your previous work so that you do better each time. Because your classmates (and often your teacher) review your games from the context of each project, a class is a useful way to improve your design prowess.

Other requirements and recommendations are generally provided by your teacher.

Creating and Managing a Class As a Teacher

If you're a teacher, you can create your own class in Gamestar Mechanic. You must be a professional instructor in a nonprofit school or registered charitable organization, or an instructor in a home-school setting. To view information about the requirements of Gamestar Mechanic teachers, go to

```
http://gamestarmechanic.com/teachers/license_agreement
```

If you don't meet those requirements, you may be able to find another person who is eligible and willing to teach. This person would manage the class, but may allow you to assist.

Before you set up a class, consider the type of class you want. All classes can hold an unlimited number of free students (students who aren't provided access to paid content). The cost of a class is determined by the number of Premium packs you (the teacher) buy. Each one is much cheaper than the Premium pack in the store, at $2 per package instead of $20.

Visit `http://gamestarmechanic.com/teachers` to find information about Gamestar Mechanic and its classes from a teacher's perspective. The Teachers' section of Gamestar Mechanic is quite different from others, as shown in Figure 16-2. Click the buttons on the left sidebar to see videos, PDFs, games, FAQs, and more about teaching a Gamestar Mechanic class.

Figure 16-2: The Gamestar Mechanic teachers' page.

Setting up a class

To set up your class, follow these steps:

1. **Go to** `http://gamestarmechanic.com/teachers/get_started`.

   Figure 16-3 shows the page that appears on the Get Started tab of the Teachers page.

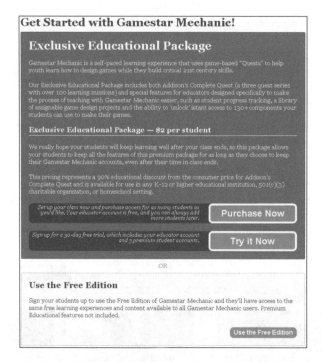

Get Started with Gamestar Mechanic!

Exclusive Educational Package

Gamestar Mechanic is a self-paced learning experience that uses game-based "Quests" to help youth learn how to design games while they build critical 21st century skills.

Our Exclusive Educational Package includes both Addison's Complete Quest (a three quest series with over 100 learning missions) and special features for educators designed specifically to make the process of teaching with Gamestar Mechanic easier, such as student progress tracking, a library of assignable game design projects and the ability to 'unlock' instant access to 130+ components your students can use to make their games.

Exclusive Educational Package — $2 per student

We really hope your students will keep learning well after your class ends, so this package allows your students to keep all the features of this premium package for as long as they choose to keep their Gamestar Mechanic accounts, even after their time in class ends.

This pricing represents a 90% educational discount from the consumer price for Addison's Complete Quest and is available for use in any K-12 or higher educational institution, 501(c)(3) charitable organization, or homeschool setting.

Set up your class now and purchase access for as many students as you'd like. Your educator account is free, and you can always add more students later. **Purchase Now**

Sign up for a 30-day free trial, which includes your educator account and 9 premium student accounts. **Try it Now**

OR

Use the Free Edition

Sign your students up to use the Free Edition of Gamestar Mechanic and they'll have access to the same free learning experiences and content available to all Gamestar Mechanic users. Premium Educational features not included.

Use the Free Edition

Figure 16-3: Check out this description of Gamestar Mechanic and its classes, as well as some purchasing options.

2. **Click the green button for the type of class you want to create. Here are your options:**

   • *Purchase Now:* Lets you create a paid class and purchase Premium packs for your students at $2 each. You must purchase a minimum of ten packages.

   When you approve the membership of a student who wants to gain Premium privileges by joining your class, you assign that person a Premium pack. These packages cannot be removed or reused, because they grant permanent bonuses to students' accounts. And as long as at least one student has a Premium pack (discussed later in this chapter, in the section "Accessing class information"), the teachers in that class have a Premium pack as well.

- *Try It Now:* Gives you an Educator account and three Premium packs. The class and premium content cost nothing, but they expire after 30 days.

- *Use the Free Edition:* An easy-to-use option that creates a free class with no Premium packs; students enter the class with whatever sprites they've earned or bought. If you're hosting a class with only free-level students, or if your students have already bought the Premium pack themselves, this option is the best one.

After you make your selection, a setup form appears on the page, as shown in Figure 16-4.

3. **Fill in the requested information to set up a Teacher account and provide information about your school.**

Figure 16-4: The setup form appears on the same page, under the options from Step 2.

4. **Select the check box to indicate that you're over 18 and that you agree to the Gamestar Mechanic licensing agreement and terms of service.**

5. **Click the Validate User and Create Your Class button.**

   Gamestar Mechanic will send you an e-mail confirming your registration.

If you return to the Get Started page after creating a class, a different page opens, in which you can purchase additional Premium packs for your class.

Accessing class information

After you create a class, it appears in your workshop with a few more options than what your students see, as shown in Figure 16-5.

Figure 16-5: The Classes section for teachers.

The Classes section contains four buttons you can click to track or edit certain qualities of your class:

- About My Institution
- Student Tracking
- Class Projects
- Student Discussions

The following sections describe how to use these options.

About My Institution

When you click this button, the Class Profile page appears, as shown in Figure 16-6. There you can see or change many universal features of your class.

Editable items have an orange button next to them labeled Edit, Enable, or Disable, depending on its function. The editable features are described in this list:

- **Class Name:** The name that's displayed for your class.

- **Class Shortname:** A series of letters and numbers (no spaces) that's used in activation links. The most convenient setting for it is your class name with spaces omitted.

Figure 16-6: The Class Profile page.

✔ **Auto-Following:** When enabled, lets all your students automatically *follow* each other, giving them updates on each other's work in the News Feed.

✔ **Collect Real Student Names:** This requires new students to enter their full names to join the class.

✔ **Unlock All Sprites:** Grants a large number of sprites to everyone who joins the class so that they don't have to complete the Quest. It also includes three sprites that are otherwise unobtainable: the Monitor and Book transmogrifier skins (new textures for the Transmogrifier sprite) and the Tombstone (a spooky, destructible block).

After these options, you see four more sections:

✔ **Quick Join Links:** Provides links for joining the class, which you may distribute to your students.

✔ **Free Students:** A list of all students in your class who don't have Premium packs. You can select students and edit their accounts by using the orange buttons at the bottom:

• *Apply Premium Pack* gives students a Premium pack for your class.

• *Remove from Class* takes away their membership in your class, placing them on the Removed Students list.

The blue Need More Premium Student Packs link takes you to a page where you can buy more packs for your students.

✓ **Students with Premium packs (used packs / total packs):** Lists the students in your class who have Premium packs. You can select students and edit their accounts by using the orange buttons at the bottom:

- *Remove from Class* moves them to the Removed Students list (but it does not mean that you can reallocate their Premium packs).

- *Report Abuse* reports users who took Premium packs when they shouldn't have.

✓ **Removed Students:** A list of students who were once in your class but have since been removed. These students have no access to class features. You can select students and click the orange Return to Class button at the bottom to reinstate their memberships.

Student Tracking

The Student Tracking option displays the names of all students in your class along with their statistics, such as number of published games, draft games, reviews, and Quest missions completed. It's a helpful way to find out how your students are using the site.

Class Projects

The Class Projects option takes you to a page similar to the Projects section of your workshop. From there, you can easily

✓ **Add new projects:** Click the Add New Project button to design a project from scratch, as described in the section "Managing Class Projects," later in this chapter.

✓ **View your projects in a vertical list:** This arrangement makes it easy to see all your projects, along with options for editing them.

✓ **Edit and delete projects:** Use the buttons to the right of your projects to edit them.

Student Discussions

The Student Discussions page shows the reviews and comments that your students have left on other games. Gamestar Mechanic has no built-in chat system, so the only on-site student discussion is by way of these reviews and comments — students usually communicate directly in person or over other social media. Use this section to view your students' progress in game design and media literacy through the context of Gamestar's extensive game database.

Setting Up a Project for Your Class

Class projects are useful for Gamestar Mechanic teachers and important for students. They're helpful for teaching important concepts that can complement the material from the Quest. Though projects can be used in many different ways, they always offer these benefits:

- ✔ **Students have room to be creative while still being guided toward certain educational goals.** If students aren't working toward the goals of the class, the class is ineffective; however, if students have no room to be creative, it defeats the purpose of game design. Projects are a useful way for you to direct your students' journey while still letting them hold an interest in learning.

- ✔ **You can use projects to teach and prepare lessons between classes.** Projects are often used to complement lectures and discussions, but they can easily be prepared and tested well beforehand.

- ✔ **Students can complete projects and peer-review other entries without your intervention.** Using class projects, you can give students any level of independence you want.

To create a new project for your class, follow these steps:

1. **Click the Class Projects button in the Classes section of your workshop.**

   The My Projects page appears.

2. **Click the orange Add New Project button.**

   This button appears below the list of your active projects. Clicking the button opens the Project Catalog page. The Project Catalog page displays a number of project templates, each with a lesson plan and a template for students to design entries.

3. **Find a project that looks interesting; click the View button underneath a project to see details about it.**

   Clicking the View button lets you see what these projects can do for your class. Every project has a few paragraphs detailing its motive and summary, as shown in Figure 16-7. Also, the gray Rewards box shows the sprites your students gain by completing the project. The Rewards box usually reads *None,* unless you're using a project that resembles a challenge in the Challenges & Contests section of the Workshop.

   You may want to start with projects that support a fundamental level of understanding, such as the Elements of Game Design project or the Easy-Hard-Balanced Game project. You can also use the Make Your Own Project option to create one from scratch, giving your students an expansive template and inventing the rubric yourself.

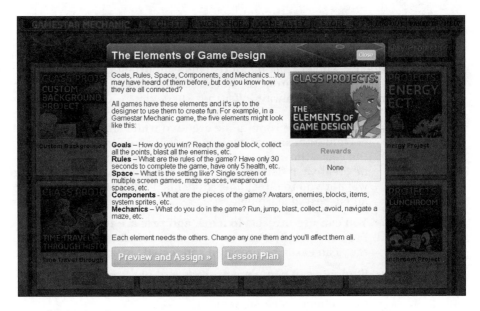

Figure 16-7: Viewing the description for a project template.

4. **(Optional) After you find a template you want to use, click the orange Lesson Plan button to view a general lesson plan for the project.**

   Although this step is optional, it's a helpful way to understand how you can use the selected project well. The *lesson plan* includes notes about the project, suggestions for questions to ask your class, and an outline of a lesson plan that includes discussion, playing, and designing. You can use the Back button or Previous Page button on your browser to return to the menu in Step 4.

5. **Click the Preview & Assign button next to the Lesson Plan button.**

   The project page appears, where you can start designing your project.

After you select a project, you see the page where you set it up. This process has several steps — after you finish a step, click the orange button in the upper right corner to move on. I discuss each of these steps in the following three sections.

Step 1: Customize the project page

The project page, shown in Figure 16-8, is the same project page your students see except that you can edit the various fields. This list describes, from top to bottom, the sections on the page:

Figure 16-8: Every editable section has an orange Edit button in it.

✏ **Title:** The title of the project is displayed at the top of the page, next to the Edit button. Use the button to change the title, if you want.

✏ **Instructions:** The instructions for the project aren't supplied by the site, but rather by you. Click the orange Edit button, and in the box that appears, write a message to your students, explaining how they should complete the project.

✏ **Important Dates:** The Important Dates box, which appears to the right of the instructions, contains a date on which the project starts (in the green box) and a date when it ends (in the red box). You can edit both dates by clicking the orange Edit button and then entering a date. You can enter the date in year-month-day format or click on a day by using the provided calendar. If you edit the Project Ends date, you can use the Never button to keep the project running unless you close it manually. Remember to click the orange Save button after editing each date.

✏ **About This Project:** This project overview is provided to your students and cannot be edited.

✏ **Project Goals:** This text, which cannot be edited, tells your students what they should be thinking about and what the project is trying to teach them.

✏ **Project Games:** These games teach the concepts of the project. You can try playing the games to see what exactly your students will experience.

Step 2: Determine the project settings

The second step, determining the project's settings, lets you change how the project functions in general, setting the parameters for submitting entries. This step consists of a series of choices, with buttons for each option:

- ✓ **Allow Draft Submissions:** If you select Yes, students' *draft* games (games they have saved but not published) count as submitted. The students can still work on the games, but others in the class can see each draft as it's saved. Then the students don't have to satisfy the restrictions of a complete game in order to finish the assignment.

- ✓ **Allow Late Submissions:** If you select Yes, students can submit games — or edit their submissions — even after the due date has passed.

- ✓ **Message Students When Project Begins:** If you select Yes, you send a reminder to every student's Messages box whenever the Project Begins date passes.

- ✓ **Receive a Message Whenever a Student Submits a Project:** This option can notify you when students submit entries to this project. The Workshop Message Only option sends the message to your Messages box, the Email and Workshop Message option also sends you an e-mail, and the Don't Message Me option does nothing.

- ✓ **Remind Students Before Project Is Due:** If you select Yes, enter a number in the next box, next to your options. If the project is about to end in the selected number of days, your students receive a message reminding them to complete the project.

- ✓ **Project visibility:** This option determines the parameters for when students can view each other's entries. The Never Show Entries option doesn't let them do so, whereas the Always Show Entries option does. The Show Entries after Project Due Date option makes students' submissions invisible to classmates until the due date passes (at which point they may be unable to edit their submissions).

Remember to click the orange Save Settings button at the bottom of the page before proceeding to the next step.

Step 3: Assign the project

In Step 3, assigning the project, you can select the group of students to whom you want to assign the project. The Add Students box allows you to select a number of students. (Click the orange Select All and Select None buttons for mass selecting and deselecting.) After selecting the students you want, click the orange Assign Project button to give them the project.

You can also assign the project to teachers with a similar box, labeled Add Teachers, allowing teachers to provide their own entries among the students'.

As you add people to the project, their usernames appear in the Assigned Students box. After you have assigned the project to whomever you want to receive it, you have successfully completed the creation process.

If you start designing a project but abandon the process, your project still appears in the My Projects page — however, it is not assigned to anyone, so your students can't see it. You can always edit or delete these projects later.

Using HTML tags in the project instructions

When you're typing the instructions for your project, it's good to know that Gamestar Mechanic supports basic *HTML tags,* which let you format text by applying special features. To use the basic HTML tags that are allowed on the project page, you type < . . . > in front of the modified text and type </ . . . > following the text. The ellipses represent certain strings of text that apply different effects to the text.

This overview of HTML explains some of the styles you can use on your project page. For more information on the programming language, check out *HTML, XHTML & CSS For Dummies,* by Ed Tittel and Jeff Noble (Wiley Publishing).

The strings available in Gamestar Mechanic are described in this list:

✔ **<b> Boldface:** This emphasizer makes the text thicker.

✔ **<i> Italic:** This emphasizer makes the text slanted.

✔ **<u> Underline:** This emphasizer adds a line under the text.

✔ **<h1> Header 1:** Header 1 HTML is used to show a title, or main, header. If this chapter had been written in HTML, for example, the title of the chapter would be <h1>, and the section headers would be <h2>.

✔ **<h2> Header 2:** A Header 2 is used as a subhead to a Header 1.

✔ **<p> Paragraph:** This tag defines a paragraph.

Other tags follow a different format. For these, you type something like this:

```
<a href="http://gamestarmechanic.com">Gamestar Mechanic</a>
```

The a refers to the type of command you're using, href refers to a property of this command, and http://gamestarmechanic.com is the setting for that property.

Remember: These tags work only with straight quotation marks. Curly quotation marks, such as the ones used by certain word processors, do not work. If you type code directly into the Gamestar Mechanic text box, this shouldn't be a problem, but be sure to copy and paste carefully.

(continued)

(continued)

Gamestar Mechanic supports the following tags of this form:

✔ **<a>: Link** — The preceding example shows the use of the `<a>` tag. When compiled, it produces the words *Gamestar Mechanic,* which readers can click to access the page at `http://gamestarmechanic.com`. You can then make clickable text that provides nicely formatted links for your students. To do so, set the text in quote marks to the link you want to use, and set the text inside the tag to the words that you want to be clickable — for example, `<a href="dummies.com">Click Here For Dummies</a>`.

✔ **<font>: Font** — This tag allows you to change the font of the enclosed text. Gamestar Mechanic supports the `face` and `color` attributes, which change the font and color of the text, respectively. For example, you can use `<font face="times new roman">Fancy Text</font>` or `<font color="red">Red Text</font>`. To change both the font and the color, separate the settings with a space, like this:

```
<font face="times new roman" color="red">
```

The `face` setting of the enclosed text can be set to the name of a recognized font, changing the style of the text. The `color` setting changes the color of the text. You can use common color names, or if you know how to use color codes, you can use a hexadecimal number, such as #FF8800.

By using these tags, you can make your assignments look more attractive and be more organized for your students.

Managing Class Projects

After you create a project, you can edit any of the settings you chose when setting up the project. Click the Class Projects button in your workshop, under the section labeled with the name of your class. This action opens the My Projects page where you created your first project.

Each project on the My Projects page contains four orange buttons and a red Delete Project button, which removes the project from your class. You can use these four orange buttons, which are described in the following list, to modify and examine your project:

✔ **Student Tracking:** Clicking this button opens a page that shows information about your students' work on the project, as shown in Figure 16-9. The page lists each student's name, the status of the students' entries, the date when the entries were submitted (if applicable), and text containing your feedback and evaluation for the entry.

Use the orange Edit buttons to change your feedback (notes on the student's entry) and evaluation (the student's grade, if applicable). In addition, you can select any number of students and click Remove Project to remove the project from their workshops, or add new students to the project, similarly to when the project was created.

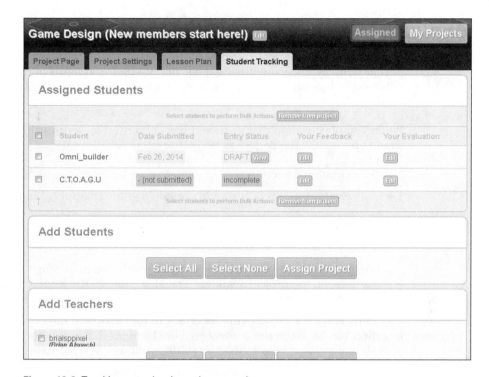

Figure 16-9: Tracking a student's work on a project.

✓ **Project Page:** Clicking this button opens a page showing your instructions, the starting and ending dates of the project, some information provided by the site, and the playable Project Games. From this page, you can modify your instructions, and change the project dates to start the project or end the project, or simply revise the due date.

✓ **Project Settings:** Clicking this button takes you to the Project Settings page, which you used to create the project. There, you can edit any of the settings you previously selected.

✓ **Lesson Plan:** Click this button to display the recommended lesson plan for your project. You can copy or print the information on this page for reference in your class.

Clicking any of the orange buttons described in the preceding list opens a page with four tabs at the top that link to the other pages that are accessible by clicking the orange buttons. Use these tabs to quickly check several components of your project quickly.

Analyzing Your Students' Games

When your students design games, you can help them improve their game design skills by analyzing their games, finding their strengths and weaknesses, and helping them expand their strong characteristics and improve their weak areas.

When you play a game that a student has submitted for a project, the box where you review the game has two other sections above it:

- ✓ The **Feedback** section should contain a verbal assessment of the game.

- ✓ The **Evaluation** section should contain a grade (if applicable).

These messages can be saved and edited at any time. Using the feedback system is important, for these reasons:

- ✓ **You can keep all your feedback organized.** When managing a project, you can see, on the project's Student Tracking page, all the feedback you've given to students.

- ✓ **Only teachers can provide feedback in this way, and only one evaluation can be given per game.** Feedback from teachers, therefore, greatly simplifies the review system by setting your assessment apart from others.

- ✓ **Feedback and evaluations are private.** Other people can see a game's reviews, but teacher evaluations can remain private. Then students don't have to worry about embarrassment or competition, and they can focus solely on the creative process.

Providing helpful feedback to students

As a teacher, giving students good feedback and advice for their games is vital. Follow these tips to provide helpful feedback to students:

- ✓ **Think of one good aspect and one not-so-good aspect of the project.** Don't let students think of their games as entirely perfect or entirely bad. Every complete game has at least one aspect that was done well and one that could be improved. As long as you point out these factors as well as you can, you can help your students start thinking about how they can progress in game design.

- ✓ **Evaluate how well the game achieves the goals of the project.** When a student submits a game for a class project, the quality of the game itself is not the only metric. If a student is working on a certain concept of game design, focus heavily on that concept. If the student is designing a game that models a certain system, assess the game based on how successfully it connects with the system. In a way, project games are easier to review, because you can focus specifically on the metric determined by the prompt.

Grading your students

Sometimes, whether you're told to or you decide to, you need to provide a short evaluation to each of your students. It means that you have to grade them, which can be a difficult task when teaching a creative field.

Often, a good way to give evaluations is by adding short bits of text, such as "Good concept" or "The story needs improvement." These statements summarize your feedback using a metric that marks improvement rather than absolute skill (because you may have a class of students with varying levels of expertise). However, you can use this strategy only if you aren't expected to give strict number or letter grades — use with caution.

If you have to use a strict letter-or-number system for grading, make sure that you know your metrics well. Have a good grasp of what characteristics you're looking for in the students' games, and remember that different projects require different metrics for evaluation. As long as you reward both creativity and application of the class topic, you can ensure that your grading rubric encourages ideals that are educational, constructive, and fun.

Using the CHEAT commands

If you're a teacher, you can use special cheats to complete any game more easily. Then you can completely analyze students' games, whether or not you're able to complete them on your own. Some students create difficult games, and draft submissions are often unbeatable, so cheats are useful for seeing the full expanse of the game and being able to give complete reviews to students.

If you complete a game but you used a cheat at some point during the game, the site doesn't count it as a victory in the game statistics.

If you're playing a game, you can access cheats at any time by pausing the game and clicking the Cheat button. A menu opens, as shown in Figure 16-10, with several options for manipulating the game.

Figure 16-10: Use the Gamestar Cheats dialog box to complete games more easily.

The Gamestar Cheats dialog box lets you perform actions that make your experience in the game much easier while still allowing you to examine it. Here's a rundown of the buttons and what they do:

- **Win Game:** Immediately opens the You Win page at the end of the game.

- **Win Level:** Automatically clears all level goals, displays the Level Complete screen, and advances you to the next level.

- **Avatar Is Untouchable:** Puts your avatar in a constant "hurt" state, effectively making it invincible. After taking damage, your avatar normally flashes red and cannot be damaged for a short time, ensuring that enemies damage you only once with a brief collision. Your avatar becomes immune to health damage — however, you can still lose the game if a VIP sprite is fragged or if you run out of time or energy. Click the button for this cheat a second time to turn it off.

- **Avatar Teleports to Mouse:** If you activate this cheat and return to the game, you can click anywhere on the game screen and cause your avatar to instantly move there. If you teleport the avatar into a wall, the avatar is pushed into the first empty space it finds. This cheat is especially useful for navigating games quickly and seeing everything that the designer has composed.

Using Projects Effectively in Your Class

After you know how to create and edit projects, as described earlier in this chapter, you need to think about how to effectively use them in your class. Doing so can require a difficult balance of educating your students while allowing them to play creatively and constructively. This section helps you use projects to maintain that balance.

Using a project in a standard classroom environment

Lesson plans in Gamestar Mechanic are constructed for classroom environments (either virtual or in person, as long as they have active discussions), making them invaluable resources for teachers who aren't sure how to apply the project. Most lesson plans are divided into these main sections:

- **Learning Goal:** A learning goal is a sentence describing the goal of the class. It's always a good idea to give your students an idea of the lesson's goal, so they can understand the point of the discussion, which helps with participation and designing skills.

- **Warm Up:** Although this is the lecture portion of the class, it still revolves around active participation and innovation. To introduce the prompt for the lesson, discuss the systems behind it, allowing students to put up their own ideas for consideration. If you're looking at a certain type of game, discuss ideas for building such a game. If you're teaching a specific value of game design, let students think of their favorite games with respect to that value. If you're basing games on a topic such as math or biology, discuss systems that the students know, and try to apply them to the field of game design. Be sure to leave lots of time for the next step.

✏ **Activity:** You may find that this is the part your students look forward to. Have them prepare however you see fit and start designing. Allow lots of time for this activity, and consider allowing students to do more work at home, if they want. The Allow Draft Submissions setting is helpful in this regard because it doesn't pressure students to finish quickly.

Rather than lecture your class, start moving around the room, periodically evaluating students' work and providing help when needed. Take questions — the best time to help students is while they're in the designer's seat.

✏ **Wrap Up:** To conclude your class, have students play and review each other's games. Then they get to have their games peer-reviewed right away, and they can learn a lot about game design by analyzing and reviewing other students' games. Ask the students what they've learned and what they might want to share.

✏ **How Did It Go?** This part is just for you. After class, examine how it went. Did students work well within the restrictions? Did they find new ways to be creative? Did the class flow well, both between you and the students, and among the students themselves? This step helps you make changes to your technique for future classes.

The preceding list presents a recommended class structure, but you don't have to do it this way. If you prefer a different structure, just remember the values of a good Gamestar Mechanic class. Most importantly, game design is all about creativity, so give your students room to work on their own ideas.

To find lots of sample lessons that cover tons of topics, from general technique to specific design exercises, visit the page at

```
https://sites.google.com/a/elinemedia.com/gsmlearningguide/
              getting-started-teacher-pack
```

Using a project in a self-paced online class

Some teachers may prefer to run their classes online, allowing students to work on their own for much of the time. This method is becoming increasingly popular. Although students may have classes or due dates or e-mail groups, most of the process consists of students designing and reviewing on their own time.

If your class has one of these self-paced components, follow these tips:

- ✔ **Provide detailed instructions.** Let your students know when each project is created, and clearly state the guidelines and metrics on the project page. Try to make sure that your students can complete the work on their own.

- ✔ **Make yourself accessible.** Use a form of communication such as e-mail, office hours, or discussion forums to allow students to contact you with any questions they may have. Stay connected with your students, and don't make them work out major difficulties alone.

- ✔ **Set up a means of communication and identity.** Online classes are greatly improved by an element of humanity behind the usernames and games of the students. Make sure that students can build identities with each other, having some way to talk or express themselves. Gamestar Mechanic users can do this via their games, but sometimes there just isn't enough time to build a complete personality within a class. Find ways for students to introduce themselves, whether by a profile picture, a verbal or written introduction, or a special game.

- ✔ **Provide resources for learning between projects.** In addition to having students learn from experience, point them toward books, tutorials, or other interesting materials to read, videos to watch, discussions to engage in, or other resources to use to help them understand the concepts of your class.

- ✔ **Keep track of your students' progress.** Play your students' games and use the Student Tracking mechanisms (described earlier in the chapter) to see how your students are working. Look for areas where you can discuss improvement with them, and use their general progress to pace your lesson plan.

Part VI
The Part of Tens

Enjoy an additional Part of Tens article about ten interesting sprites you should know at www.dummies.com/extras/gamestarmechanic.

In this part . . .

- ✔ Explore ten classic types of games.
- ✔ Discover ten common mistakes you should try to avoid.

17

Ten Types of Gameplay

In This Chapter

▶ Exploring ten ways to build a game

▶ Creating fun via different processes

▶ Connecting different types of games

Despite the simple look of the Gamestar Mechanic website, you can use the available tools to make many different types of games. Although the elements of game design comprise an excellent starting point for understanding what makes a game fun to play, a game can produce a sense of fun by way of many different processes. This chapter describes ten of the most prominent types of games, each with a different look and feel, for you to draw inspiration from.

As a mechanic, it's your job to

✔ Use some or all of these ten types of gameplay to their full extent.

✔ Develop new concepts to practice and publish.

✔ Combine and build on the ideas of common types of gameplay.

Navigator

The *navigator* game involves an avatar working its way toward a goal by maneuvering through spatial puzzles, as shown in Figure 17-1. Top-down games often create this experience via mazes or dungeons, whereas platformer navigators are often referred to as *run-and-jumpers*. This simple but fun gameplay type can be expanded in a number of ways, since it can work along with most any arrangement of goals, rules, and challenges. You can add a score keeper so that the player must reach multiple destinations, you can break up the maze with enemies and puzzles — you can even place a blaster partway through, so that the player has to run back through the level with a new mindset (fragging enemies). The versatility of this sort of game makes it a good starting point for new users.

Figure 17-1 shows two navigator games: a top-down one and a platformer one.

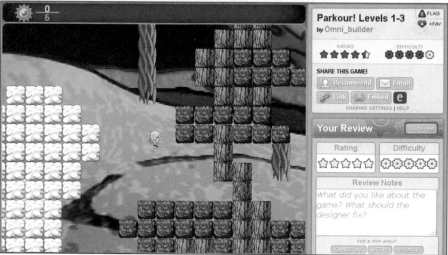

Figure 17-1: Two navigator perspectives introduce basic navigation challenges.

Enemy Gauntlets

The *enemy gauntlet* is a simple and effective way to provide a challenge in a game. Like the navigator, it is often applied by inexperienced users, but can be useful to veterans as well. An enemy gauntlet is a level, or a portion of a level, consisting of well-placed enemies attacking the avatar through various methods and motion paths, as shown in Figure 17-2. In platformer games, one or more enemies often guard a platform by pacing back and forth on top of it, whereas top-down games allow for much more complexity, such as using intricate motion paths to design powerful guillotines or barricades.

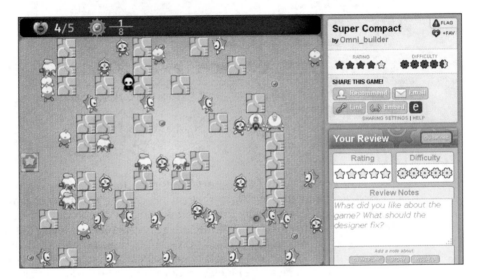

Figure 17-2: A player navigating a difficult gauntlet.

Frag the Foes

As with many video games, Gamestar Mechanic players often love a good action romp. Because the avatar is armed with a weapon and set loose in a level full of enemies, the frag-the-foes concept is popular among thrill seekers. There are many ways to apply this type of game incorrectly, but it's quite rewarding to get it right: Because enemies follow simple motion patterns, you should ensure that they always pose a threat to the avatar rather than turn into useless goons that aren't interesting to the player. Every designer seems to accomplish this goal in a different way. For example, in Figure 17-3 the designer has enemies set up on platforms, requiring the player to jump and shoot between the enemies' attacks.

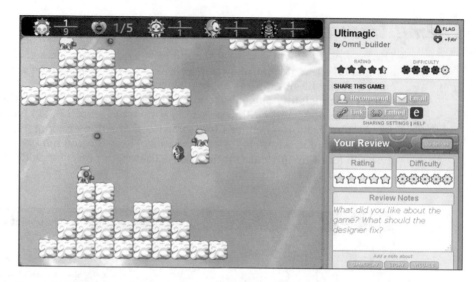

Figure 17-3: A frag-the-foes-style game that requires the player to ascend through the clouds while fighting shooters.

Storyteller

Lots of designers enjoy telling stories in their games, and they sometimes use a *storyteller* game to focus their work on a narrative. This type of game focuses on using a game specifically to tell a story, usually via a series of message blocks or the introductory and winning messages on each level. The designer tells a story by way of segments of text spaced appropriately through the level, usually with gameplay and visual elements illustrating the events. For example, you might place a message block at every room or an important character in a level to write about what takes place there. However, it's always helpful to add supporting gameplay.

Grand Adventure

A popular type of game among both new and experienced designers, the *grand adventure* is a game that has everything — a lengthy gameplay, an intricate story, and detailed visual elements. It takes a bit longer to design, and it often needs to be combined with other types, but it's a game to be proud of. The disadvantage is that this type of game is easy to lose interest in, and some players prefer a shorter challenge. Keep the gameplay, story, and visual elements new and interesting throughout the game. You may also find it useful to design shorter games to balance out your grand adventure projects.

Virtual Economy

One of the many fields relevant to game design is economics. Whether by points or keys or other forms of measurement, designers have found ways to implement complex systems of value in their games. A *virtual economy* is a game based around one or more of these systems. A game centering on a virtual economy is interesting: It can implement elements of complexity and strategy because players have to work with dynamic elements in order to play the system and win. For example, Figure 17-4 shows a game where you play a predator trying to survive while functioning along with a prey population and a limited plant population.

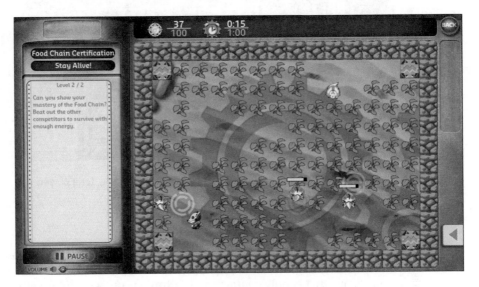

Figure 17-4: An economy of plants, prey, and predator.

Puzzle

The *puzzle* game, consisting of a player having to use her wits to clear a challenge, can be applied in many different ways, whether by telling a riddle or unleashing an advanced gameplay trick. For example, some players use sprites such as enemy generators and transmogrifiers, to manipulate populations, requiring players to toggle or destroy the proper machines to satisfy a number of population counters. You can find many ways to build an interesting puzzle in Gamestar Mechanic. Usually, you need a lot of practice and experience to come up with a challenging puzzle, but a single puzzle can often be expanded into an entire game. In Figure 17-5, you can see a level of the Phoenix Machine, a timing-based puzzle based around a moving block. By anticipating its motion path and breaking the pieces of glass that obstruct it, the player guides the motion block into the enemy lancers.

Figure 17-5: A puzzle game can be challenging, but interesting, for a player.

Showcase

A *showcase* is a display of your abilities in Gamestar Mechanic, to show off your techniques, backgrounds, thoughts, stories, or sprites. The simplest showcase game is one that simply contains all the sprites you own, put together in a room. Though this sort of game is often used by designers, it isn't particularly popular among players, so be careful using it. Whether showcasing your sprite library or your various ideas, always combine this type of game with another one, giving players some gameplay to keep them interested.

Timer Rush

In the *timer rush* type of game, shown in Figure 17-6, the player must complete certain objectives within a time limit. Whether by way of an expiring timer, energy meter, or population counter — or the actions of other sprites — a time constraint adds a sense of urgency to your game.

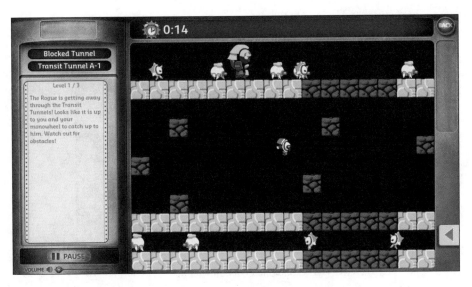

Figure 17-6: Using a timer creates a sense of urgency, adding excitement to a game.

Innovations and Combined Personalities

After you have experience with game design, you can try to build on classic elements of video games to produce more unique content. There's nothing wrong with following the other structures in this chapter, but to gain a deeper understanding of the game system, try inventing your own game mechanics.

Game mechanics are derived from patterns, and patterns can be found everywhere, including the world of Gamestar Mechanic. To develop your own innovations, try these tips:

✔ **Expand a lesser-used component.**

Certain components in Gamestar Mechanic may not always be used to their full potential. Take full advantage of complex sprites — such as the transmogrifier, which can have many different applications — and play around with simple components to find new uses for them. Figure 17-7 shows a game that takes advantage of an innocuous concept that's present in many classic video games: When the avatar is damaged, it cannot be damaged again for about a second. This universal rule prevents the avatar from taking ridiculously rapid damage. By requiring the player to contact lower-damage enemies in order to move through higher-damage ones, the game inverts the spaces of safety and danger.

Figure 17-7: Expanding on a component.

✔ **Find synergy between different game types.**

Many compelling games apply multiple components and mechanics at one time. For example, combine the navigator and timer rush game types to make the player escape a labyrinth before time runs out. Or, use puzzle, showcase, and storyteller game types to show off a number of challenges provided by a mysterious villain. Single mechanics don't have to stand alone — add anything that brings your game closer to your personal vision.

✔ **Adapt a non–Gamestar Mechanic concept.**

Many users enjoy designing adaptations of popular video games in Gamestar Mechanic, and no two independent adaptations are completely alike. Even if you don't want to copy a game you like, use it for inspiration — think about classic mechanics you know, and then consider which sprites or settings you can use to re-create such an idea. This is a great way to use your sprite library to its full potential, and to produce the sort of games you know and love. It's also good practice for beginners because all the elements of fun are provided — you only have to practice the technical skill of creating them.

18

Ten Pitfalls of Gamestar Mechanic Projects

In This Chapter

▶ Recognizing classic design errors in Gamestar Mechanic

▶ Avoiding common mistakes in design

▶ Benefiting from negative examples

*I*n Game Alley, you can find many good design techniques on display, but you can also find many poor ones — in order to create fun content on the website, you should learn from these examples and see how to avoid them. In this chapter, I describe ten important yet common pitfalls that can endanger the balance, pacing, or player interest in a game.

Luck-Based Elements

Luck is sometimes good in a game, adding an element of randomness to a game so that it doesn't appear to follow a script. However, a luck-based challenge in place of a skill-based one can be irritating for players.

Players who finish long challenges don't want to have their victories determined by chance. For example, make sure that one last challenge at the end of your level can be predicted and surpassed on the first try, rather than inevitably sending the player all the way back to the beginning of the level. Similarly, when players face challenges that can be solved only by trial and error, they grow more frustrated in proportion to the number of choices they have.

An example of a luck-based game is a room full of randomly moving enemies. Whether the goal is navigation or fragging, the open space and chance-based patterns make the game rely more on randomness than on the actions of the player. A game such as this one needs more of an identity, a more skill-provoking challenge, in order to be expanded.

Adding a bit of randomness to a game is acceptable as long as the game is primarily one of skill. Randomness can sometimes make difficult games more enjoyable — if a player has to keep retrying a level, he can occasionally get some help if he has a burst of luck.

Loopholes

Loopholes can be hard to spot, but you *must* check for them in your game. You might design a level, and a player then discovers a "trick" that solves it quite easily. Perhaps you've misplaced a key in your design or overlooked a simple technique. These types of loopholes can make or break a game, so if a player finds one, edit your game as soon as possible.

For example, the game featured in Figure 18-1 is an unbounded level in which the avatar must navigate its way to the goal against a stream of enemies. However, because the level is unbounded, the player can easily run off the side of the screen (as the avatar is ready to do in the figure), move around the outside of the level, and then trigger the goal blocks from the right. In this way, the player is exploiting a loophole that the designer didn't notice, allowing her to win easily.

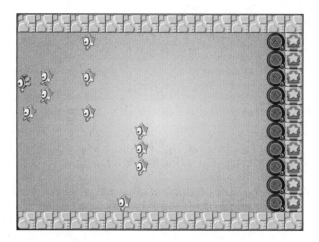

Figure 18-1: A player exploiting a loophole.

Loopholes in Gamestar Mechanic can emerge in a few different ways:

✓ **Imperfect enemy patterns:** If you have a group of enemies that is supposed to challenge the player, there may sometimes be a trick that players can use to outmatch them easily. This problem is common in shooter games: Sometimes, a game has a spot where the player can shoot at enemies without fear of retribution. Try to find these loopholes before publishing so that you can fix them. Look for every safe spot and imperfection that a player might use to beat the game as easily as possible. If you find this type of loophole, revise your game space to force the avatar into the heart of the game.

If part of your level includes a room with a major battle, drop the avatar into the room with a ledge or a one-way teleporter. This prevents the player from easily clearing the gauntlet from a safe location or from escaping the room when the avatar's health runs low.

✔ **Breakable mazes:** Sometimes, you build a maze system with keys and locks or a large, open world with nonlinear puzzles and challenges. These elements can be tricky to design, because a single loophole can break them. If players find a trick to cut through part of the level, such as using a key where you wouldn't expect or running off and finding a shortcut, they skip over a lot of your level. To prevent this situation, maintain a clear outline of your map and test it critically before publishing.

✔ **Unrestrictive rules:** Your game should have enough rules to guide the player through the route you've set. For example, if you give the avatar a blaster and no frag counter, be prepared for players to simply evade your enemies rather than fight.

Loopholes aren't always bad! If you add one that's difficult but doable, you can give experienced players an interesting challenge and offer an alternative route past a difficult segment. Players like to feel clever.

Misused Message Blocks

Message blocks are useful tools, displaying as many as 40 short lines of information to the player. Some designers are also accustomed to placing multiple message blocks in series to provide more information. However, there are several ways to use message blocks improperly, resulting in either irritating the player or compromising the content of your message.

Sometimes, players have to touch a single message block many times to get where they need to go. This can happen if a message block is unavoidable or if the player has to pass by it multiple times or jump meticulously to avoid hitting it twice. This process can become annoying to players, especially when the message block has several pages of content. For example, the message blocks shown in Figure 18-2 are unavoidably triggered whenever the avatar passes through the middle of the level. Because the avatar is engaged in a battle that potentially takes it all around the level, the message blocks become a recurring annoyance. To fix this problem, you can delete some white blocks in the middle so that the player can jump over the message blocks, or place the message blocks in a separate level that serves as a transition. Train yourself to notice arrangements like these (if you hit the same message block many times, you know there's a problem), and revise them to make the game run smoother.

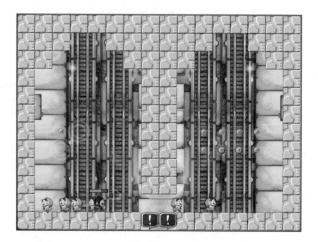

Figure 18-2: Poorly placed message blocks can frustrate players.

Another problem with message blocks is the "wall of text." If you try to simply copy a long spiel into a message block, the text pours over from page to page, and the result is intimidating text that may turn away readers and cause them to skip over the information, if they care more about the flow of the gameplay than the text between levels. To ensure that most of your players read the content in your game, try breaking the message block into smaller chunks of information. For example, use only a few words per page or use multiple blocks and custom backgrounds to display the information piece by piece.

Inconsistent Writing

Any game that involves text, whether it has a story or a tutorial or simply a series of encouragements, has the mechanic of messaging. *Messaging* encompasses everything that is told to the player, when it is told, and how it relates to the game. In Gamestar Mechanic, where your writing is viewable only in message blocks and level messages, you must ensure that the player's messaging is consistent.

Messaging is a difficult concept to master, though you can do so with some practice. Tell players everything they need to know, when they need to know it, and make sure that the information you provide is consistent and useful. For example, you might write, "Frag the blue sprites, and avoid the white sprites" on a message block just before this type of challenge, or you might relate segments of the game's story in the locations where they occur.

Many pitfalls can occur within this mechanic: Messages that aren't triggered in the correct order can disrupt the flow of the game, and useless information can inconveniently break apart gameplay. Furthermore, if you leave level messages at their defaults (such as `Welcome to LEVEL #` or `Way to go — that level`

was no match for you!), the game can be interpreted as insufficiently detailed. Any verbal structure behind your game must coincide neatly with the game itself.

Time Consumers

A *time consumer* is a portion of a game that takes much longer to complete than it should. Fortunately, this one is easy to solve: If you make the player run a long distance before reaching the next challenge, find obstacles to place in the avatar's way, to make the path more interesting. If a battle is slow and boring, make it more fast-paced by giving the enemies added speed and capabilities, but less health and numbers.

One of the most common time consumers is the roomful of enemies, pitting a powerful avatar against a swarm of unedited turrets or chasers. Unfortunately, only a small fraction of these enemies have truly threatening patrol routes, leading to a lengthy and boring session of holding down the Fire button while standing in place. This type of process is shown in Figure 18-3. Always consider how to make a game difficult and epic but also fast.

Figure 18-3: Time-consuming games that offer little challenge make players lose interest and become unwilling to finish the game.

 Certain avatars, such as the popular Acheron marksman (described in Chapter 6), start with very low speed, leading to potentially time-consuming situations. Be sure to increase the speed of sprites such as this one, or design the level tightly to eliminate long travels.

If you create a game where lots of action is going on, lag (which makes the game run slower when there's too much going on for your computer to handle smoothly) can cause the game to consume extra time. If a game is lagging, it can become a time consumer and detract from the flow of the game. Don't overload on sprites or cause too many game actions at a time. For example, using transmogrifiers to change more than a few sprites per second can slow down the game's frame rate.

Overloaded Enemies

Similar to the preceding section on time consumers, the pitfall of having overloaded enemies is a result of the bigger-is-better concept. If you want to build a game quickly, implementing huge swarms of enemies is a simple and tempting task. However, it sacrifices the virtue of crafting the element of fun in a game. Rather than add lots of enemies to make the game fun by coincidence, try to design the toughest gauntlets with a small number of enemies. If you truly want to give the player the satisfaction of bringing down an army of enemies, make sure that the enemies can be destroyed or dodged quickly and elegantly. Avoid designing levels in which the player just stands in place and shoots down the enemies with no real challenge, as shown earlier, in Figure 18-3.

Having lots of sprites can sometimes be beneficial, especially when you want to add visual detail. Blocks are useful for rich landscapes, whereas enemies can make crowds, villages, or armies. Just be sure that you provide quality over quantity.

Details Ignored

If you rush to complete the design process, you can easily let the pitfall of ignoring details sabotage your efforts. If you have room for detail, you should implement it — detail almost subconsciously marks a game as well designed in the minds of players. Add lots of blocks, fine-tune the settings of enemies, and tweak the gameplay so that it incorporates the five elements of game design. (Refer to the section in Chapter 5 that introduces the five elements of game design.) If you have unused space, you may also fall into the time-consumers pitfall (discussed earlier in this chapter).

Figure 18-4 shows how adding more detail can transform a game. The left image shows the first iteration of the game. As you can see, it's missing background detail and a sense of space. When you incorporate these elements into the right image, the game becomes much more interesting and appealing.

Figure 18-4: Using details such as engaging backgrounds adds interest to games.

Underused Wrench Tool

The Wrench tool may seem to be usable only for fine-tuning, but it's vitally important and must be used often. Because some sprites have thousands of combinations of options, editing them is one of the most useful techniques in the toolbox. By using the Edit and Clone tools together, you can, and should, edit almost every sprite in your game. (See Chapter 5 for the lowdown on these tools.)

Figure 18-5 shows a game in which no sprite is edited. It isn't well balanced, because the player can always attack all the enemies, but only one or two enemies at a time can attack the player — their straightforward motion patterns make them easy to defeat.

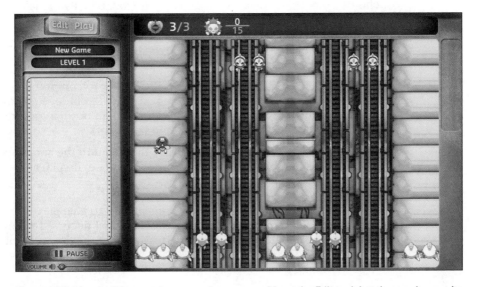

Figure 18-5: It's possible to make a complete game without the Edit tool, but the results aren't as interesting.

You can improve this game in a number of ways by using the Edit tool a few times to adjust these elements:

- **Avatars:** The avatar now has three points of health and very low speed. To make this game more interesting, you might make the avatar faster but less durable.

- **Enemies:** The slow, easy-to-frag enemies would certainly benefit from gaining more health or speed. The Edit tool also lets you change how they move — with the help of a few blocks to stop the avatar's bullets, the enemies can pose a far greater challenge to the avatar.

- **System sprites:** You now have one goal — to frag all enemies. If you want to make the game more complex, system sprites such as the energy meter have to be balanced by using the Edit tool. You can also edit the frag counter to require less than all enemies, if you want to deepen the game further with concepts such as disjoint goals or unfraggable enemies.

Sham Options

A *sham option* occurs when you give players a choice that turns out to be loaded (some options are weighted over others), uninformed (the player doesn't understand the choices well enough to make a serious decision), unnecessary, or unfair. For example, if you give the player several choices for weapons, puzzles, or challenges, you may offer one choice that's clearly better — or clearly worse — than the others. The worst of the choices is a sham option (one that no one would ever choose) that removes the element of choice from a choice-based objective. For example, if you make a level that involves two split paths, these pitfalls can occur:

- **One path is impossible for the player to complete.** The path is a sham option.

- **One path is trivial, or too easy for the player to complete.** The other path becomes a sham option. Giving paths different levels of difficulty and allowing players to select the difficulty can be an intentional feature of your game (though no path should be trivial).

- **The paths are exactly the same, and they lead to the same place.** The whole decision becomes a sham option because the player's choice doesn't affect the outcome.

Sham options show up in your game when you try to give players power over how they complete the game but the opposite effect occurs. To prevent sham options, test all choices you provide, to ensure that they're true options.

If you give players choices and only one choice results in reward, the other choices are not necessarily sham options. This setup makes players figure out which choice is correct, which is a basis for an excellent game. An option becomes a sham option when one choice is clearly better or worse than the others, and the player is fully aware of it.

Deliberate Irritations

The most important point to remember when designing a game is your motive: You want players to enjoy your work. Some people find it humorous to irritate players throughout the game, using unfair obstacles or large amounts of message blocks to make the levels drag on. This practice is simply not humorous, and you should avoid it. Annoyance isn't a substitute for fun. Fortunately, this pitfall is easy to fix: Just remember what your players want to see.

Index

• D •

• E •

● *N* ●

About the Author

Jacob Cordeiro has been discovering game design at the Gamestar Mechanic website for several years. He won an award in the 2011 Scholastic Art and Writing competition via the site, and subsequently wrote *Minecraft For Dummies, Portable Edition.* Jacob is a junior at the Stanford Online High School.

Dedication

To my family, for all their love and support.

Author's Acknowledgments

Thanks to Amy Fandrei, for all her work to make this project happen, and to Kim Darosett and Rebecca Whitney, for making this book the best it could be.

Thanks to Brian Alspach, a great game designer, with whom I had the pleasure of working in the most recent revisions of the book.

Thanks to Brenda Morris and the Davidson Young Scholars program, for organizing the Ohio University gathering, where I first learned about Gamestar Mechanic.

Thanks to Dr. Titu Andreescu, who provided many classes and opportunities that shaped my interest in problem solving. Also, thanks to the Stanford Online High School for teaching everything I needed to know to write this book.

Thanks to my family, whose values, resources, and support have made everything possible.

Lastly, thanks to everyone on the Gamestar Mechanic website, including atek7, Doublenegativeinfinity96, Elephants4Ever, FlyingForever, Iaashadow, IDrumly, Infernus, Messenger, mustelidae, Myzer, nitrox116, Omni_Chrome, Topaz1116, Walrus365, widm1999219, and zenwarrior54. This helpful community, composed of many good people and quite a few excellent designers, has been inspiring and fun to be a part of — and has been a vital factor in the creation of this book.

Publisher's Acknowledgments

Acquisitions Editor: Amy Fandrei

Senior Project Editor: Kim Darosett

Copy Editor: Rebecca Whitney

Technical Editors: Ryan W. Nelson and Emily P. Nelson

Editorial Assistant: Anne Sullivan

Sr. Editorial Assistant: Cherie Case

Project Coordinator: Rebekah Brownson

Cover Images: Courtesy of Jacob Cordeiro

Apple & Mac

iPad For Dummies,
5th Edition
978-1-118-72306-7

iPhone For Dummies,
7th Edition
978-1-118-69083-3

Macs All-in-One
For Dummies, 4th Edition
978-1-118-82210-4

OS X Mavericks
For Dummies
978-1-118-69188-5

Blogging & Social Media

Facebook For Dummies,
5th Edition
978-1-118-63312-0

Social Media Engagement
For Dummies
978-1-118-53019-1

WordPress For Dummies,
6th Edition
978-1-118-79161-5

Business

Stock Investing
For Dummies, 4th Edition
978-1-118-37678-2

Investing For Dummies,
6th Edition
978-0-470-90545-6

Careers

Personal Finance
For Dummies, 7th Edition
978-1-118-11785-9

QuickBooks 2014
For Dummies
978-1-118-72005-9

Small Business Marketing
Kit For Dummies,
3rd Edition
978-1-118-31183-7

Careers

Job Interviews
For Dummies, 4th Edition
978-1-118-11290-8

Job Searching with Social
Media For Dummies,
2nd Edition
978-1-118-67856-5

Personal Branding
For Dummies
978-1-118-11792-7

Resumes For Dummies,
6th Edition
978-0-470-87361-8

Starting an Etsy Business
For Dummies, 2nd Edition
978-1-118-59024-9

Diet & Nutrition

Belly Fat Diet For Dummies
978-1-118-34585-6

Mediterranean Diet
For Dummies
978-1-118-71525-3

Nutrition For Dummies,
5th Edition
978-0-470-93231-5

Digital Photography

Digital SLR Photography
All-in-One For Dummies,
2nd Edition
978-1-118-59082-9

Digital SLR Video &
Filmmaking For Dummies
978-1-118-36598-4

Photoshop Elements 12
For Dummies
978-1-118-72714-0

Gardening

Herb Gardening
For Dummies, 2nd Edition
978-0-470-61778-6

Gardening with Free-Range
Chickens For Dummies
978-1-118-54754-0

Health

Boosting Your Immunity
For Dummies
978-1-118-40200-9

Diabetes For Dummies,
4th Edition
978-1-118-29447-5

Living Paleo For Dummies
978-1-118-29405-5

Big Data

Big Data For Dummies
978-1-118-50422-2

Data Visualization
For Dummies
978-1-118-50289-1

Hadoop For Dummies
978-1-118-60755-8

Language &
Foreign Language

500 Spanish Verbs
For Dummies
978-1-118-02382-2

English Grammar
For Dummies, 2nd Edition
978-0-470-54664-2

French All-in-One
For Dummies
978-1-118-22815-9

German Essentials
For Dummies
978-1-118-18422-6

Italian For Dummies,
2nd Edition
978-1-118-00465-4

 **Available in print and e-book formats.**

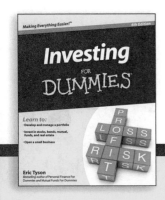 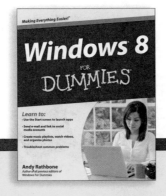  

Available wherever books are sold. **For more information or to order direct visit www.dummies.com**

Math & Science

Algebra I For Dummies,
2nd Edition
978-0-470-55964-2

Anatomy and Physiology
For Dummies, 2nd Edition
978-0-470-92326-9

Astronomy For Dummies,
3rd Edition
978-1-118-37697-3

Biology For Dummies,
2nd Edition
978-0-470-59875-7

Chemistry For Dummies,
2nd Edition
978-1-118-00730-3

1001 Algebra II Practice
Problems For Dummies
978-1-118-44662-1

Microsoft Office

Excel 2013 For Dummies
978-1-118-51012-4

Office 2013 All-in-One
For Dummies
978-1-118-51636-2

PowerPoint 2013
For Dummies
978-1-118-50253-2

Word 2013 For Dummies
978-1-118-49123-2

Music

Blues Harmonica
For Dummies
978-1-118-25269-7

Guitar For Dummies,
3rd Edition
978-1-118-11554-1

iPod & iTunes
For Dummies, 10th Edition
978-1-118-50864-0

Programming

Beginning Programming
with C For Dummies
978-1-118-73763-7

Excel VBA Programming
For Dummies, 3rd Edition
978-1-118-49037-2

Java For Dummies,
6th Edition
978-1-118-40780-6

Religion & Inspiration

The Bible For Dummies
978-0-7645-5296-0

Buddhism For Dummies,
2nd Edition
978-1-118-02379-2

Catholicism For Dummies,
2nd Edition
978-1-118-07778-8

Self-Help & Relationships

Beating Sugar Addiction
For Dummies
978-1-118-54645-1

Meditation For Dummies,
3rd Edition
978-1-118-29144-3

Seniors

Laptops For Seniors
For Dummies, 3rd Edition
978-1-118-71105-7

Computers For Seniors
For Dummies, 3rd Edition
978-1-118-11553-4

iPad For Seniors
For Dummies, 6th Edition
978-1-118-72826-0

Social Security
For Dummies
978-1-118-20573-0

Smartphones & Tablets

Android Phones
For Dummies, 2nd Edition
978-1-118-72030-1

Nexus Tablets
For Dummies
978-1-118-77243-0

Samsung Galaxy S 4
For Dummies
978-1-118-64222-1

Samsung Galaxy Tabs
For Dummies
978-1-118-77294-2

Test Prep

ACT For Dummies,
5th Edition
978-1-118-01259-8

ASVAB For Dummies,
3rd Edition
978-0-470-63760-9

GRE For Dummies,
7th Edition
978-0-470-88921-3

Officer Candidate Tests
For Dummies
978-0-470-59876-4

Physician's Assistant Exam
For Dummies
978-1-118-11556-5

Series 7 Exam For Dummies
978-0-470-09932-2

Windows 8

Windows 8.1 All-in-One
For Dummies
978-1-118-82087-2

Windows 8.1 For Dummies
978-1-118-82121-3

Windows 8.1 For Dummies,
Book + DVD Bundle
978-1-118-82107-7

e **Available in print and e-book formats.**

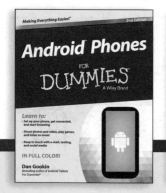

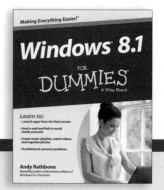

Available wherever books are sold. **For more information or to order direct visit www.dummies.com**

Take Dummies with you everywhere you go!

Whether you are excited about e-books, want more from the web, must have your mobile apps, or are swept up in social media, Dummies makes everything easier.

Leverage the Power

For Dummies is the global leader in the reference category and one of the most trusted and highly regarded brands in the world. No longer just focused on books, customers now have access to the For Dummies content they need in the format they want. Let us help you develop a solution that will fit your brand and help you connect with your customers.

Advertising & Sponsorships

Connect with an engaged audience on a powerful multimedia site, and position your message alongside expert how-to content.

Targeted ads • Video • Email marketing • Microsites • Sweepstakes sponsorship